Implementing and Managing Oracle® Databases

Check the Web for Updates:

To check for updates or corrections relevant to this book visit our updates page on the Web at http://www.prima-tech.com/updates.

Send Us Your Comments:

To comment on this book or any other PRIMA TECH title, visit our reader response page on the Web at http://www.prima-tech.com/comments.

How to Order:

For information on quantity discounts, contact the publisher: Prima Publishing, P.O. Box 1260BK, Rocklin, CA 95677-1260; (916) 787-7000. On your letterhead, include information concerning the intended use of the books and the number of books you want to purchase.

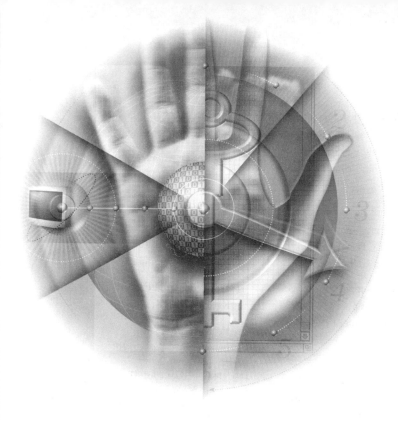

Implementing and Managing Oracle® Databases

Steve Lemme with
John R. Colby

A Division of Prima Publishing

A Division of Prima Publishing

Prima Publishing and colophon are registered trademarks of Prima Communications, Inc. PRIMA TECH is a trademark of Prima Communications, Inc., Roseville, California, 95661.

Important: Prima Publishing cannot provide software support. Please contact the appropriate software manufacturer's technical support line or Web site for assistance. This book is an independent publication of Prima Publishing and is not affiliated with or sponsored by Oracle or any other manufacturer mentioned herein.

Oracle is a registered trademark, and PL/SQL and SQL are trademarks or registered trademarks of Oracle Corporation. Microsoft, Windows 95, Windows 98, Windows NT and Windows 2000 are either registered trademarks or trademarks of Microsoft Corporation in the United States and/or other countries. All other brand and product names mentioned herein are trademarks, registered trademarks, or service marks of their respective holders.

Prima Publishing and the author have attempted throughout this book to distinguish proprietary trademarks from descriptive terms by following the capitalization style used by the manufacturer.

Information contained in this book has been obtained by Prima Publishing from sources believed to be reliable. However, because of the possibility of human or mechanical error by our sources, Prima Publishing, or others, the Publisher does not guarantee the accuracy, adequacy, or completeness of any information and is not responsible for any errors or omissions or the results obtained from use of such information. Readers should be particularly aware of the fact that the Internet is an ever-changing entity. Some facts may have changed since this book went to press.

ISBN: 0-7615-2936-5

Library of Congress Catalog Card Number: 00-106661

Printed in the United States of America

00 01 02 03 04 II 10 9 8 7 6 5 4 3 2 1

Publisher:
Stacy L. Hiquet

Marketing Manager:
Judi Taylor Wade

Managing Editor:
Sandy Doell

Acquisitions Editor:
Jawahara K. Saidullah

Developmental Editor:
Kate Welsh

Project Editor:
Elizabeth A. Agostinelli

Technical Reviewer:
David Kennedy

Copy Editor:
Kezia Endsley

Interior Layout:
Shawn Morningstar

Cover Design:
Prima Design Team

Indexer:
Sharon Shock

Proofreader:
Jeannie Smith

Dedication

To my mother and father who always said,
"If you put your mind to it, you can do anything!"

—S. Lemme

To my wife Susan, and my children, Zachary, Joel, and Tiffany,
who graciously adjusted to my frequent absence as I sat
behind my computer writing this book during the
past several months.

—J. Colby

Foreword

E-business is dramatically changing the way companies do business today. In order to do business at e-speed, traditional IT job roles are changing, one of which is the database administrator (DBA). To meet these new business demands, the DBA has to be better equipped, better educated, and better in sync with the business. This requires the DBA to know more about the business, and the business to know more about the DBA.

Database administration starts before the software is ordered. Most often, planning and selection of the database software, architecture, procedures, and processes are overlooked. A vast majority of database installations occur on an existing platform because of available space. Then, once the application is in production, performance issues, administration problems, and bottlenecks appear. Most often, these issues are viewed as the DBA's responsibility. The DBA tries to tune the database, but usually yields minor tuning improvements of less than 15 percent. Is this primarily due to a lack of expertise on the part of the DBA? Usually not. Like a company, all database systems grow in usage, size, and complexity. To address these issues, database systems must be properly planned, developed, and refined through a set of methods and processes. This methodology is the database system's lifecycle. The purpose of this book is to discuss the decisions, processes, and techniques you should consider when deploying an Oracle RDBMS.

Acknowledgments

With this book five years in the making, I could pen a whole chapter on all those who have inspired me, but content—not pages—makes a good book.

First and foremost is the support from my loving and tolerant wife who had to put up with a laptop on vacations, midnight e-mails, and those last night 24×7 pages and phone calls. Without her and the support of our three young children, Nicole, Shelby, and Justin, I would have never finished. In fact, all three are DBAs in training.

Gary Benedict from Allied Signal was my first mentor and planted a seed in my mind by allowing me to participate in his book.

Very important is all the support and encouragement I have had over the years in the Oracle User Group community. People like Buff at The Primary Key bookstore, John and Peggy King at King Training, as well as Tony Jambu, Leng Kaing, Kevin Loney, Ari Kaplan, Merilee Nohr, Rich Niemiec of TUSC, Brian Laskey, Michael Abbey, Michael Corey, and a cast of many others.

I must also thank those at Prima Publishing as well as my co-author, John Colby. Without their perseverance and hard work, this book would have never seen the light of day.

—Steve Lemme

About the Authors

Steve Lemme is currently a vice president of Database Management Solutions for Computer Associates International. He has over 10 years of experience with mission-critical Oracle system design and e-business system and network architectures. Prior to joining Computer Associates from the Platinum technology acquisition, Mr. Lemme designed, deployed, and maintained business-critical systems for several Fortune 50 companies.

Mr. Lemme is also president of the Arizona Oracle Users Group, a volunteer with the International Oracle User Group, and a featured speaker across the world at IOUG-A, EOUG, CAWORLD, HPWorld, and Oracle OpenWorld.

John R. Colby is currently a Senior Software Engineer/Oracle DBA for TYBRIN Corporation in Fort Walton Beach, Florida. He has written several articles on topics such as software engineering, configuration management, quality assurance, and many Oracle papers on issues concerning analysis, design, implementation, tuning, and performance. John has developed countless full-scale database applications using Oracle development tools, Delphi, Java, and Visual Basic/VBA, as well as other tools and programming languages.

He earned a B.S. in Computer Engineering from Wright State University in Dayton, Ohio, and also has an M.S. in Software Engineering from the University of West Florida in Pensacola, Florida. His hobbies include computers, music, muscle car restoration, outdoor activities, and his family—not necessarily in that order!

Contents at a Glance

Contents

Introduction

I never dreamed that one day I would actually write a book. This all started when I was faced with Oracle database problems as a DBA and wasn't sure where to turn—the telephone hold music didn't do much for me. As I learned and networked with others in the industry, I found that others were also "recreating the wheel" time and time again. Consequently, I started on a quest to learn as much as I could with a promise to share what I learned with others.

Like most other IT professionals, my library grew but I started to notice a trend in the materials I had collected. Everyone seemed to be addressing the database issues once the application was already in production: YAT books (Yet Another Tuning book). What about before deployment? What about architectural considerations? What about the people who are the assets in enabling the business solution? Too often, the starting point for a database is installing it on an existing server. Then folks wonder why there are so many performance issues. What about impact analysis and risk mitigation?

I have assembled this book with the database lifecycle in mind. This is a book that a company considering Oracle technology can use, a book a DBA can use, and a book an HR professional can use to better understand what DBAs do so that they can better attract and retain professionals in this hot job sector.

I hope all my readers will benefit from this book by learning at least one thing. If you don't find a particularly helpful tidbit here that you learned elsewhere, please let me know so that I can add it in the next edition.

—Steve Lemme

Steve_Lemme@yahoo.com

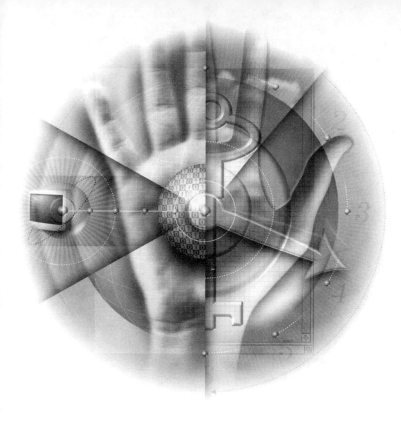

PART I

Implementing Your Oracle Database

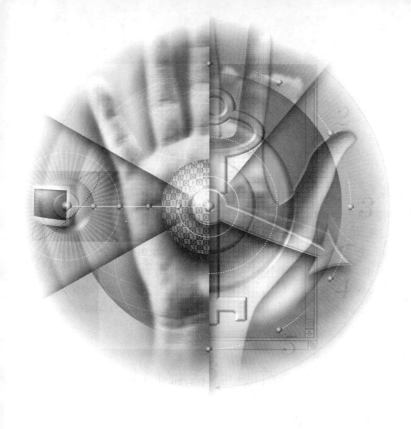

Chapter 1

This chapter is geared toward anyone who is involved with Oracle's Relational Database Management System (RDBMS). If you have been assigned to manage a team of Oracle professionals and want an overview of Oracle, this book was written for you. If you are assigned the task of administrating an Oracle database from scratch, this book is tailored for you as well. *Implementing and Managing Oracle Databases* was written for all levels of Oracle personnel in mind—from the beginner to the professional, for the manager or the database administrator.

The following sections describe in detail these concepts:

◆ What an Oracle database is made up of, including physical and logical components

◆ The history of where Oracle started

◆ Products that belong to Oracle

◆ How to get started

It makes sense to start by defining an Oracle database.

What Is an Oracle Database?

Oracle defines a database in its simplest form as:

◆ A set of operating system files, treated as a unit, in which an Oracle server stores a set of data dictionary tables and user tables. A database requires three types of files: one or more database files, one or more control files, and two or more redo log files.

◆ The disk space corresponding to this set of files.

◆ A subset of database objects necessary to support a single database application.

Okay, you say, but how do I implement and manage one of these databases?

How Do I Implement an Oracle Database?

The dictionary defines implement as to put into practical effect; carry out. This is a good definition and can be used in reference to Oracle. To implement an Oracle database is to put the database into practical use, and then carry out this implementation for your customers to use. Throughout this book, you will see more and more practical definitions that will help you understand what implementing an Oracle database is all about.

How Do I Manage an Oracle Database?

The word manage means many things to many people. Again, the dictionary can help to define the word for the purposes here. Manage means to "direct or control the use of; handle." This word plays nicely in with Oracle databases and this book. In order to "manage" an Oracle database, one must "oversee" and "direct" how Oracle is conducted throughout its lifecycle.

But first, before you can "implement and manage," you need to be familiar with the concept of an Oracle database, commonly referred to as the *Oracle server*. The following information will help you understand more about an Oracle database or server. Some of the following material was taken from *Oracle's Server Concepts* manual that comes with Oracle8, and is worth repeating here.

The Oracle Server

The Oracle server is an object-relational database management system that provides an open, comprehensive, and integrated approach to information management. An Oracle server consists of an Oracle database and an Oracle server *instance*. The following sections describe the relationship between the database and the instance.

An Oracle Instance

Every time a database is started, a system global area (SGA) is allocated and Oracle background processes are started. The *system global area* is in an area of memory used for database information shared by the database users. The combination of the background processes and the system global area (sometimes referred to as a memory buffer) is called an Oracle *instance*.

An Oracle instance has two types of processes:

◆ A *user process* executes the code of an application program or an Oracle tool.

◆ *Oracle processes* comprise server processes that perform work for the users and background processes that perform maintenance work for the Oracle server.

The Physical and Logical Database Structures

An Oracle database has both a physical and a logical structure. Because the physical and logical server structures are separate, the physical storage of data can be managed without affecting access to the logical storage structures.

Logical Database Structure

An Oracle database's logical structure is determined by

◆ **One or more tablespaces.** A *tablespace* is a logical area of storage.

◆ **The database's schema objects.** A *schema* is a collection of objects. *Schema objects* are the logical structures that directly refer to the database's data.

The logical storage structures, including tablespaces, segments, and extents, dictate how the physical space of a database is used. The schema objects and the relationships among them form the relational design of a database.

The following sections explain logical database structures, including tablespaces, schema objects, data blocks, extents, and segments.

Tablespaces

A database is divided into logical storage units called *tablespaces*. A tablespace is used to group related logical structures together. For example, tablespaces commonly group an application's objects to simplify certain administrative operations. The following are key items that relate to tablespaces:

◆ Each database is logically divided into one or more tablespaces.

◆ One or more datafiles is explicitly created for each tablespace to physically store the data of all logical structures in a tablespace.

◆ The combined size of a tablespace's datafiles is the total storage capacity of the tablespace.

◆ The combined storage capacity of a database's tablespaces is the total storage capacity of the database.

A tablespace can be *online* (accessible) or *offline* (not accessible). A tablespace is normally online so that users can access the information within it. However, sometimes you can take a tablespace offline to make a portion of the database unavailable while allowing normal access to the remainder of the database. This makes many administrative tasks easier to perform.

Schemas and Schema Objects

A *schema* is a collection of objects. *Schema objects* are the logical structures that directly refer to the database's data. Schema objects include such structures as tables, views, sequences, stored procedures, synonyms, indexes, clusters, and database links. (There is no relationship between a tablespace and a schema; objects in the same schema can be in different tablespaces, and a tablespace can hold objects from different schemas.)

Data Blocks, Extents, and Segments

Oracle allows fine-grained control of disk-space use through the logical storage structures, including data blocks, extents, and segments.

Oracle Data Blocks

At the finest level of granularity, an Oracle database's data is stored in *data blocks*. One data block corresponds to a specific number of bytes of physical database space on-disk. A data block size is specified for each Oracle database when the database is created. A database uses and allocates free database space in Oracle data blocks.

Extents

The next level of logical database space is called an extent. An *extent* is a specific number of contiguous (or adjacent) data blocks, obtained in a single allocation, and used to store a specific type of information.

Segments

The level of logical database storage above an extent is called a segment. A *segment* is a set of extents allocated for a certain logical structure. For example, the different types of segments include the following:

◆ **Data segment.** Each *non-clustered table* (a cluster is a means of storing data from multiple tables together when the data contains common information that is likely to be accessed concurrently) has a data segment in whose extents all the table's data is stored. Each cluster has a data segment; the data of every table in the cluster is stored in the cluster's data segment.

◆ **Index segment.** Each index has an index segment that stores all its data. An *index* is a general term for an Oracle feature that speeds execution when searching for specific data within a table.

◆ **Rollback segment.** One or more rollback segments are created by the database administrator so a database can temporarily store "undo" information. This information is used during database recovery, and to roll back uncommitted transactions for users.

Oracle dynamically allocates space when the existing extents of a segment become full. In other words, when the existing extents of a segment are full, Oracle allocates another extent for that segment as needed.

Physical Database Structure

The operating system files that constitute the database determine an Oracle database's physical structure. As stated in the beginning of this chapter, each Oracle database is made of three types of files: one or more datafiles, two or more redo log files, and one or more control files. The files of an Oracle database provide the actual physical storage for database information.

The following sections explain the physical database structures of an Oracle database, including datafiles, redo log files, control files, alert files, and trace files.

Datafiles

Every Oracle database has one or more physical *datafiles*. A database's datafiles contain all the database data. The data of logical database structures—such as tables and indexes—is physically stored in the datafiles allocated for that database.

The following are characteristics of datafiles:

◆ A datafile can be associated with only one database.

◆ Database files can have certain characteristics that allow them to automatically extend when the database runs out of space.

◆ One or more datafiles form a logical unit of database storage called a tablespace, as discussed earlier in this chapter.

The data in a datafile is read, as needed, during normal database operations and stored in the memory cache of Oracle. For example, assume that a user wants to access some data in a table of a database. If the requested information is not already in the *memory cache* (which is Oracle's readily available memory area, or SGA, for quickly accessing commonly used data), the information is read from the appropriate datafiles and stored in memory.

Modified or new data is not necessarily written to a datafile immediately. To reduce the amount of disk access and increase performance, data is pooled in memory and written to the appropriate datafiles all at once, as determined by the database writer (DBWR) background process of Oracle. The DBWR process can be tuned to account for how often the data is written to the datafiles.

Redo Log Files

Every Oracle database has a set of two or more *redo log files*. The set of redo log files for a database is collectively known as the database's *redo log*. The primary function of the redo log is to record all changes made to data. Should a failure prevent modified data from being permanently written to the datafiles, the changes can be obtained from the redo log; thus, work is never lost.

The information in a redo log file is used only to recover the database from a system or media failure that prevents database data from being written to a database's datafiles. For example, if an unexpected power outage abruptly terminates database operation, data in memory cannot be written to the datafiles and the data is lost. However, any lost data can be recovered using the redo log files once the database is opened, after power is restored. By applying the information in the most recent redo log files to the database's datafiles, Oracle restores the database to the time at which the power failure occurred.

Redo log files are critical in protecting a database against failures. To protect against a failure involving the redo log itself, Oracle implements a *multiplexed redo log* so that two or more copies of the redo log can be maintained on different disks.

Control Files

Every Oracle database has a *control file*. A control file contains entries that specify the physical structure of the database. For example, it contains the following types of information:

◆ Database name

◆ Names and locations of a database's datafiles and redo log files

◆ Time stamp of database creation

Every time an instance of an Oracle database is started, its control file identifies the database and redo log files that must be opened in order for the database operation to proceed. If the physical makeup of the database is altered (for example, a new datafile or redo log file is created), Oracle automatically modifies the database's control file to reflect the change.

Like the redo log, Oracle allows the control file to be multiplexed for protection of the control file.

Alert Files and Trace Files

To complete a discussion on Oracle files, the alert and trace files should also be described.

The alert file, which is located in the directory specified by a parameter called BACKGROUND_DUMP_DEST, logs significant database messages and events. The alert file is a text file and can be viewed using a standard word processor. The alert file records each time the database instance starts up and shuts down. The alert file also logs messages and errors that are normally written to a console that trigger trace files to be written.

The trace files are specific to certain server and background processes. If an internal error is detected by a process, then the information concerning the error is dumped into the associated trace file. This information is compiled so that either the Oracle DBA or Oracle support personnel can "trace" through the file and hopefully understand the cause of the error.

Structured Query Language (SQL)

SQL (pronounced "sequel") is the programming language that defines and manipulates the database. SQL databases are *relational databases*; this means simply that data is stored in a set of simple relations. A database can have one or more tables, and each table has columns and rows. A table that has an employee database, for example, might have a column called "employee number" and each row in that column might contain an employee's employee number.

SQL Commands

You can define and manipulate data in a table using SQL commands of two types:

◆ You use data definition language (DDL) commands to set up the data. DDL commands include commands that create and alter databases and tables.

◆ You can update, delete, or retrieve data in a table with data-manipulation commands (DML). DML commands include commands that alter and fetch data. The most common SQL command is SELECT, which allows you to retrieve data from the database.

In addition to SQL commands, the Oracle Server has a procedural language called PL/SQL. Oracle's procedural language extension to SQL, or PL/SQL for short, enables the programmer to program SQL statements. It allows you to control the flow of a SQL program, to use variables, and to write error-handling procedures.

Issuing SQL Commands through the SQL*Plus Application

SQL*Plus is a command-line SQL and PL/SQL language interface and reporting tool that ships with the Oracle database server. It can be used interactively or run from text files containing its commands (referred to as scripts).

Table 1.1 shows some common commands that you can execute from SQL*Plus.

Table 1.1 Basic SQL*Plus Commands

Command	Description
Accept	Gets input from the user.
Define	Declares a variable or a word used to represent a value (short: DEF).
Describe	Lists the attributes of tables and other objects (short: DESC).
Edit	Opens an editor so you can edit a SQL command (short: ED).

(continued...)

Exit or Quit	Disconnects from the database and terminates SQL*Plus.
Get	Retrieves a SQL file and places it into the SQL buffer, which is an area in memory used to hold SQL commands.
Host	Issues an operating-system command.
List	Displays the last command executed/command in the SQL buffer.
Prompt	Displays a text string on the screen.
Run	Lists and runs the command stored in the SQL buffer (short: /).
Save	Saves the command in the SQL buffer to a file (for example, save x creates a script file called x.sql).
Set	Modifies the SQL*Plus environment (for example, Set Pagesize 66).
Show	Shows environment settings.
Spool	Sends output to a file. For example, spool x will save your work to a file called x.lst, which is short for a "listing" file called "x".
Start	Runs a SQL script file (short: @).

From VMS to Unix and NT

Oracle first appeared in the mid 1980s, on Digital's VAX minicomputer running the Virtual Memory System, or VMS operating system (OS). Oracle software was developed for VMS and then ported over to Unix a few years later. Around 1989, Oracle jumped heavily on the open systems/Unix bandwagon that dominated the midrange computer environment. By 1995, the majority of Oracle installations were Unix-based, and most of the VMS Oracle DBAs (database administrators) traded their VMS hats for the more popular Unix hat. Over the last few years, however, Microsoft NT has gained considerable market share, and Unix and NT are now sharing the market as the platform of choice for Oracle. Even so, Unix systems continue to hold the high ground and constitute the majority of mission-critical and Very Large Database (VLDB) implementations.

In the following sections, you will see how Windows NT/2000 compares to Unix as an Oracle server platform with some details on some common Oracle administration tasks under both Unix and Windows NT/2000.

On both types of systems (Unix and Windows NT/2000), Oracle implements a common architecture that includes the following components:

◆ The area of memory known as the *system global area* (SGA) is available to all Oracle sessions. This area of memory includes recently accessed data blocks (called the buffer cache), SQL and PL/SQL objects or commands (known as the library cache), and transaction information, which takes the form of redo log buffers.

◆ Oracle datafiles contain the tables, indexes, and other segments that make up what's known as an Oracle instance.

◆ Tasks that perform dedicated database activities, including the database writer (DBWR), the redo log writer (LGWR), the system monitor (SMON), the process monitor (PMON), and the log archiver (ARCH), are present. Other tasks can be configured if required to support Oracle options such as a distributed database, a parallel query, or use of multi-threaded servers. All these tasks are considered background tasks, more commonly referred to as *background processes*.

◆ Redo logs, which record critical transaction information, are present in case of an instance failure.

◆ A separate task is created to perform database operations on behalf of each Oracle session, or for each Oracle user logged into the system. This process is referred to as the *dedicated server*, meaning that the server is dedicated to each user. If the multithreaded server option is implemented in Oracle, shared servers can then support these sessions. For each logged in user, several servers implement the user's commands.

◆ A SQL*Net listener task, which is Oracle's connection between the database and your computer network, establishes connections from external systems so that applications can connect to your database.

Figure 1.1 shows the components that comprise the common Oracle structure. Next, you can focus on the differences between the two systems because of the structural differences of their operating systems.

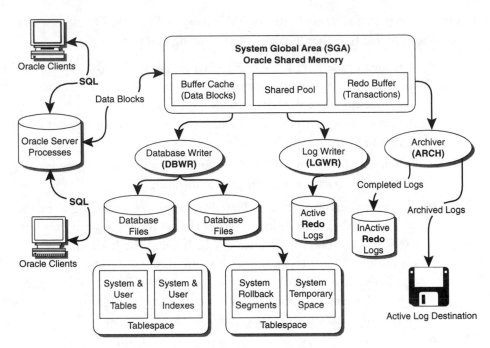

FIGURE 1.1 *Common database structure of Oracle.*

Oracle's Architecture on Unix Platforms

In Unix, each Oracle task is implemented as a separate Unix process. Accordingly, a process is created for each Oracle background task and for each (dedicated or shared) server task. The SGA exists within Unix shared memory, which any of the background or server tasks can access.

Figure 1.2 illustrates the Oracle/Unix architecture.

 NOTE

When the term Unix is used in this book, Linux can be substituted. Oracle has dedicated much research and development into developing Oracle for Linux. Linux, which is growing rapidly in popularity, is similar to Unix and follows the same architecture.

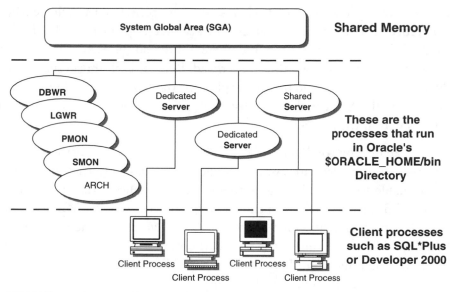

FIGURE 1.2 *Unix-specific Oracle database structure.*

Oracle's Architecture on Windows NT/2000

The architecture of Oracle in a Windows NT/2000 environment is somewhat different from that of Unix. Oracle takes advantage of Microsoft NT's strong support for *threads*. In almost all operating systems, a process is forbidden from accessing memory belonging to another process. Threads belonging to the same process, however, share a common memory address space and can therefore share memory easily.

 NOTE

The word thread comes from the term multithreading. A thread is basically a path of execution through a program. It is also the smallest unit of execution that Microsoft's Windows programs schedule. A thread consists of a stack, the state of the CPU registers, and an entry in the system scheduler's execution list (which is a list of commands waiting to be run). Each thread shares all the process's resources.

On Windows NT/2000, the Oracle instance is implemented as a single Microsoft NT process. This process includes threads that implement each of the tasks required for the instance. Therefore, there is a thread for each of the background and server tasks plus a two-thread overhead. Because each thread shares the same memory space, there is no need to implement the SGA in shared memory. If you implement the SGA within the instance's process memory, it is available to all threads within the process.

Oracle's architecture on Windows NT/2000 is well suited for Microsoft's NT/2000 process/thread model. However, the single process model restricts the total memory available to threads belonging to an Oracle instance. Prior to Windows NT version 3.51, the memory limit for a single process was 256MB. This in itself caused a severe limitation for Oracle databases, which was the main reason that Windows NT at the time was not a good option for large databases. (Unix does not have this limitation.) Now, in Windows NT version 4.0, an Oracle process can address up to 2GB of virtual memory.

One way to overcome this limitation is to use Oracle's multithreaded server option, which allows multiple client processes to share a smaller number of Oracle's server processes. The multithreaded server is available on Windows NT, but only starting with version 8 of Oracle. Using the multithreaded server under Windows NT version 4.0 can reduce the number of threads in the Oracle process as well as reduce overall memory requirements. With the release of Windows 2000, the process memory limit was increased to 32GB, which should be sufficient for most Oracle installations. See Figure 1.3 for details on the Windows NT/2000 structure.

In summary, Oracle is available on several platforms and can use several operating systems. This book concentrates on the more popular Unix and Windows NT/2000 environments.

What's Included with Oracle?

When you think about what is included with Oracle, do you automatically think database? Do you think development tools or administration tools? Oracle is touting itself as more than just a database program. If you were to break Oracle into two parts—the database and an environment for developers—you would see the Oracle products listed in Table 1.2.

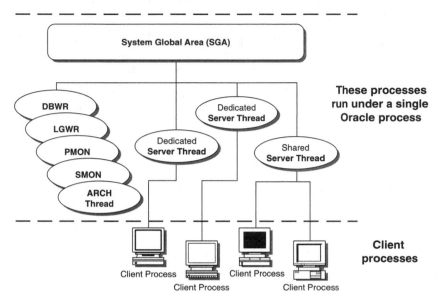

FIGURE 1.3 *Windows NT/2000–specific Oracle database structure.*

Table 1.2 Oracle Products

Oracle RDBMS (Oracle 8i Products)	Oracle Developer Server
Oracle8i Enterprise Edition	CDE2 Database Tables
Oracle8i Standard Edition	GUI Common Files
Oracle8i Personal Edition	INTERSOLV DataDirect Driver
Oracle Developer Server	Open Interfaces
Oracle E-mail Server	Oracle Forms
Oracle Enterprise Manager with Change Management Pack	Oracle Graphics
Oracle Enterprise Manager with Diagnostics Pack	Oracle Information Navigator
Oracle Enterprise Manager with Standard Management Pack	Oracle Installer
Oracle Enterprise Manager with Tuning Pack	Oracle JDK
Oracle Express Server and Oracle Express OLAP Client	Oracle Procedure Builder
Oracle Fail Safe	Oracle Reports Developer

(continued...)

Oracle Installer	Oracle Wallet Manager
Oracle Management Pack for Oracle Applications	Oracle(R) ODBC Driver for RDB
Oracle Management Pack for SAP	Project Builder
Oracle Message Broker	Required Support Files
Oracle WebDB	SQL*Net
Oracle Workflow Cartridge and Workflow Client	SQL*Plus
Oracle Warehouse Builder	System Support Files
Oracle Internet File System	Tools Utilities

That doesn't seem like a lot of products for such a large company as Oracle. Well, Oracle8i's Enterprise, Standard, and Personal editions also include the products listed in Table 1.3.

Table 1.3 Oracle8i's Enterprise, Standard, and Personal Edition Products

Advanced Security Export Edition	Agent Paging Extensions
COM Automation	Developer Server Forms Manager
Enterprise Security Manager	Generic Connectivity
interMedia Audio	interMedia Image
interMedia Locator Service	interMedia Text
interMedia Video	Java Runtime Environment
Java Virtual Machine Component	Legato Storage Manager
Net8	Net8 Assistant
Net8 Client	Net8 Configuration Assistant
Net8 Server	Object Type Translator (OTT)
Oracle Administration Assistant for Windows NT	Oracle Application Manager
Oracle Applications Server Manager	Oracle AppWizard for Microsoft Visual C++
Oracle Call Interface	Oracle Configuration Assistant
Oracle Connection Manager	Oracle Data Gatherer

(continued...)

Oracle Data Migration Assistant

Oracle Database Administration Management Pack

Oracle Database Collection Cartridge

Oracle Database Configuration Assistant

Oracle DBA Studio

Oracle Directory Manager

Oracle Documentation

Oracle Enterprise Manager Client

Oracle Enterprise Manager Migration Assistant

Oracle Enterprise Manager Web site

Oracle for Windows NT Performance Monitor

Oracle Home Selector

Oracle Instance Manager

Oracle Intelligent Agent

Oracle interMedia

Oracle interMedia Client

Oracle interMedia Text Manager

Oracle Internet Directory

Oracle INTYPE File Assistant

Oracle Java Utilities

Oracle JDBC Thin Driver for JDK 1.1

Oracle JDBC Thin Driver for JDK 1.2

Oracle JDBC/OCI Driver for JDK 1.1

Oracle JDBC/OCI Driver for JDK 1.2

Oracle JServer Enterprise Edition

Oracle Management Server

Oracle Migration Workbench

Oracle Named Pipes Protocol Support

Oracle Names

Oracle Objects for OLE

Oracle ODBC Driver

Oracle Parallel Server

Oracle Parallel Server Management

Oracle Parallel Server Manager

Oracle Partitioning

Oracle Provider for OLE DB

Oracle Remote Configuration Agent

Oracle Remote Operations

Oracle Replication Manager

Oracle Schema Manager

Oracle Services for Microsoft Transaction Server

Oracle Spatial

Oracle Spatial Index Advisor

Oracle SPX/IPX Protocol Support

Oracle Storage Manager

Oracle TCP/IP Protocol Support

Oracle Time Series

Oracle Universal Installer

Oracle Universal Installer Libraries

Oracle Utilities

Oracle Visual Information Retrieval

Oracle Visual Information Retrieval Client

Oracle Web Publishing Assistant

Oracle8i Client

(continued...)

Oracle8i Client Release Notes	Oracle8i Enterprise Edition for MS Windows NT
Oracle8i Server	OS Collection Cartridge
PL/SQL	Pro*C/C++
Pro*COBOL	Pro*COBOL
Programmer	SQL*Plus
SQLJ	SQLJ Runtime
SQLJ Translator	SQLPlus Worksheet

So, once again, the Oracle DBA has many products to keep track of and have some familiarity with. But enough already, that's too many tools to keep track of! Fortunately, most Oracle DBAs and managers don't have to worry about the details of each of these products. Usually there is a small subset of products specifically tailored to your database application. So rest easy and begin to absorb this Oracle experience.

Summary

This chapter has given you an idea of what Oracle is all about. As you can see from just this first chapter, Oracle is not a simple database, and will take plenty of time to actually master the concepts presented in this chapter.

You can approach the implementation of your Oracle database from different points of view—either by overseeing an entire Oracle database project or by being the lucky Oracle DBA who must install the database.

Managing an Oracle database can also take on two meanings. One can mean watching over a team of Oracle DBAs and having a good understanding of what's going on so you can brief your database team's progress each week at staff meetings. A second can mean plunging into the heart of the system and monitoring the progress of the Oracle database yourself.

As stated in the beginning of this chapter, this book is ideal for all levels of involvement and should serve as a valuable guide and reference for implementing and managing your Oracle database!

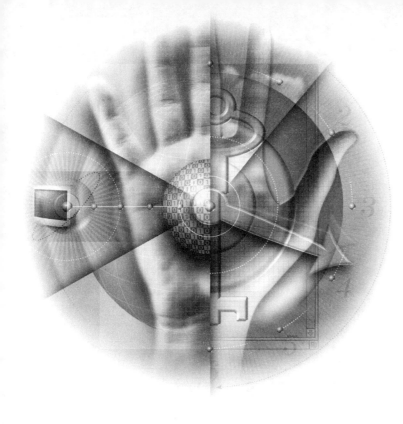

Chapter 2

**Administrating
the Lifecycle
of an Oracle
Database**

Chapter 1, "Overview of Oracle Databases," explained what Oracle is and how it is put together. This chapter steps you through the different phases involved in administering an Oracle database. Whether you are looking for the guidance to administer and implement your first full database project or application, or the knowledge to maintain an ongoing Oracle database project, or a combination of both, this chapter will help steer you in the right direction.

The areas that this chapter highlights include the following:

◆ The business requirements for achieving *scalability*, which entails being able to tailor your requirements to any size business

◆ Analysis, design, and how the database lifecycle fits in with the architecture

◆ Hardware and network options

◆ Maintenance of uptime and availability

◆ Installation and deployment

◆ Backup and recovery

◆ Change management and documentation

◆ Training and support

◆ Web and Internet deployment

The first logical step is to better define the lifecycle for administering an Oracle database.

The Oracle Database Lifecycle

Almost all database systems grow in usage, size, and complexity. To address these issues, database systems must be properly planned, designed, and refined through a set of methods and processes. This is called the *database administration systems lifecycle*. Figure 2.1 shows the critical phases in administrating your Oracle database's lifecycle in sequential order; a more detailed description for each of the phases follows.

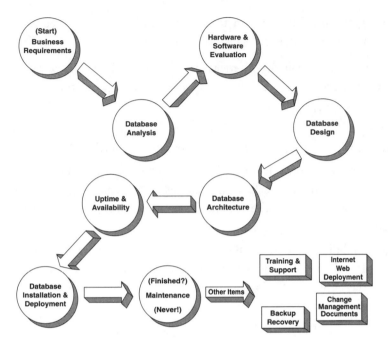

FIGURE 2.1 *Administrative phases of an Oracle database lifecycle.*

Business Requirements for a Scalable Solution

An understanding of companies' strategic business objectives is key to helping identify practical, scalable, enterprise database solutions. Without an understanding of the business you are in and how the software and database applications are used, you are caught in a never-ending downward spiral of frustration when trying to define business requirements. A well-defined and properly configured scalable database platform is one that has enough capacity to handle the application's estimated or measured workload, without bottlenecks. In other words, it is easy to throw together a database solution, but without knowing how the system will be used, it is hard to measure how *much* the system will be utilized.

Scalability is the capability of a system to grow in one or more dimensions. In the database arena, these dimensions include the amount of data accessible to the application, the number of concurrent users supported, the number of transactions processed in a given unit of time, and the breadth of functionality that the application encompasses. To fully understand and plan for scalability is to truly understand the requirements, the application, and the users who access your database.

When you are gathering information to aid in defining business requirements, consider these important database decision drivers:

◆ **Average query complexity.** A measure of how complex the average queries of your system are. The more complex the query, the longer the time needed to process it.

◆ **Expected data access response time.** Users' estimation of how much waiting time is acceptable when they perform a query or search.

◆ **Number of concurrent user queries.** A measure of the number of users on the system who are performing queries at the same time. The database must be able to handle concurrent requests and process them within a reasonable amount of time.

◆ **Data availability.** The insurance that the data is available when the users need it. In other words, does the database need to be available 24 hours a day, 7 days a week? Or is availability during normal business hours sufficient?

◆ **Security model.** What type of security is needed for the system?

◆ **Integration with other applications or systems.** Will the system need to integrate with other existing systems. If so, how?

◆ **Skill sets.** Can be a crucial element when defining your database. If the system is a simple non-mission critical database application, the skill set will be smaller than compared to a system deployed for, say, NASA.

After you have addressed these decision drivers, you are ready to consider the analysis, design, and preliminary architecture of the database.

Analysis and Design

Distributed systems are critical in delivering mission critical solutions to companies of all shapes and sizes. Because companies are so dependent upon the data and the systems on which it resides, proper analysis and design are crucial when selecting dependable and scalable database servers. To initiate the analysis process, consider compiling information from sources such as industry standard benchmark results, analyst reviews, vendor reference accounts, and results of custom in-house benchmarks. This information will assist you in making educated purchasing decisions.

A sound technical analysis and design centers on understanding the business requirements, designing the system to meet the requirements, and then making various predictions about future application use. After you gather the business requirements, you can then employ technologies to meet these requirements. The following criteria are important to consider in a distributed database architecture because they affect the analysis and design of the system:

◆ Ability to support change

◆ Ability to support growth

◆ Well-defined usage and capacity planning

◆ Elimination of data redundancy

◆ Elimination of process redundancy

◆ Price and performance

◆ Implementation and integration planning

◆ Automating the administration tasks

◆ Server, client/server, n-tier, and Web-based architectures

Now that you've established the analysis and design criteria, you are ready to discuss the database's architecture.

Hardware and Network Architecture Options

A database environment should provide a quality, high-performing system with extensibility for growth. Lack of or incorrect architecture decisions can cause one or more of the following problems:

◆ Poor performance

◆ Limited functionality

◆ High total cost of ownership

◆ Complex administration

◆ Lack of scalability

◆ Poor support

◆ Poor reliability/availability

To prevent problems like these, as well as others, be sure to address these key hardware areas:

◆ Availability of the hardware

◆ Backup technology

◆ Network bandwidth
◆ Processor technology
◆ Storage and I/O subsystems

Considering Uptime and Availability

With more and more companies depending on computer systems to run their businesses, the applications and database systems become mission-critical to the organization. The inability to access the application or the database system on which it runs translates to lost opportunity or revenue. System uptime and availability comprise a combination of process, software, and hardware issues.

Achieving dependability and availability requires effort at all phases of development. You must use risk-reduction and avoidance techniques at design time, implementation time, and execution time, as well as during the maintenance phase. The three primary techniques are as follows:

◆ **Fault avoidance.** Use of techniques and tools to minimize the introduction of *faults*, which are problems within the system.
◆ **Fault recognition and removal.** Monitoring and testing techniques to actively locate faults and quickly address their root cause.
◆ **Fault minimization.** In spite of efforts to avoid or remove them, there are bound to be faults in any system. Taking those into account and handling them with risk-assessment and fault-minimization planning can maintain operations.

A highly available database system provides substantial benefits, but can require a significant investment in terms of dollars and resources. Like any other investment, ensuring that the proper strategy and products are in place to protect those systems is the cornerstone to successfully maintaining the environment.

Installation and Deployment

For many organizations, installation and deployment can prove to be more work than anticipated. One primary reason for this is a lack of planning. To properly install or deploy Oracle requires more than just spinning a tape (after all, an organization can have Oracle on a tape, but no tape drive). Prior to installation, it's critical to perform an environmental audit and system overview. DBAs (database administrators) have lost many hours of precious installation time dealing with lack of disk space, or with performance problems caused by an overloaded system. Prior to any installation, upgrade, or deployment activity, you should review the system and connectivity environments with the appropriate team members.

 TIP

If it hasn't become obvious yet, you need to develop a project plan to detail each of these phases and to outline everyone's responsibilities. Weaving a schedule into this plan is also a great idea. You never know when management will start asking how long and how much.

Backup and Recovery

Backup and recovery are among the most critical administration tasks that you must regularly perform as part of your database administration. Creating working backups after the installation of the database usually involves a lot of initial effort, but once backups are functioning, your time is often redirected to other tasks. As a result, a majority of organizations never test or even assemble a recovery plan. Of course, this is usually realized after data has been lost, after the backup tapes are found to be blank or overwritten, or after a disaster such as a flood occurs.

Because of the importance of backup and recovery, Chapter 13, "Planning for Disaster Recovery," is dedicated to these topics.

Security

Security is a component of backup and recovery. With great security and a perfect system, backup and recovery become moot. Because the world we live in is imperfect, this is not the case. Thus, security plays an important role in administrating the database.

As the Oracle DBA, you should establish, maintain, and monitor sound database security policies and procedures. It's best to write down and adhere to these policies at all times. Careful planning during this phase will ensure better security in the future.

Change Management and Documentation

Without giving serious effort to consistent standards and procedures, your database project will decline into an indecipherable hodgepodge of various styles, techniques, and naming conventions. In addition, without documentation, you run the risk of having no one left on the team who understands the riddle of code left behind. Standards, procedures, and documentation for the database systems environment cover the following major topics:

- ◆ **OS standards and procedures.** Includes file system layouts, kernel parameters, system backup/recovery, security, performance monitoring, installation, and upgrades of the operating system.
- ◆ **Database standards and procedures.** Includes instance parameters, object sizing, storage and naming, procedures for installation and upgrades, security, and backup/recovery.
- ◆ **Applications development standards.** Includes techniques for managing change procedures, detailed coding standards including source code control, change control, naming conventions, and table/index creation.
- ◆ **Network standards and procedures.** Defines network addressing and protocols supported for database and application communication.

Of course, it's best to consider these and other similar concepts in the early planning stages and to include them in your project plan. Now is a good time to catch up on the documentation of the administration of your Oracle database. Although keeping good documentation is an afterthought on many occasions, it is definitely one of the most important things you can do to improve reliability and maintainability. Start now with documentation and continue throughout the entire lifecycle and well into maintenance by documenting problems and changes to your system.

Training and Support

Support is critical to sustaining and maintaining an Oracle database environment. Dependent upon business requirements, availability, and service level agreements, support can make or break the business. Understanding and maintaining the appropriate vendor contracts is part of database administration.

With technology and product feature updates leapfrogging every six months, you need to determine which features and upgrades map to business requirements. In order to do that, you have to have some level of understanding of the relevant features or technology. Annual Oracle training, as well as participation in user groups, can assist you in keeping abreast of issues, features, and technologies.

Training is not just for the DBA. Database users and management staff should be trained on Oracle at regular intervals so that they are better educated about the factors involved.

TIP

A good training plan will help with training and support issues. Update the plan period-ically and hold regular training sessions to keep everyone abreast of system changes.

Internet and Web Deployment

Another business driver that changes database availability and scalability require-ments is Internet access and Web deployment. More and more companies are providing Web interfaces to its applications and data. Providing a Web interface usually results in higher numbers of concurrent users and transactions per second. In addition, new functionality that might not have been planned for in the origi-nal implementation can add to the load as well.

The perception is that e-commerce will reduce costs and increase responsive-ness, thus improving overall efficiency. Partners and customers involved in the e-commerce implementation directly connect to the core business applications and expect a timely response, or business will be lost. Therefore, both e-commerce and Internet initiatives generally have a major impact on an application's system resources, making scalability extremely important.

Summary

A good overall understanding of how to administer the Oracle database lifecycle is critical to a successful and properly maintained Oracle database. For full-circle database administration, distributed database availability and scalability cannot be an afterthought. It is impossible to add scalability to an application or system that was not designed to handle the anticipated load. All components must be tightly integrated, from the computer hardware and operating system to the database software, application layer, network, and interfaces. In addition, the need for tighter integration between database applications and the database systems they support has become more apparent with data volumes, transaction volumes, and usage.

Other affected areas include response times, backup, and recovery. Especially for distributed systems, it's important that the transaction load is evenly distributed across all the processing resources in order to keep any one resource from becoming the bottleneck. For backup and recovery, it is vital that backing up the database and other data on the system has a minimal impact on the availability and throughput of your system.

Most DBAs never make it through their database's entire lifecycle, because they are too busy handling database issues. For Oracle database administration, however, you cannot just expect to install the database and have it run forever. A set of processes and tools is required to properly deploy and sustain it.

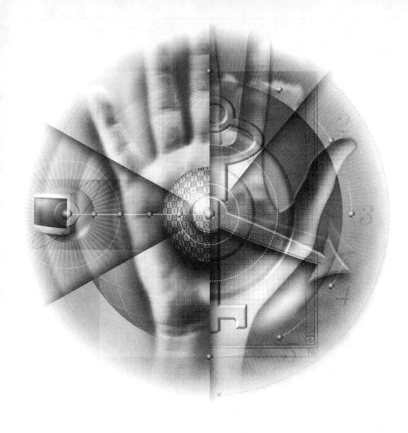

Chapter 3

**The Oracle
Database
Administrator**

An exact list of an Oracle database administrator's (DBA's) responsibilities is hard to find in print. It would be great if those responsibilities could be easily bundled into a nice package like that of an accountant or an elementary school reading teacher. However, differences among companies and the distributed enterprise has made that seemingly impossible.

The Skill Set of the DBA

The position of database administrator seems to mean different things to different organizations. The duties of the DBA in smaller organizations are much broader than in major corporations. Whether a company is performing development or using third-party packages will further define the role of the DBA. Knowing what is expected of the role and how the position fits within the company's business operations are critical.

An important factor to defining the DBA's role and responsibilities is ensuring there is an infrastructure in place to support existing and new business processes. For most organizations, confusion arises when the skills of the IT staff overlap without a clear delineation of responsibility. To be most productive, the skills of the staff should intersect with the responsibilities being clearly defined. It is important to define, establish, and communicate these roles and responsibilities to all parties involved.

What a DBA Is Not: Other Responsible Parties

Many jobs outside the role of DBA, but within the IT team, empower the DBA to be fully effective in the job:

- ◆ System administrator
- ◆ Network administrator
- ◆ Desktop administrator
- ◆ Developer
- ◆ Application administrator
- ◆ Business analyst

System Administrator

The system administrator is responsible for server maintenance and configuration. This administrator installs, upgrades, and tunes the operating system. Responsibility for implementing the backup and recovery plan falls into system administration, as does the development and implementation of a disaster recovery plan. The system administrator works closely with the DBA and the network administrator.

Network Administrator

The network administrator is responsible for the network architecture, as well as for the maintenance, performance, and monitoring of the network. The network administrator works closely with the DBA, system administrator, and desktop administrator.

Desktop Administrator

The desktop administrator is responsible for the PC network at the workgroup level, for setting standards for LAN software and hardware, and for testing and configuring the network software on the client and fileservers. The desktop administrator maintains fileservers and terminal servers, and troubleshoots PC and LAN issues. The desktop administrator works closely with the system administrator, DBA, and network administrator.

Developer

The development staff is responsible for the design and creation of the various programs making up the business application. Developers should be familiar with forms, PL/SQL, fourth-generation languages (4GL), and client/server development. Developers work closely with the business analyst, the application administrator, and the application DBA (you'll learn about the application DBA later in this chapter).

Application Administrator

The application administrator has in-depth knowledge of the use of the applications. The application administrator is responsible for the configuration of the application from the users' viewpoint, enrolling users, and troubleshooting problems for the help desk. The application administrator works closely with the business analyst, developer, DBA, and desktop administrator.

Business Analyst

The business analyst is responsible for implementing the applications and facilitating any transition required from legacy systems. The business analyst has in-depth knowledge of the business functions of the corporation and other areas of the system. The business analyst works with the project managers, developer, users, and application administrators.

What a DBA Is: Traits and Responsibilities

Qualifications for the role of DBA are quite diverse. The DBA must possess technical knowledge in the interpretation of database design models. The DBA must also possess a knowledge of the company's security, data-retention, and disaster-recovery requirements. Knowledge of the database performance and administration requirements of the application systems is also required. Business skills such as multitasking, analytical thinking, active listening, and effective oral and written communication are significant requirements, as are technical skills in operating systems, networking, and database-management software. A DBA should be familiar with the software tools and languages used by the organization that interact with Oracle. A DBA must also have an understanding of tools used to test, monitor, tune, and administer the company databases.

In the mainframe environment of old, the typical duties of a DBA consisted of talking with a few analysts supporting a single operating system, along with a few programmers who supported the transaction processing applications. In a distributed open systems environment, the role of the DBA is expanded by various operating systems and applications, combined with a greater number and diversity of people. A typical DBA must deal each day with groups in many functional areas, including network management, systems management, training, and application development. DBAs must be knowledgeable enough to determine where in the system a problem actually occurs. DBAs should assist with incorporating consistent adherence to standards and naming conventions. Not having standards and procedures leaves a project more susceptible to security risks and confusion.

Responsibilities are numerous when a DBA is involved. The following are some of the basic responsibilities:

◆ **Architecture.** The DBA must be familiar with sizing, file placement, and specification of storage media. Expertise in Redundant Arrays of Independent Disk Drives, or RAID, fail over, networking, disk shadowing, solid state disks, and their application to the Oracle database environment are important. The DBA needs to be familiar with installation and updates for the database server platform. For the Unix operating system, DBAs should be familiar with the drawbacks and benefits associated with use of raw devices.

♦ **Availability and maintenance.** One of the jobs of a DBA is monitoring and tuning the database. Monitoring and tuning requires a detailed understanding of the architecture of Oracle.

♦ **Backup and recovery.** A DBA must understand all the backup and recovery options, including use of the Import and Export utilities, and cold and hot backups. Recovery scenarios are subject matter that a DBA must understand.

♦ **Business processes and requirements.** A DBA should possess a sound understanding of business requirements and how they map to database methods and systems.

♦ **Security.** An understanding of Oracle security is critical to the DBA role. Knowledge of roles, profiles, system design, and object-level privileges is essential for a DBA. In addition, understanding how the operating system security interacts with Oracle is equally important.

Many organizations tend to concentrate on technical knowledge and overlook personal skills. Like most IT roles, the role of the DBA is customer-service oriented. The DBA has to interface with a variety of people—users, developers, administrators, vendors, and managers. Consequently, these traits should be considered when filling the DBA role:

♦ Communication skills

♦ Confidence

♦ Curiosity

♦ Attention to detail

♦ Determination

Critical Factors for Success

There are several factors that are critical for success in the DBA role:

♦ **Adaptability.** Configuring systems and software as business needs dictate while maintaining the production environment and servicing the user community (not an easy task without an Oracle crystal ball).

◆ **Availability.** DBAs must be prepared to respond rapidly to issues. Here again the Oracle crystal ball would help, but with proper monitoring of the database, a DBA is more prepared to respond to potential problems.

◆ **Control.** DBAs must be in control of the database and data at all times. Controlling the metadata (metadata is data about data), the data definition process, and access to the database are key points.

◆ **Tools.** Probably the most important factor in determining a successful DBA is the DBA's tools and the knowledge to use them. Without proper tools to implement and maintain the database, a DBA might be overwhelmed with no hope to control the database. With proper tools, a DBA can be available, can adapt to database changes, and can take control.

Demands on DBAs

Many demands are placed on DBAs, as follows:

◆ According to a recent *Computerworld* survey, the average information technology professional works over 50 hours per week.

◆ Over half of the surveyed IT workers said they "occasionally" miss getting home for dinner, with 28 percent saying "frequently."

◆ Almost half work an average of six hours on Saturdays and Sundays and said they work while on vacation. Also, 61 percent of IT professionals interrupt their vacations to check on things at work, with 25 percent of them bringing along a laptop computer, pager, or cellular phone to stay in touch with the office.

Types of Oracle DBAs

As the scope, size, and complexity of systems expand, the DBA role can be into several areas of responsibility, called specialties. In smaller organizations, this might not be necessary, but in larger organizations, DBAs tend to occupy areas of specialty.

Database Operator

The database operator manually monitors the database console, tape mounting, and critical jobs. The database operator verifies that backup or archives ran correctly, restarts the backup or archives if necessary, and monitors the available space in the backup and archive directories. The database operator can be supported by existing staff or filled using a third-party tool.

System DBA

The system DBA's role is critical for the initial database architecture, for new projects or application upgrade analysis, and for capacity planning. A system DBA not only has experience with Oracle and advanced features such as replication, parallel servers, and partitioning, but also has a background in system and network architecture. Without a system DBA, many organizations find themselves against a wall with I/O, performance, storage management, backup, and capacity problems.

Application DBA

The application DBA provides database modeling support and development of the logical database. The application DBA develops applications architecture, performs SQL tuning, and supports the applications. The application DBA works closely with developers, the system DBA, and business analysts.

Fundamental Practices of DBAs

These fundamental practices are required of all DBAs:

- ◆ **Identify the root cause of the problem, resolve database problems, and develop methods for preventing the problem.** This involves the following:
  - Reviewing databases on a periodic basis with developers, users, and management to detect system or operational problems.
  - Coordinating on a timely basis to resolve current problems.
  - Implementing and maintaining methods and procedures for monitoring and maintaining database systems.

- ◆ **Maintain and improve technical skills, environment knowledge, and application knowledge.** This involves the following:
  - Identifying areas that need improvement and attending training as directed.
  - Reviewing available Web sources or trade publications.

- Reviewing existing applications by studying documentation and through discussions with application developers.

- Developing a knowledge base of the database, environment, and associated software.

- Assisting with support for all application development.

- Reviewing reports/logs/dumps and other data and recommending corrective actions to maintain database performance and efficiency.

- Coordinating performance and tuning actions with database developers.

◆ **Review and evaluate status of assigned projects and their impact upon the database systems.** This involves the following:

- Monitoring project progress and discussing major problems with other analysts and management.

- When discovered, resolving delays affecting project completion.

- Providing status reports to management.

- Conducting database walkthroughs with programmers, analysts, and users prior to finalization of major recommendations.

- Reviewing databases thoroughly before recommending new systems or system changes.

◆ **Provide user support through meetings, presentations, and documentation.** This involves the following:

- Establishing and maintaining effective communication with the user community.

- Participating actively in meetings with staff and users, and demonstrating the ability to interpret user needs.

◆ **Prepare and review database specifications, including testing and controls.** This involves the following:

- Reviewing database recommendations thoroughly with users and management, and resolving problems or differences before final recommendations are made.

- Studying new database design principles, and developing knowledge of database principles by applying them in projects.

- Gathering information from users and staff when required by project tasks, to be evaluated by supervisors through review of work, discussion with users, and review with other analysts.

◆ **Prepare budgets and planning documents, and maintain service contracts.**
This involves the following:

- Preparing requested material for the fiscal year and other requested material by stated deadlines.

- Designing, creating, and maintaining physical and logical databases.

- Participating in logical model design or walkthroughs of the logical model design to gain an understanding of it. Presenting physical implementation concerns to the design teams and management.

- Creating physical databases using sound design principles including documentation of the creation and access procedures.

- Creating, testing, and monitoring backup procedures for the physical or logical databases.

- Maintaining the physical database by monitoring and recommending changes as needed to management. Creating quarterly reports of physical storage needs, memory requirements, and database upgrades projected for a two-year time span.

What Type of DBA Is Required in Your Organization?

A DBA's skill set ranges from operators to senior system or application DBAs. With all these choices, you might find yourself wondering what type of DBA, and how many, you need. If an experienced DBA is hired only to monitor Oracle and to ensure the completion of backups and jobs, such a person might become bored and leave. On the other hand, if you hire a single DBA to administer not only the databases, but the systems and applications for the 20 or more servers, burn-out is eminent.

If your organization simply requires an additional person to monitor a database application using a monitoring tool and to react when the tool reports a problem, it's best to employ a junior DBA or to outsource the function. A person whose resume is full of Oracle projects, most involving third-party applications with Oracle installed as the back-end repository, makes a good junior DBA. Junior DBAs are too inexperienced to address recovery issues or database internals, but are competent when monitoring database health.

A more senior individual might be needed to participate fully in the company's IT lifecycle. A senior DBA will have the broad range of skills needed to map to business operations and architectures. The senior DBA can focus entirely on one subject matter such as performance tuning, whereas another team member can be responsible for backups and recovery.

Top 99 Responsibilities of a DBA

The following outline is a comprehensive listing of the DBA's responsibilities. The intent is not to assign every one of these responsibilities to the role of the DBA, but to allow an organization to choose and staff only the activities that fit its business requirements.

Database Architecture Duties

1. Planning for the database's future storage requirements
2. Defining database availability and fault management architecture
3. Defining and creating environments for development and new release installation
4. Creating physical database storage structures after developers have designed an application
5. Constructing the database
6. Determining and setting the size and physical locations of datafiles
7. Evaluating new hardware and software purchases
8. Researching, testing, and recommending tools for Oracle development, modeling, database administration, and backup and recovery implementation, as well as planning for the future
9. Providing database design and implementation
10. Understanding and employing the optimal flexible architecture to ease administration, allow flexibility in managing I/O, and to increase the capability to scale the system
11. Working with application developers to determine and define proper partitioning

Backup and Recovery

12. Determining and implementing the backup/recovery plan for each database while in development and as the application moves through test and onto production
13. Establishing and maintaining sound backup and recovery policies and procedures

14. Having knowledge and practice of Oracle backup and recovery scenarios

15. Performing Oracle cold backups when the database is shut down to ensure consistency of the data

16. Performing Oracle hot backups while the database is operational

17. Performing Oracle import/export as a method of recovering data or individual objects

18. Providing retention of data to satisfy legal responsibilities of the company

19. Restoring database services for disaster recovery

20. Recovering the database in the event of a hardware or software failure

21. Using partitioning and transportable tablespaces to reduce downtime, when appropriate

Maintenance and Daily Tasks

22. Providing adjustment and configuration management of INIT.ORA parameters

23. Adjusting extent size of rapidly growing tables and indexes

24. Administering database-management software and related utilities

25. Automating database startup and shutdown

26. Automating repetitive operations

27. Determining and setting critical thresholds for disks, tablespaces, extents, and fragmentation

28. Enrolling new users while maintaining system security

29. Filtering database alarm and alert information

30. Installing, configuring, and upgrading Oracle server software and related products installation

31. Logging Technical Action Reports (TARs); applying patches

32. Maintaining the "Database Administrator's Handbook"

33. Maintaining an ongoing configuration for database links to other databases

34. Maintaining archived Oracle data

35. Managing contractual agreements with providers of database-management software

36. Managing service level agreements with Oracle consultants or vendors
37. Monitoring and advising management on licensing issues while ensuring compliance with Oracle license agreements
38. Monitoring and coordinating the update of the database recovery plan with the site's disaster recovery plan
39. Monitoring and optimizing the performance of the database
40. Monitoring rollback segment and temporary tablespace use
41. Monitoring the status of database instances
42. Performing "housecleaning" tasks as required; purging old files from the Oracle database
43. Performing database troubleshooting
44. Performing modifications of the database structure from information provided by application developers
45. Performing monthly and annual performance reports for trend analysis and capacity planning
46. Installing new and maintaining existing client configurations
47. Performing ongoing configuration management
48. Performing ongoing Oracle security management
49. Performing routine audits of user and developer accounts
50. Performing translation of developer modeled designs for managing data into physical implementation
51. Performing correlation of database errors, alerts, and events
52. Planning and coordinating the testing of the new database, software, and application releases
53. Providing a focal point on calls to Oracle for technical support
54. Working as part of a team and providing 24×7 support when required

Methodology and Business Process

55. Coordinating and executing database upgrades
56. Coordinating upgrades of system software products to resolve any Oracle/operating system issues/conflicts
57. Creating error and alert processes and procedures

58. Creating standard entry formats for SQLNet files

59. Creating processes and procedures for functional and stress testing of database applications

60. Creating processes and procedures of application transport from DEV, to TEST, to PROD

61. Defining and maintaining database standards for the organization to ensure consistency in database creation

62. Defining database standards and procedures to cover the instance parameters, object sizing, storage, and naming. The procedures define the process for install/upgrade, corporate database requirements, security, backup/recovery, applications environment, source code control, change control, naming conventions, and table/index creation.

63. Defining the database service levels necessary for application availability

64. Defining methodology tasks for database software integration

65. Defining a methodology for developing and improving business applications

66. Creating a process to determine whether a new release is "stable" enough to be placed on the development system

67. Developing data-conversion processes for customization, testing, and production

68. Developing database test plans

69. Developing database administration procedures and responsibilities for production systems

70. Developing production migration procedures

71. Establishing and providing schema definitions, as well as tablespace, table, constraint, trigger, package, procedure, and index naming conventions

72. Facilitating design sessions for requirements gathering and defining system requirements

73. Providing database problem reporting, management, and resolution

74. Providing final approval for all technical architecture components that manage and exchange data, including database management software, server hardware, data distribution management software, transaction processing monitors, and connecting client applications software

75. Providing processes for the setup of new database environments

76. Providing risk and impact analysis of maintenance or new releases of code

77. Providing standards and methods for database software purchasing

78. Providing standards and naming conventions

79. Handling multiple projects and deadlines

Education and Training

80. Attending training classes and user group conferences

81. Evaluating Oracle features and Oracle-related products

82. Understanding the Oracle database, related utilities, and tools

83. Understanding the underlying operating system as well as the design of the physical database

84. Understanding Oracle data integrity

85. Knowing the organization's applications and how they map to the business requirements

86. Knowing how Oracle acquires and manages resources

87. Knowing enough about the Oracle tools' normal functional behavior to be able to determine whether a problem lies with the tool or the database

88. Possessing sound knowledge in database and system performance tuning

89. Providing in-house technical consulting and training

90. Staying abreast of the most current releases of Oracle software and compatibility issues

91. Subscribing to database trade journals and Web sources

Communication

92. Interfacing with vendors

93. Disseminating Oracle information to the developers, users, and staff

94. Training application developers to understand and use Oracle concepts, techniques, and tools that model and access managed data

95. Assisting developers with database-design issues and problem resolution, including how to run and understand the output from both TKProf and the Explain Plan utilities

96. Training interim DBAs and junior-level DBAs

Documentation

97. Creating and maintaining a database operations handbook for frequently performed tasks

98. Defining standards for database documentation

99. Creating documentation of the database environment

Summary

It is so easy for a DBA to become overwhelmed with tasks for which they were unprepared. The DBA must always be prepared to promptly address issues and requests. With the rate of technology changing every six months, DBAs need to be trained often. Oracle training is not effective if attended all at once. A DBA's training has to occur prior to installation of the hardware, database, or applications. To stay proficient, the DBA has to practice and refine those skills learned in training.

This chapter has presented a comprehensive set of tasks that a DBA can perform within a company. Tasks unique to a company's environment might not be listed in this chapter. In addition, there are tasks mentioned in this chapter that might be assigned to another job role. In either case, it is important that the tasks are performed by someone.

When examining a DBA's tasks, there are normally two perspectives: an applications perspective, and a systems perspective. An application DBA works closely with the developers and users of the application, and places emphasis on application optimization. A systems DBA is more involved at the hardware level, looking at I/O, system, and network database performance issues, backups and recovery, and technologies such as parallel server and replication. Both types of Oracle DBAs are critical to the success of implementing and maintaining your company's Oracle database.

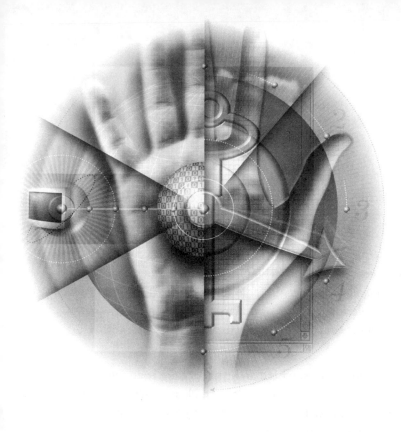

Chapter 4

**Understanding
Oracle Licenses**

Most companies understand physical information-system asset-management concepts such as servers, desktops, network equipment, and other hardware-related items. In most cases, software licenses for the systems and the applications that run on that equipment are not effectively managed or understood as business assets. Software licenses comprise a significant portion of a company's assets that managers are responsible and accountable for. It is not uncommon for an organization to be responsible for millions of dollars of hardware, software, or both. In addition, annual support and maintenance usually tacks on another 20 percent annually.

Unlike physical assets, such as computers, where an inventory tag is attached and inventoried each year, software is much more difficult to track and manage. Additional complexity occurs in decentralized organizations that have no standards or communications between groups. In many cases, a company has one group responsible for the hardware assets. With software assets, however, there can be hundreds of people responsible for purchasing and maintaining them.

This chapter helps you understand more about software licenses and, in particular, Oracle's way of licensing. The first part of this chapter focuses on the management, administration, challenges, and costs associated with software licenses. The next part explores areas related to software audits, hoarding, gauging peak demand, and service-level agreements. Finally, the remainder of this chapter guides you through Oracle's licensing process.

Managing the License Process

Software-asset management is defined as the processes, policies, and technologies established for the procurement, deployment, administration, and management of network, client, or server assets. Even if companies apply standard asset-management practices—lifecycle planning, tracking, budgeting, and procurement—there still may be more to invest to ensure proper management of the software. Distributed client/server, multitier, and heterogeneous computing environments add complexity to license management. When taking a closer look at software assets, many companies have discovered that their software assets exceed their hardware assets.

The four key ingredients of license management are as follows:

◆ **Audit readiness and audit exposure.** This is the dreaded software audits that companies talk about. Be ready to prove you have properly licensed your software for the number of users using the software.

◆ **Software asset investment.** This is the investment made in software purchases. This can be a very large company asset.

◆ **Cost effective license reuse.** If possible, try to be efficient when re-issuing software licenses. There is more about this topic later in this chapter.

◆ **User satisfaction.** Don't license software that your users don't use. Satisfy your user by licensing the appropriate software.

Challenges Associated with Licensing Software

Having a clear understanding of license agreements, how a company has deployed software, and how a company uses the software is the only way to establish accurate counts of the installed software base. However, determining the license baseline is only half the work. Proper license management requires usage and trend data to facilitate the planning, budgeting, and acquisition of software. Analyzing license use and interpreting the data can be complicated, but it is the only way to properly determine whether an organization has properly licensed and deployed software.

Managing software is challenging for most organizations because of these factors:

◆ Software is replenished and updated at a faster rate than any other fixed company asset.

◆ Software is intangible and is easily copied across networks.

◆ Software is everywhere and is more broadly distributed than any other type of asset.

Costs Associated with Licensing Software

The Gartner Group addresses software license management within a Total Cost of Ownership (TCO) model. TCO addresses the hard and soft costs, or the initial and the continual costs, associated within a distributed network-computing environment. TCO focuses on operating costs versus Return On Investment (ROI). The TCO model focuses on costs attributed to four main areas:

◆ **Capital.** The initial investment of your software.

◆ **Support.** The cost to support your software (upgrades, new versions, and so on).

◆ **Administration.** Similar to support, but deals with the cost related to the administration of the software, including the costs to pay the administrator.

◆ **End users.** The cost to license users.

The majority of software costs can be grouped into six categories:

◆ **Time of use.** When the licenses are being used.

◆ **Initial license cost.** The initial contract price and quantity.

◆ **Update and maintenance fees.** Software bug fixes, updates, and upgrades.

◆ **Support contracts.** Product technical support services.

◆ **License administration.** Designating someone to the role of software administration, the systems and processes that are in place, and the time it takes to track the licenses.

◆ **Yearly budget reviews.** Review of licenses in use, reordering, and reallocation for planned projects.

Software continues to have costs after the initial purchase with items such as support and version upgrades. Software license administration includes soft costs such as the frequency of purchases, report analysis, and the software order placement. Many organizations routinely pay annual software fees without reviewing or auditing their existing inventory. In many instances, the software may not even be in use. Abandoned licenses might even hold a value when used as a trade-in or as a competitive upgrade. All these and more are reasons enough for companies to spend a little more time and money getting a handle on their software assets.

Administering Software Licenses

The majority of software licensing issues and costs can be grouped into nine categories:

◆ **License compliance.** The costs of managing and limiting software licensing from a legal standpoint.

◆ **Software tracking.** The costs associated with tracking purchased licenses, trial licenses, licenses in use, and available unused licenses.

◆ **Software licensing accounting methods.** Designating software as an expense instead of a capitalized asset leads to software being forgotten or lost. With capitalized assets, the asset is inventoried, tracked, depreciated, and eventually written off.

◆ **Software deployment delays.** Costs incurred while waiting for software. Without electronic distribution, or Right-To-Copy media duplication, there can be a considerable time between the initial software purchase and deployment. Of course these questions can be answered ahead of time with proper software licensing management.

◆ **Lost licenses and software salvaging.** Costs due to repurchasing licenses that can't be located. Lost licenses occur due to inadequate tracking or lack of software reclamation when an employee, department, or business reorganizes or leaves. Lost licenses can be attributed to:

  • Same software licensing but from different vendors

  • Licenses personally expensed by employees that are not reported to the company

  • Bundled software packages

  • Illegally copied software

  • Licenses from acquisitions and reorganizations within companies

◆ **Lack of communication across organizations.** Costs incurred because of duplication, no standardization, or no software reuse within a company. Within the typical decentralized organization, many versions, vendors, and products are more costly to support. This has always been a problem, and until more software-management processes are in place, as well as basic communication protocols, this cost will continue to hamper big businesses.

◆ **Contract confusion.** Costs incurred when companies don't utilize existing volume purchase agreements because of complexity or lack of communication.

◆ **Bundled licenses.** Costs of handling bundled licensing specials. Additive costs can be associated with the lack of communicating bundled licensing specials.

◆ **Software vendors.** Costs incurred when vendors change or alter licensing schemes from release to release. Normally these are encountered during an update or upgrade for the software.

Auditing Software Licenses

The need for a software audit is often a sign that software license management is lacking. After an audit takes place, companies usually implement a process and a baseline for software license management. Companies with a process or baseline already in place prior to an external audit typically fare better because of their due diligence. External audits of companies with unauthorized software and no software licensing management practices have sometimes lead to penalties totaling millions of dollars.

For most organizations, internal software audits can assist in establishing an initial software baseline. It is easy to lose track of software that has already been purchased.

There are several software process improvement models. If your company wants to avoid high penalties, you should look hard into establishing stricter guidelines and processes for controlling software and tracking the licenses. For more information, look for software process improvement models such as the Compatibility Maturity Model (CMM) or ISO 9000. Both of these processes have software configuration models to help you track and audit your software.

Gauging Peak Demand

With tightening budgets and the risks associated with audits, companies are paying closer attention to their software assets. After looking more closely at the licensing issue, many companies find that they are using out-of-date metrics and license numbers. Whether software assets are insufficient or in excess, both are costly to the bottom line.

A good rule of thumb is to have at least 90 percent of your licenses in use. More than 95 percent can lead to user dissatisfaction, and fewer than 90 percent can be wasteful. Purchasing licenses based on peak demand can lead to idle assets, whereas under-licensing can foster license contention or liability. Typically, companies should license for average use.

To measure use, companies must look at how their licenses are being used. Desktop or client licenses are usually interactive, whereas server-based licenses are normally CPU intensive. For a majority of interactive applications, the application server performance has minimal effect on the work accomplished over a specific period of time. For these types of applications, concurrent usage is primarily independent of processor performance.

For computer-intensive server-based applications, processor performance significantly affects the amount of work accomplished in a period of time. Many software vendors sell their products on a user concurrency basis, but the cost changes based on the system size and performance. Consequently, you should consider the tradeoffs between performance, concurrency, and cost.

Many companies are considering "network" or "floating" licenses. These licenses require a greater level of administration. Without usage metrics or trends, it is difficult to determine the number of licenses required. The key to appropriate metric selection is in choosing the metric that approximates the work accomplished during the period of time that the software is used.

If current license use is high, consider software leveling, which involves tracking the number of true users, before purchasing new licenses. A quick internal company audit might yield employees who do not exit out of applications, thus depleting precious resources. A "following the sun" methodology uses unused licenses by time zone or country regions. In a network or floating license, time of use becomes important. If normal system processing is 8a.m. to 5p.m. in the United States, it might be possible to use existing licenses for overseas use.

Hoarding Licenses

In many decentralized organizations, licenses are stashed or hoarded. Even when a project has been completed, a group holds on to unused licenses in expectation of another project that might require the licensed software. Consequently, another group that could have reused those licenses is now forced to purchase additional licenses. Obviously, this is not cost effective. Hoarding is minimized through data collection, reporting, and centralized budgeting practices.

A good practice that might help prevent hoarding is to include a plan to turn in the software licenses once the project ends. Also, the project plan should list the required software licenses (during the planning phase perhaps), and these issues should be resolved before the software is needed.

Leveraging and Standardization

Managing and leveraging licenses across an enterprise can yield significant savings but can be difficult to organize. Within a centralized organization, leveraging and utilization is usually easier than within decentralized organizations. A centralized organization typically has a baseline of approved products along with a standard set of policies and procedures. However, within a centralized organization, departments sometimes have little or no input as to what or how software is licensed.

It is not uncommon for one part of an organization to have a decline in the use of a product while another part of the organization sees an increase. However, it requires proper license management to rotate or share licenses within a company. Within a decentralized organization, sharing is discouraged because of departmental budgets and hoarding. A decentralized organization typically purchases licenses from many department budgets. By doing so, license sharing is viewed as having no benefit as one department bears the burden of the license purchase and depreciation, whereas the other department shares the license without sharing the cost.

Whether centralized or decentralized, companies can significantly improve their license management through application standardization. Significant costs can be associated with a custom application solution, whereas an "off the shelf" product can be better leveraged. In addition, considerable time and effort is expended to manage hundreds of products from many developers and vendors. A common example of this is the word processor. It makes economical sense for a company to dictate that everyone in the company use the same word processor. Many employees might be accustomed to using another word-processing program, but with a little "on the job training," eventually everyone will adjust. This one standardization can save a big company thousands, if not millions, of dollars in software licensing costs and administration.

Effective license management requires accurate and meaningful data. Proper data analysis assists in quick, effective business decisions. Reliable data assists in making the decisions and tradeoffs in purchasing additional software licenses, updates, or support, as well as maximizing the value received from the software investment. Effective license management also minimizes the staff time required to manage software assets and improves accountability of software costs.

A license management framework should minimally consist of:

◆ Software storage, retrieval, check-out, and check-in procedures

◆ Compliance reporting, which ensures that the licenses are up-to-date

◆ License request reporting

◆ License usage reporting

◆ Used and new software license tracking

Obtaining and Managing Licenses

In many companies, a technical professional will place a purchase order or make a request for software, at which point the request is forwarded to a buyer or supply-management department. These personnel then try to get the product for the best price and terms. Most often, to get the best price, the vendor requests additional information about how the product will be used and on what systems. However, most procurement organizations are not technical, and need to call upon the original requester for this information. In complicated distributed architectures, it is not uncommon for the procurement specialists to throw their hands up and the technical professional to then become involved to finish the negotiation. If this happens enough, technical professionals might decide to perform the majority of the negotiation and procurement themselves, leaving the final dotted line signature to the procurement specialists.

There are many that believe the work is done after the software is installed. With most software products, there is normally a maintenance or support contract to administer. This contract has to be budgeted, reviewed, and renewed, most often annually. Many companies leave this up to the procurement specialist or contracts organization. Like the initial purchase negotiation, most of these people are not technical, and need to refer to the original requester each year. In other companies, the systems administrator or DBA must administer those contracts. What happens to that knowledge base and those contracts after that individual leaves? This again is why documentation is so important. Instead of having a few individuals who have and understand this information, spread the wealth. One of the best ways to do this is to write it down.

Using Service-Level Agreements

How can companies gauge whether their software is meeting expectations? A service level agreement (SLA) is a document that defines measures of expectations, quality, performance levels, and the roles and responsibilities of all personnel involved with the software. An SLA is a contract between all involved parties to meet an agreed-upon set of expectations.

A key factor to using an SLA is the sponsor. The role of the sponsor should be well-defined, because interpretation of the SLA is not only technical but also political. As such, the SLA sponsor needs to be empowered to make key business decisions.

In order for SLAs to be truly effective, there needs be a feedback mechanism for problems and issues. Without such a mechanism, vendors might not get a chance to address the root of the problem before their product is thrown out. A good way to implement a feedback mechanism is to use a software tracking database that is reviewed weekly for problem areas. These areas can then be assigned to the appropriate parties as action items to ensure that the problems and issues are resolved.

Licensing Oracle's RDBMS

Primarily based upon the number of concurrent users, Oracle RDBMS licensing is fairly straightforward in smaller to midsized installations. Concurrency can be primarily gauged from the *license high watermark*, which is the maximum number of known users. However, in large corporate, multitier, or Web-enabled environments, the database license high watermark becomes meaningless. In many of those cases, it is best to meet with an Oracle representative for clarification on your company's specific licensing needs.

To give you a sense of how Oracle licenses are handled, the next two sections cover types of Oracle licenses and the licensing options you have.

Types of Oracle Licenses

There are many types of Oracle licenses. This section will help you understand some of these areas and allow you to pick the best one for your circumstances.

Oracle Application Licensing

Licensing of Oracle applications is primarily based upon the number of concurrent users. In most instances, one user equals one application license. It is not common for Oracle applications to be based upon named users (you'll learn more about named users in a bit). Because Oracle application products use the Oracle RDBMS as well, you need to take application use into account when considering RDBMS license concurrency.

Oracle Development Tools Licensing

Licenses for Oracle tools such as Designer 2000 or Developer 2000 are primarily based on the number of developers. In most instances, one developer equates to one tool license. But if the tool in question uses the Oracle RDBMS as well, you need to consider that use in your RDBMS license concurrency.

 TIP

After you purchase the appropriate number of concurrent Oracle licenses, replace the default value of 0 for LICENSE_MAX_USERS in the Initialization Parameter file of your Oracle database with this number. Use the Instance Manager to find your instance and scroll down in the list of Initialization Parameters until you find this parameter, as shown in Figure 4.1.

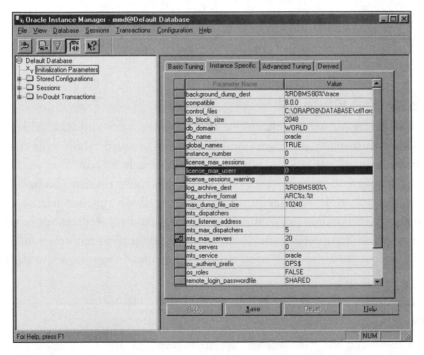

FIGURE 4.1 *Initialization parameters in Windows NT/2000 Instance Manager. Be sure to change the* LICENSE_MAX_USE *parameter to the appropriate number of users.*

Oracle Database Administration Tools Licensing

Licensing Oracle Enterprise Manager administration tools is no different from licensing other tools. Despite what you might have heard, Oracle Enterprise Manager (OEM) is not free, and is available in different configurations. OEM is licensed based upon RDBMS concurrency as well as any additional OEM modules purchased.

Oracle Web-Enablement Licensing

In multitier and Web-enabled environments, licensing can become quite complicated. Depending on how the RDBMS data is Web-enabled, additional licensing can cost thousands of dollars. If you use Oracle to generate applications that are deployed or accessed from your company's intranet browser, you can accrue additional deployment licensing costs. If you enable the RDBMS data using Java tools or as an Oracle Forms application, no additional licensing is required from the end users, but remember the initial development tools require a development license.

Oracle uses the Universal Power Unit (UPU) method (described later in this chapter) when Oracle tools are used for Internet or e-commerce purposes. For large Internet or e-commerce projects, contact Oracle for information about custom licensing schedules.

Third-Party Licensing

Many third-party software packages use Oracle as the back-end RDBMS. When purchasing a third-party package, you not only need to understand how the software application is licensed, but understand the Oracle RDBMS as well. Most often, the software application is bundled with an Oracle runtime license or sold with a full Oracle RDBMS license. An Oracle RDBMS runtime license can be used only with its bundled application and schema. Adding applications or objects or performing ad hoc queries outside the bundled application requires a full-usage RDBMS license. In either scenario, you should be clear about how the RDBMS is supported.

Support Contracts

In many instances, the first year of support is bundled into the software license. But thereafter, each software product is usually billed annually at approximately 20 to 50 percent of the original purchase price.

In many companies, support contracts are handled by accounts-payable or supply-management personnel. However, without a technical liaison, those folks might become out of touch with ever-changing software usage, and might continue to pay support on unused licenses. Centralized organizations that can pool vendor support contracts to better leverage and negotiate annual support contracts have the advantage.

For proper contract implementation and deployment to occur, there must be focused processes, sufficient resources, and ongoing training.

Oracle Customer Support Identifier (CSI) Consolidation

For many small to midsized companies, CSI consolidation doesn't necessarily apply. However, in larger companies, especially ones going through acquisitions, CSI consolidation can help you get a handle on software assets. Having hundreds or even thousands of Oracle CSIs can prove unmanageable. It is usually the best strategy to use one CSI per platform with a clearly identified primary and secondary technical contact.

Oracle's Licensing Options

At this time, Oracle's pricing is based on where the products will reside and how they will be used. Beyond the initial purchase, the burden of license management rests on the company that purchased the product. A thorough understanding of Oracle licensing and a good Oracle licensing contact can be the key to effective Oracle license management. Oracle offers custom licensing solutions as well as these licensing options:

- ◆ Named users (single server and multiserver)
- ◆ Universal Power Unit (UPU)
- ◆ Trial licenses
- ◆ Network licenses
- ◆ Site licenses

Named User—Single Server or Multiple Servers

In this case, individual users, authorized by the program developer, can use the programs installed on a single server, regardless of whether the individuals are actively using the program(s) at any given time. An automated device, such as a nightly automated backup program on the Oracle server, is also counted as a named user if the device can access the programs. If you use multiplexing hardware or software (for example, a TP monitor or a Web server product), you must measure the number of named users at the multiplexing front end.

Universal Power Unit (UPU)

In this type of licensing, one license is required for each unit of platform-dependent processing power you have. To determine the number of UPUs required for each Intel/CISC or Intel/CISC-compatible processor, multiply the total number of MHz on which the programs run by 1.0. (This type of platform is the base platform, therefore these machines' base number is 1.0.)

To determine the number of UPUs required for each RISC or RISC-compatible processor (including Intel/RISC), multiply the total number of MHz on which the programs run by 1.5. To determine the number of UPUs required in a mainframe environment, multiply the total number of MIPS, or machine instructions per second, on which the programs run by 24. You then add the number of UPUs for all your computers to determine your total. Programs licensed on a UPU basis can be accessed by your internal users and by third-party users through Internet networking protocols.

The following examples help clarify the UPU method for calculating licenses.

Example 1

You are licensing the Oracle8i Enterprise Edition for a computer containing two 400MHz RISC processors. How many UPUs do you need?

> 1 computer × 2 processors × 400MHz × 1.5 (RISC factor) = 1,200 UPUs for each program that you license for this computer

Example 2

You are licensing Oracle8i Enterprise Edition for your entire environment. It is composed of four Intel computers, each with a 550MHz Intel processor, and one computer with eight 400MHz RISC processors. How many UPUs do you need?

> 4 computers × 1 processor × 500MHz × 1.0 (Intel factor) = 2,200 UPU
>
> 1 computer × 8 processors × 400MHz × 1.5 (RISC factor) = 4,800 UPU
>
> 2,200 UPU + 4,800 UPU = 7,000 UPUs to cover all needed licenses

Example 3

You have a mainframe computer that has 200 MIPS and are licensing Oracle8i Enterprise Edition. How many UPUs do you need?

1 computer × 200 MIPS × 24 (mainframe factor) = 4,800 UPUs to cover all needed licenses

Trial Licenses

Trial licenses allow you to evaluate Oracle software programs for a 30-day period, commencing on the delivery date. If the developers or DBAs decide to use any of the programs after the 30-day trial period, they must obtain a non-trial license for each program. No technical support or warranties are provided for the programs during the 30-day period.

Network Licenses

After acquiring Oracle licenses over a period of time, you will find that your company has made a significant investment. Once you reach this threshold of investment, consider a volume licensing agreement. Volume licensing agreements (VLAs), also called network licenses, usually offer simplified procurement, provide structure to upgrade strategies, and assist in reducing costs. However, if not properly defined, VLAs can have a significant amount of administration associated with procurement and compliance tracking. A well-defined VLA typically includes the following:

◆ Relaxed annual measurement of licenses

◆ Flexibility to negotiate contract clauses

◆ Rights to current and future versions throughout the organization

◆ A strategic business relationship with the software publisher

◆ Purchase reporting

Expect to pay 10–30 percent more for a network license based on the value of this increased flexibility. A well-defined network license agreement reduces orders, payments, and administrative duties.

Site Licenses

Unlike volume license agreements and their associated administration costs, site licenses apply to a specific business location, or can span across a company's enterprise.

A site license can facilitate the copying and distribution of that vendor's software without the overhead of procurement and compliance tracking. However, the site license is usually negotiated based upon a specific numbers of users. As that number fluctuates, you need to understand those ramifications and consider if and how adjustments can be made to the contract.

Oracle Minimums for Licensing

In general, user minimums apply to Oracle databases and their options. User minimums do not apply to specific products, including Oracle8i Personal Edition, Oracle8i Lite, and Oracle Development Tools. To ensure that you fully understand your license and have met the user minimum requirements, it's best to review the user minimums with an Oracle sales representative.

Key Oracle License Contacts

In most cases, there is not one set of rules for software licensing and administration. Many licensing questions are specific to a company or situation. Consequently, it is best to contact Oracle with questions specific to your needs. You can either contact your local Oracle office or representative, or contact Oracle client relations at (650) 506-1500.

Named User Minimums

The required minimum Oracle licenses are as follows:

◆ **Oracle8i Standard Edition and RDBMS Standard Edition.** The required minimum is an initial transaction of five named users.

◆ **Oracle8i Enterprise Edition.** The required minimum is one named user for every 30 UPUs.

If you are licensing by named user, follow these instructions to calculate the minimum number of named user licenses required for your intended hardware configuration:

1. Determine the number of MHz on each server.

2. Calculate the total number of UPUs for your intended hardware configuration (add the MHz on all processors on all servers).

3. Divide the total number of UPUs by 30.

4. The result represents the minimum number of named user licenses required for your intended hardware configuration.

For example, suppose you have three computers, each with two 400MHz processors:

◆ The number of MHz on each server is 800 (2 processors × 400 MHz processors = 800MHz).

◆ The total number of UPUs is 2,400 (3 computers × 800 MHz = 2,400 UPUs).

◆ The minimum number of named user licenses required is 80 (2,400 UPUs/30 = 80 named users).

UPU Minimums

If you are licensing by UPU, there is an initial transaction minimum of 200 UPUs.

Option Minimums

Options must match the license level and number of users of the associated database licenses on a per-server basis.

Oracle CRM and ERP Application Minimums

To ensure that you fully understand your license grant and have met the user minimum requirements, be sure to review the user minimums for Oracle CRM and ERP applications with an Oracle sales representative.

Summary

Consolidating and standardizing software licensing and administration are the first steps towards effective management of client/server assets. Maximizing any asset requires controlling an asset's cost while maximizing its use. With distributed, multitier architectures, licensing administration and delivery methods have become complex. Therefore, effective software management involves input from organizations, evaluation and deployment processes, and policies and tools.

The primary goals of effective software license management are to:

◆ Maximize software asset investment value

◆ Ensure the purchase of the right software

◆ Provide efficient software license administration with minimal resources

◆ Provide accountability and tracking

◆ Address strategic business strategies

◆ Provide efficient software administration reporting

To meet these goals, you should put these processes and procedures in place:

◆ Established standards across the organization

◆ Standard procurement practices

◆ Established policies for software distribution

◆ Processes for handling arriving and departing employees' software assets

◆ Electronic software distribution

◆ License reclamation and reissue standards

It is important when partnering with the vendor that the vendor have the technological infrastructure necessary to automate such enterprise agreements and be able to address issues such as purchasing practices, electronic software distribution, piracy prevention, moves, deletes, and add policies.

It is not necessarily cost effective to have system administrators spend hours every week managing software licenses and generating reports. You might want to look for integrated tools to help provide a common and centralized mechanism for the acquisition and administration of licensed software products. Coupled with trends in downsizing and outsourcing, companies are finding that software management tools provide a competitive advantage for monitoring, deploying, distributing, and administering software across the enterprise.

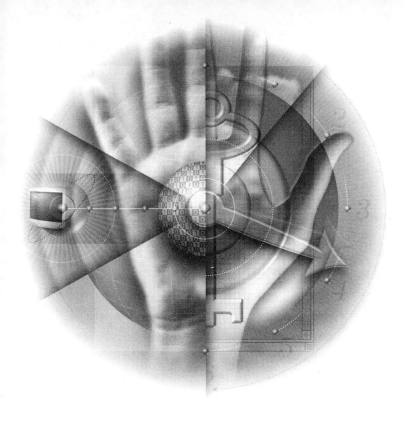

Chapter 5

What's Oracle8i All About?

Today, the Internet is considered a primary business driver. Companies are being challenged to maintain computing availability and scalability. At the same time, everyone is touting that e-business will somehow reduce the costs and increase the profits for those companies that go online. In fact, some analysts believe that if your company fails to establish an e-business presence, your business will suffer.

This pressure has encouraged more companies to provide Web browser interfaces to their applications and data. By providing a Web interface, companies believe they will see a much greater demand on their data, thus resulting in higher numbers of concurrent users and transactions. Therefore, both Web enablement and e-business initiatives have a major impact on those applications' system resources, making scalability extremely important. In addition, an Internet/intranet-enabled application works only when all the components are available all the time. Web-based access must perform at a higher level than conventional client/server systems, be continuously available, and have great scalability features. In many implementations, the new functionality is being added to the existing infrastructure without consideration to the original architecture, design, and implementation. Consequently, many companies are plagued with downtime, slow response times, or service interruptions that often result in customer loss.

Interestingly enough, even Oracle notes that the ongoing maintenance costs of many individually managed servers, and the cost of acquiring and keeping trained technical personnel to operate and maintain such systems, is much higher and more problematic than a centralized Internet-based server approach. As a result, Oracle is now promoting the Oracle8i architecture. It simplifies the deployment and upgrade of Internet/intranet applications, as well as improves the management and storage of data. Database administrators are faced with an ever-changing business environment where the challenge of getting the databases online, operational, and on schedule has become a daily heroic event. This activity is then followed by continual installations. It is easy for a DBA to become so occupied with reacting to current problems that there is no time for real database administration, let alone the additional load brought on by the Internet.

There are many choices to be made in implementing Oracle8i; with over 150 new features, where should you begin? The purpose of this chapter is to jumpstart the process by providing an overview of Oracle8i's features.

Understanding Oracle8i

From how it is marketed and advertised, it sounds like Oracle8i is a database server, Web server, fileserver, e-mail server, application server, and Java server. It slices, it dices, and everything in between! At least one thing is for certain: Oracle8i has a much larger marketing team than Oracle7 had. With all this hype, how can you unearth the real technical benefits of this database wonder?

The following section contains the Oracle8i features that you'll want to thoroughly evaluate when planning any new Oracle8i installation:

◆ Advanced replication

◆ Content and file management

◆ Oracle interMedia

◆ Dropping and setting unused columns

◆ Materialized views

◆ Function-based indexes

◆ Partitioned tables and indexes

◆ Temporary tables

Advanced Replication

Oracle's advanced replication option allows you to replicate any combination of master data sources and their updateable snapshot replications instead of just one master data source. Oracle's replication functionality was introduced in Oracle7, but is much improved in Oracle8i. With the release of Oracle8i, replication imposes a substantially lower performance hit. Oracle8i continues by moving more of the replication code into the database kernel. Implementing and administering the replication option is still not easy, and probably never will be based on its goals and architecture.

Because advanced replication is such a complex and important concept when implementing and managing Oracle databases, an entire chapter covers this matter—see Chapter 14, "Replicating Oracle Databases."

NOTE

Oracle8i's advanced replication feature is also supported by Oracle Lite so organizations can deploy their applications on a mobile database. Oracle Lite includes a transparent replication facility that enables users to connect to the server and replicate a subset of applications and data without any technical knowledge or expertise in either the application or data structure. Oracle Lite allows Web-based applications written for Oracle8i to automatically deploy for connected as well as disconnected users. Mobile users bring a whole new paradigm to database administration and you must consider their ramifications during planning, deployment, and administration.

Content and File Management

Oracle8i allows you to easily manage and store all your information from the Internet in the database. It can manage application content that incorporates text, images, and audio/video (native support for JPEG, MPEG, and GIF is included). Oracle8i (version 8.1.6) has an IFS (Internet file system) that stores, alters, and deletes pages, spreadsheets, word-processing files, images, e-mail, HTML pages, and XML.

Oracle8i's iFS can interact with any 32-bit Windows client as if it were a file-server, presenting its contents as a Windows-style file structure. Because the database is presented as a virtual drive equivalent to an NT file-system structure, the database content can be browsed topically through Windows Explorer, which represents tables as files of type "table" and other data content as files.

Oracle8i's IFS enables users to access database contents with more than just SQL. Other options include the following:

◆ **Through the desktop file system.** For tables, folders are generated to represent each valid traversal of foreign key relationships.

◆ **Through HTML pages.** The contents available in the NT file system format are also available with equivalent topical search capability through an HTML-based user interface such as a browser.

◆ **Through SQL or ODBC.** These means can be combined with conventional searching based on index or row contents using SQL or ODBC, Microsoft's Open Database Connectivity programming interface.

Using Oracle's IFS, the database becomes a generalized fileserver that is easily accessible from any desktop. This mass use can mean increased load for you in the form of space-management activities.

Oracle interMedia

Another great feature of Oracle8i is interMedia. Information management goes well beyond managing simple records, especially on the Internet, which is the natural environment for multimedia applications. Oracle's interMedia specialized data types, which are similar to Java or C++ classes, let you store rich data types, including text, audio, and video, along with traditional relational data right in the database.

Oracle interMedia enables standard SQL access using native text, image, audio, and video data type services. Oracle's interMedia includes Internet support for Web authoring tools and servers, and text-search features. Vendors of electronic document archiving systems, e-commerce systems, and Internet publishing applications are currently taking advantage of the features in interMedia. These and other features are likely to be well used in the future; therefore, it's important to understand interMedia when working with Oracle8i.

Dropping and Setting Unused Columns

Oracle8i adds a new feature that can save you space by dropping or setting unused table columns without having to export or import data or recreate indexes, constraints, or statistics. You can mark columns as unused and they are treated as if they were dropped, even though their column data remains in the table's rows. Dropping a column from a large table to reclaim space can take some database effort, depending upon the size of the table. Consequently, unused columns are better dropped when system resources are available.

 NOTE

Be aware that when the drop column clause is used, it also drops any columns that were previously marked as unused. Just as for any new functionality, you need to understand all the restrictions that go with a feature.

NOTE

To view the columns that are currently marked as unused, select all from the SQL prompt in either the DBA_Unused_Col_Tabs or User_Unused_Col_Tabs views. See the following code snippets:

```
SQL> select * from dba_unused_col_tabs
SQL>/
```

Or

```
SQL> select * from user_unused_col_tabs
SQL>/
```

Materialized Views

Oracle8i introduces *materialized views*, which are stored summaries of queries containing precompiled results that can improve large query processing. They can be used to summarize, replicate, and distribute data. Materialized views can be beneficial for data warehousing, decision support, and distributed or mobile computing. In many ways, a materialized view is like an index. The materialized view consumes space, it must be refreshed when the master data changes, and when used, it improves the performance of a SQL execution. However, unlike indexes, materialized views can be accessed directly using a SELECT statement and, dependent upon the type of refresh, they can also be accessed using INSERT, UPDATE, or DELETE statements.

You need to set up procedures to refresh the materialized views whenever the data is changed in the underlying tables. The refresh method can be incremental (fast refresh) or complete. The incremental method repopulates only the changed data, whereas the complete method truncates and rebuilds the view.

Materialized views can improve performance, but the overhead and space consumption associated with materialized view management can become a significant problem. Materialized view management activities include the following:

◆ Identifying the required materialized views

◆ Indexing the materialized views

◆ Ensuring that all materialized views and materialized view indexes are refreshed properly each time the database is updated

- Monitoring and tuning each materialized view with respect to workload performance
- Measuring and monitoring the space being used by materialized views

Function-Based Indexes

Oracle8i introduces the capability to index functions and use these indexes in a query. A function-based index is an index on an expression. An application developer or DBA can create function-based indexes for any repeatable SQL function. Oracle recommends using function-based indexes for range scans and for functions in ORDER BY clauses. You can define function-based indexes almost anywhere you use an index on a column. Prior to this feature, every row in the table had to be scanned, made uppercase, and compared.

Application developers and DBAs should evaluate this feature if slow ORDER BY or range scan performance is an issue.

Partitioned Tables and Indexes

Oracle8 introduced partitioning that allowed administrators to store large tables and indexes in pieces, instead of as one big unmanageable object. When you use the partitioning feature, you can perform maintenance tasks on one partition at a time, thus permitting the bulk of the data to remain available during maintenance.

Oracle8i adds parallel execution to help perform most operations more quickly, as well as two new partitioning types: hash and composite. Hash and composite partitioning can enable a mechanism for data corruption, independent backup and recovery of partitions, or for striping data across devices.

 NOTE

Don't set up all tables or indexes as partitioned, because partitioned objects have some overhead issues that traditional tables do not. A table's partition strategy is very important and should be determined by the application design. Also, designing a table's physical characteristic for a specific application goes against traditional database design.

Other issues related to partitioning that you should be aware of include:

◆ Batch deletions are quicker and consume fewer resources by truncating a single partition instead of deleting a range of data.

◆ Batch routines such as data loading need to be rewritten to take advantage of parallelism, multiple processors, or running in multiple threads if available.

◆ By assigning data to a partition, you can control whether an update or insert goes to a specific tablespace.

◆ Partition elimination allows you to avoid the cost of going after the whole table when you need just a small subset. Queries that use specific portions of the table by using the partitioning columns in the WHERE clause benefit from not having to access the unnecessary partitions.

◆ Ordinarily, Oracle acquires locks to ensure that no operation (DML, DDL, utility) interferes with an individual DDL statement, such as ALTER TABLE...DROP PARTITION. However, if a partition maintenance operation requires several steps, it is your responsibility as the DBA to ensure that applications or other operations do not interfere with the multistep operation in progress.

Partitioning has a great many benefits that yield some significant performance increases. But implementing and administering partitioning is not something you do in a day. In most cases, to use the partitioning functionality, applications have to be rewritten. Once applications do take advantage of partitioning, you have additional administration to perform in monitoring and maintaining those partitions.

Temporary Tables

Oracle8i introduces a new concept called *global temporary tables*. This feature permits you, as the DBA, to create temporary tables that hold session-specific data. You specify whether the data is specific to a session or to a transaction. A temporary table has a definition or structure that persists like a regular table, but the data it contains exists only for the duration of a transaction or session.

Data in a temporary table is private to the session. Each session can see and modify only its own data. DML locks are not acquired on the data of the temporary tables. Indexes created on temporary tables are also temporary, and the data in the index has the same session or transaction scope as the data in the temporary table. You can create views and triggers that access both temporary tables.

To improve performance of complex queries, you can cache the values from a more complex query in a temporary table, and then run SQL statements, such as joins, against those temporary tables. Otherwise, the conventional process requires querying the table multiple times for each row returned.

When considering using temporary tables, you should understand these issues:

◆ Designating temporary tablespaces exclusively for sorts helps eliminate serialization of space-management operations involved in the allocation and de-allocation of sort space.

◆ DML statements on temporary tables do not generate redo logs for the data changes.

◆ Data from the temporary table is automatically dropped in the case of session termination, either when the user logs off or when the session terminates abnormally such as during a session or instance crash.

◆ Troubleshooting can be more difficult because the information no longer persists after a session disconnects or crashes.

Reorganizing and Defragmenting Your Database with Oracle

A common cause of downtime or degraded transaction response time is poor database performance. Proper database administration can improve data availability, query performance, response time, and disk space utilization, which are all important to the 24×7 Internet enterprise operation. However, they usually require downtime to perform.

Although the Internet makes it easy to share data globally, it also brings new challenges and requirements for data availability. As global users access data 24 hours a day, maintenance windows have all but evaporated. Planned downtime is becoming as disruptive as unplanned downtime, because there are no longer any windows of time when users are not affected. Compounding this is the fact that when the volume of data stored in a database becomes very large, maintenance operations become time consuming. It is important that these operations be performed without affecting users of the data. Oracle8i introduces new features and functionality that assist you in keeping the database available for the 24×7 Internet world.

Online Index Creation, Rebuild, and Defragmentation

After numerous inserts and deletes, indexes become fragmented, wasting space and affecting performance. Oracle8i now provides two facilities to help defragment an index: online rebuild and in-place coalesce. While the index is online, Oracle8i can rebuild it completely to recover space and relocate the index. Changes to the base table and index during the build are recorded in a journal table, and merged into the new index upon completion of the operation.

Index-Organized Tables (IOTs)

Oracle8 introduced the Index-Organized Tables (IOT) feature. An index-organized table differs from an ordinary table in that the data for the table is held in its associated index. Changes to the table data—such as adding, updating, or deleting rows—result only in updating the index.

Oracle8i now allows index-organized tables to be moved and reorganized while users are accessing and updating the data in the table. Oracle can only reorganize indexes or index structures online. Changes to the table during the operation are recorded in a journal table and merged with the table upon completion of the operation.

When considering using index-organized tables, you should understand these issues:

◆ Oracle recommends that you use the index-organized option on all new tables that might become fragmented or require reorganization.

◆ Because index-organized tables are primarily stored in a B*-tree index, a DBA might encounter fragmentation as a consequence of incremental updates.

◆ Before converting an index-organized table to a regular table, be aware that index-organized tables cannot be exported using pre-Oracle8 versions of the Export utility.

Database Resource Manager

Oracle database availability and manageability are directly affected by how resources are used on the server as well as how the applications access the database. Oracle8i introduces the Database Resource Manager to assist with allocating and managing Oracle CPU resources among users and applications. The Database

Resource Manager is a PL/SQL package that allows you to create, update, and delete resource plans and resource consumer groups. You define a user's default consumer group and what privileges the users have.

To use the Database Resource Manager, you must define the following:

◆ **Resource consumer groups.** A means of grouping user sessions that have similar processing and resource usage requirements.

◆ **Resource plans.** A means of allocating resources among the consumer groups.

◆ **Resource allocation methods.** A policy used when allocating any particular resource.

◆ **Resource plan directives.** A means of assigning consumer groups or subgroups to resource plans and allocating resources among consumer groups by specifying parameters for each resource allocation method.

Transportable Tablespaces

Oracle8i provides a new feature for copying tablespaces between identical systems and allowing the same data to be accessed by both systems. You transport a tablespace by copying the datafiles and moving the dictionary information to another database. By having to export only the system tablespace information, or only the data dictionary information, you can save a considerable amount of time. You can also transport indexes using this feature. This can save you additional processing time on a large table. Here is the basic sequence of events that occur:

1. Place the tablespace in read-only mode to guarantee that a consistent image of the data is captured.

2. Export from the source database dictionary, the metadata describing the tablespace.

3. Copy the tablespace files to the destination database using any operating system facilities (copy command, FTP, and so on).

4. Import the metadata describing the tablespace. If desired, the imported tablespace can be placed in read-write mode.

When implementing Oracle8i's Transportable Tablespace functionality, be aware of these issues:

◆ The need to connect as SYS or SYSTEM while exporting or importing the data dictionary information

- ◆ The granularity of a tablespace
- ◆ The tablespaces must be self-contained, meaning that all the objects in the tablespace must be contained wholly in the tablespace.
- ◆ The source and the target database must be on the same platform—for example, between Sun Solaris and Sun Solaris but not Sun Solaris and NT.
- ◆ The source and target database must have the same block size.
- ◆ The same tablespace name should not be used by the target database.

Locally Managed Tablespaces

Prior to Oracle8i, administration of used and free extents relied heavily on the DBAs' experience and their knowledge of the data dictionary. Oracle8i has now introduced the Locally Managed Tablespaces feature in an attempt to get a handle on space-management issues. A locally managed tablespace manages its own extents by maintaining a bitmap in each datafile that tracks the free or used status of blocks in that datafile. Each bit in the bitmap corresponds to a block or a group of blocks. When an extent is allocated or freed for reuse, Oracle changes the bitmap values to show the new status of the blocks. These changes do not generate rollback information because they do not update tables in the data dictionary (except for special cases such as tablespace quota information).

This new tablespace type sizes new extents using either a uniform or system policy. The system policy is consulted at the time of tablespace creation, or when you issue the CREATE TABLESPACE command. If the tablespace uses the uniform policy, all extents are uniformly the same size, so no fragmentation *should* occur. If the tablespace uses the system policy, there are only small and large extents. Small extents are automatically used for small objects, and large extents are used for large objects. Small extents are then packed together in a group the size of a large extent. By separating small and large extents, fragmentation is further reduced.

When implementing Oracle8i's Locally Managed Tablespace functionality, be aware of these issues:

- ◆ Oracle recommends using locally managed tablespaces for all new tablespaces.
- ◆ Tablespace quota information changes generate rollback information.
- ◆ After the tablespace type is created, you cannot alter the type.

◆ For system-managed extents, you can specify the size of the initial extent. Oracle then determines the optimal size of additional extents, with a minimum extent size of 64KB.

◆ For uniform extents, you can specify an extent size or use the default size, which is set at 1MB.

Internet Application Support

One of the most significant areas of change with the Oracle RDBMS is in Java and Internet support. Oracle is seeking to attract application developers by adding Java to Oracle's internal system or kernel. By doing so, Oracle has repositioned itself as the Internet database. Developers should not have to worry about where and how they store their data. This functionality can actually add database administration load to the DBA. With just about anyone being able to easily back-end their application to an Oracle database, it will become an increasing challenge to control the management and performance of the database. This is also directly related to the n-tier application server environment, which comprises the different application levels that make up a complete system.

Oracle8i comes with an engine that can process HTTP requests and serve Web pages. Java stored procedures and functions are also stored in the database. Oracle has also implemented SQLJ (SQL Java), an embedded SQL language for Java. Java developers can now write stored procedures in either Java or PL/SQL and deploy and execute the applications directly in the database.

Oracle8i's Java offering includes:

◆ **Oracle Jserver.** A Java Virtual Machine (JDK 1.1.6 compliant) that runs within the Oracle8i database server address space

◆ **Oracle JServer Accelerator.** A native code compiler that speeds up the execution of Java code by eliminating interpreter overhead (scheduled for Oracle8i, release 8.1.6)

◆ **JDBC SQLJ.** Programmatic interfaces

Oracle Java implementation targets different segments of application developers:

◆ Database programmers can write database-stored procedures, triggers, and object-relational methods in Java.

◆ Enterprise Java Beans (EJBs) developers can write reusable server-side scripts or mini-applications called Enterprise Java Beans (EJBs).

◆ CORBA server developers can implement CORBA servers in Java on the database's Java Virtual Machine (VM).

When implementing Oracle8i's Java functionality, be aware of these issues:

◆ When to use Java and when to use PL/SQL. Oracle has stated that there are times when a DBA or developer should use Java, and there are times when PL/SQL is more appropriate. Unfortunately, there hasn't been anything released from Oracle on the specific details.

◆ JServer comes with Oracle8i Enterprise Server. If the DBA installs a default or custom database, the setup routines automatically initialize, configure, and enable Java in the database.

◆ When planning to use JServer, the DBA needs to consider a footprint of approximately 40KB for each Java Virtual Machine. When the Java Virtual Machine is initialized, 4000+ classes are loaded; the shared pool is used to load and resolve all those Java classes.

Web Site Development

Oracle also offers WebDB, a tool designed to build and personalize Web sites for Oracle8i. The tool provides the facilities to easily build and browse database objects, and to build HTML database applications and Web Sites into the database without any programming. By using a browser, just about anyone can create simple database queries to more complex, dynamic database applications.

Although this sounds wonderful, a tool like this can pose some important technical issues in the enterprise environment. In many large organizations, there is tight control on code, change management, and system usage. Any tool that can easily attach to the databases and uses system and network resources while offering an outcome that could easily become a production application could burden the administration staff. Without knowledge of the created applications, their activity can create additional burden and risk for administrators trying to resolve documented issues. With the proper procedures and tools used by the DBA, applications, databases, servers, and even networks can be monitored to minimize any impact these quickly developed Web sites have on the administration staff. Chapter 9, "Choosing Manual or Automatic Database Management," includes more information on proper procedures and tools.

Oracle Enterprise Manager 2.0

Along with all the changes in the Oracle RDBMS, Oracle's basic administration tools have changed as well. The Oracle Enterprise Manager (OEM) base product now includes a lightweight console, a management server, and distributed agents that execute tasks and monitor conditions on each managed system.

The Intelligent Agent is a process that runs on nodes. It is responsible for service discovery, event monitoring, and job execution. The Intelligent Agent supports the Simple Network Management Protocol (SNMP), enabling the addition of third-party applications to Oracle Enterprise Manager's lightweight architecture.

Base OEM comes with only three events. These events are written in a language called TCL (Tool Command Language). TCL has been customized and licensed by Oracle and named OraTCL. OraTCL is an extension to the original TCL that provides access to an Oracle database server. OraTCL adds TCL commands that log in to an Oracle server, pass SQL code, read results, and more.

Oracle Enterprise Manager has significantly changed; in addition, its price has increased substantially. The latest version of OEM requires its repository and Java components to be installed in an Oracle8i environment, but you can still monitor certain older Oracle releases.

Oracle Parallel Server

Oracle8i brings improvements to Oracle Parallel Server with cache fusion technology. Cache fusion is a new ping architecture that provides copies of blocks directly from the holding instance's memory cache to the requesting instance's memory cache using a cluster interconnect for establishing cache coherence across nodes, thus eliminating disk I/O. Cache fusion copies blocks directly from the holding instance's memory cache to the requesting instance's memory cache.

Cache fusion is particularly useful in databases where updates and queries on the same data tend to occur simultaneously and where, for whatever reason, the data and users have not been isolated to specific nodes so that all activity can take place on a single instance. Cache fusion helps alleviate the need to concentrate on data or user partitioning by instance.

Oracle8i's Backup and Recovery Features

Backup and recovery are critical administration tasks that must be performed regularly as part of database administration. There is usually a lot of effort in getting operational backups after the installation of the database. However, after backups are functioning, your critical time is usually then redirected to other tasks. As a result, a majority of organizations never test or even assemble a recovery plan. Of course this is usually realized after data has been lost, the backup tapes are found to be blank or overwritten, or a disaster such as a flood has occurred.

Many times, DBAs assume that a basic system backup will take care of database needs. However, many DBAs discover that shrinking maintenance windows or improper backup techniques end up equating to no backups and the loss of data. Consequently, you need to employ the proper practices and tools to protect the business and ensure the data. Again Oracle8i has made improvements to this issue with items such as the ones discussed here.

Media Failures and Data Corruptions

It is extremely important to design and administer a plan that protects against and recovers from media failures and corruptions. Chapters 8, "Understanding Problems, Risks, and Errors," and 13, "Planning for Disaster Recovery," both include ideas about managing risk and preparing for a disaster. A system or network fault can prevent users from accessing data, but media failures or corruptions without proper backups can lead to unrecoverable data. A large database server can connect to hundreds of disk drives. Even though today's disks are very reliable, such a large number of disks makes the issue of disk failure a statistically likely event. In addition, a variety of events including human errors and rogue applications can corrupt data.

Recovery Manager

With Oracle8, Oracle introduced Recovery Manager (RMAN) to assist you in backing up, copying, restoring, and recovering data files, control files, and archived redo logs.

New Oracle8i functionality for Recovery Manager now allows you to duplicate backup sets to multiple I/O devices. Oracle8i also includes a media-management layer so that users can direct media management software to perform the copy operation on Oracle's behalf.

Like Oracle7's Enterprise Backup Utility (EBU), RMAN doesn't drop right in and magically start working. You need to look at business requirements, map out a backup strategy, and then configure RMAN to execute that strategy. You need to learn RMAN's syntax, and perform some form of integration to media management software. RMAN's syntax is covered in various places on Oracle's home page (**www.oracle.com**).

When working with RMAN, you should understand these issues:

◆ A recovery catalog is an optional schema containing information about RMAN operations. RMAN does not store backups in the recovery catalog; rather, it stores information about backups and copies in the recovery catalog.

◆ RMAN is not compatible with Oracle databases prior to release 8.0.

◆ RMAN is not compatible with EBU (Oracle7's Enterprise Backup Utility).

◆ RMAN obtains the information it needs from the control file of the target database.

If you have a mixed environment of Oracle7 and Oracle8, consider a third-party product for backup and recovery. Chapter 10, "Maintaining Your Oracle Database with 5-Nines," includes more information about tools that help in backup and recovery processes.

Automated Standby Database

Oracle did not officially support the standby database feature until Oracle 7.3. Prior to Oracle8i, the archived redo logs were manually transported or copied to the standby database and manually applied by the DBA.

With the Automated Standby Database feature in Oracle8i, the archived redo logs can be automatically transferred and applied. This eliminates the need for manual procedures to copy and transmit the redo logs and for the DBA to manually specify which logs to apply. Additionally, in Oracle8i, the standby database can be taken out of recovery mode and opened for read-only query processing to offload a production database. When the query processing is complete, the standby database can return to standby mode without re-cloning the production database.

Using standby databases creates additional administration responsibilities. You need to design, plan, and monitor these new instances. In addition, you need to make sure the data is in sync. Also, because logs are transferred only after a redo log fills and log switch occurs, it is possible that up to two logs' worth of transactions (the current and the one previously archived but not yet transferred) can be lost in the event of a disaster.

Detecting and Repairing Data Corruptions

Oracle8i includes a new package, DBMS_REPAIR, which helps detect and repair block corruption on tables, indexes, and other objects. DBMS_REPAIR assists you in detecting and reporting corruptions, making corrupt objects usable, repairing corruptions, and reporting on any lost data.

DBMS_REPAIR is not a general-purpose tool. Only those who are experienced and understand whether the repair approach provided by this package is appropriate for a specific corruption problem should use the tool. Prior to using DBMS_REPAIR, you must weigh the benefits of its use in relation to the liabilities. Depending on the nature of the repair, data may be lost and logical inconsistencies can be introduced. Possible issues that can occur include:

◆ There may not be access to rows in blocks marked corrupt.

◆ A block may be marked corrupt even when it contains rows that can be accessed.

◆ Referential integrity constraints might be broken when blocks are marked corrupt.

◆ Logical corruption can occur when there are triggers defined on the table.

◆ Indexes and tables can be out of sync.

Fast Fault Recovery

In addition to human fault, another common cause of downtime is outages caused by power glitches, hardware failures, server crashes, and network or operating system failures. The focus in the face of such an event is getting the database operational as soon as possible. Oracle8i includes enhanced recovery to get the database back online faster with System Fault Recovery.

You can define Oracle8i System Fault Recovery, thus enabling predictable recovery time. A DBA can now define an upper limit on the number of I/O operations (the parameter is called FAST_START_IO_TARGET) that Oracle needs to perform during instance recovery.

With Oracle8i, the rollback phase of fault recovery has been replaced with non-blocking rollback. New transactions can begin immediately after roll forward completes. When a new transaction accesses a row locked by a dead transaction, the new transaction will roll back only the changes that block its progress. In addition, the database server now has the capability to roll back dead transactions in parallel.

SQL-Based Log Analyzer

Oracle8i introduces the LogMiner 8i feature, which allows you to view the contents of the transaction log files. You can now see what SQL DML and DDL operations were executed, by whom, and at what time. The LogMiner also creates the SQL necessary to back out of any operation that was inadvertently executed by a user.

The log files to be analyzed are mapped to a dynamic performance view (such as V$ tables) and are then accessed using standard SQL, or programmatically from any supported language. LogMiner is based upon a set of PL/SQL triggers with a Graphical User Interface (GUI) front end.

You'll find this functionality to be useful when an object has been accidentally dropped or when auditing the database.

Oracle8i Management and Security Features

With so many means of accessing the database—locally, remotely, and most notably through the Internet—server-enforced and granular access control becomes crucial. Security implemented in applications is no longer sufficient, because one only needs to access the data from outside the application (through SQL*Plus, for example) to bypass security.

Oracle8i features a centralized registry for all system information called the Oracle8i Internet Directory or "iDirectory." It supports the definition of user identities and privileges, application components including CORBA objects, network configurations, and system resources such as clients, servers, Net8 listeners, and connection managers.

Security policy can now be directly tied to a table or view. To implement this fine-grained access control, you create a function to implement a security policy and associate the function with a table or view. The server then enforces these access policies no matter how users attempt to access data. The Oracle-supplied DBMS_RLS package associates security policy functions with the table or view. When a query or subquery that affects that table or view is executed, the server dynamically appends a WHERE condition generated by the function implementing the security policy.

This new functionality is a great improvement in security over previous versions. As before, you need to understand and work closely with application developers and security administrators in defining these security polices to be stored in the database. It must be determined whether the DBA or the security administrator is the one who maintains, monitors, and audits these items.

Oracle Optimizer

Every SQL statement submitted to the database is processed by a component of the database server called the *optimizer*. The optimizer constructs an execution plan that specifies the most efficient way the requested data can be retrieved from the database.

Part of this analysis is based on statistics that describe the underlying data in the table and indexes. After upgrading the database or application, the optimizer can generate a different execution plan than was used in the past. Queries running with these new execution plans can exhibit different performance than they exhibited before the change was introduced. This effectively reduces the predictability and increases the risk associated with database and application upgrades and can inhibit use of new features in the database.

Oracle8i provides two new features that address this issue. First is the capability to store existing execution plans and insulate an application from upgrades. Plans can remain consistent using `analyze` commands, creation of new indexes, new releases of Oracle, and other changes. The optimizer uses the stored plan to create an equivalent execution plan for the query. Multiple stored plans can be created for experimentation, and a phased rollout of an application can be done with more predictable results.

Oracle8i also has enhanced the collection and management of the statistics used to generate execution plans. Statistics can be automatically generated as an index is created with minimal overhead. Statistics-gathering can also now be done in parallel. Statistics can be extracted from the dictionary and stored in a user table. They can then be modified and reinserted into the dictionary. This process can be used to transfer statistics to or from a test database or to experiment with different versions of dictionary statistics.

With Oracle8i, it is now possible to upgrade applications and Oracle releases with more predictability, thus improving the performance and availability of applications.

INIT.ORA *Parameters*

For Oracle8i and Java, there are some initial parameters located in the INIT.ORA to be aware of. These include:

◆ **Shared_Pool_Size, Java_Pool_Size.** Greatly affect the performance of the Java VM.

◆ **Java_Soft_Sessionspace_Limit.** Has a default value of 1MB and permits the DBA to set a soft limit on Java memory usage in a session. This parameter also generates a warning in the trace file when a user's session state exceeds the value.

◆ **Java_Max_Sessionspace_Size.** Sets a maximum limit and kills the program when the Java state exceeds this size.

Obsolete Parameters

As with any new Oracle database version, Oracle includes parameters that have been deemed unneeded or that have created support problems. To identify parameters that have become obsolete in Oracle8i, you can query the information stored in the v$obsolete_parameter table. This table has the parameter name and a flag indicating whether the parameter has actually been set. Underscored parameters are parameters that Oracle doesn't want you to use unless you are instructed to by support. To see the list of parameter names and whether they have been specified in the INIT.ORA, use the following command:

```
SQL> SELECT name, isspecified FROM v$obsolete_parameter;
```

To check whether a parameter is obsolete or underscored, perform a query to the `v$obsolete_parameter` view. The value in the `ksppoflag` column identifies whether the parameter has been eliminated or underscored. Underscored values are parameters that are not documented and should not be used unless absolutely necessary. The term underscored means that the parameters are preceded with a "_" character. Eliminated values are identified by a flag of 1, and underscored values are identified by 2. To see these values, try the following command:

```
SQL> SELECT kspponm, ksppoflg, FROM v$obsolete_parameter;
```

Implementing Oracle8i Successfully

Production database migrations and upgrades are usually done under considerable time pressures and are quite challenging. Each company runs the risk of losing precious company assets and time when a problem is encountered or an error is introduced. Migrating or upgrading an organization's database is a big project and one that cannot be completed successfully by you alone. Application developers, system and network administrators, and even users need to be involved for the duration of the project.

You should develop the entire project plan including all tasks, milestones, and ownership of each item that requires attention prior to beginning the implementation. You should include time to meet with all organizations that will be affected by the project.

A majority of the time scheduled in the project plan should be allocated to preparation and testing. It is crucial to develop a fallback strategy as well as a comprehensive test plan to be carried out during pre-implementation as well as post-implementation. From the business perspective, it is important that application owners work with you to determine when certain tasks can be executed so that the project will minimally affect the production environment.

The application development staff also needs time allocated to verify and test application functionality with the new database version. This testing is performed prior to the migration or upgrade, and checkpoints should be in place to stop the project should major problems be identified. After the database migration or upgrade is completed, application developers need to run the tests again on the new database and compare the results to the test environment. Developers should review the migration guide that comes with the Oracle installation documentation.

Be sure to perform database backups before and after the actual migration or upgrade. The starting point is to identify the version number of the existing production Oracle database, patch, or revision level. Oracle defines three paths to reach Oracle8i. They are as follows:

◆ If currently using version 6 or 7, you need to follow what Oracle calls the "migration" steps.

◆ If you are using Oracle8 databases, you need to use the "upgrade" path.

◆ The third path is a new installation.

Whether performing a new installation, migration, or upgrade, you should always have a strategy and plan. Consider these items as part of such a plan:

◆ Read planning documentation including the "readme" file.

◆ Define the requirements.

◆ Identify risks and issues, such as how long the production database can remain offline without disturbing business operations, how quickly the production environment can be restored, and so on.

◆ Define the strategy—a migration, upgrade, or new installation.

◆ Define roles and responsibilities—who does what and how (the plan).

◆ Perform an analysis of current system resources versus required system resources.

◆ Define a plan.

◆ Define a test plan. Validate data and applications in a pre-implementation test environment as well as post-installation prior to going live with Oracle8i. Perform functional testing performance and stress testing.

◆ Define a fallback plan.

◆ Practice the plan. Test the backup and recovery procedures prior to attempting an Oracle8i implementation.

◆ Identify issues and workarounds for issues discovered during testing.

◆ Refine the plan.

◆ Perform full backup and clean shutdown.

◆ Execute the plan.

◆ Post-installation: Analyze the installation and perform a full backup.

◆ Post-installation testing.

◆ Record and document any changes in the plan.

◆ Review the procedures with other involved parties at the end of the installation.

Once a proper architecture and design has been deployed, it is important to maintain environment stability and availability.

Summary

There are many choices to be made when implementing Oracle8i. An entire book could be dedicated to the subject of how to make that decision. However, the intent of this chapter is to gain an overview of the Oracle8i features and make decisions as to which features are best for your site. To select the right Oracle8i strategy for your company, you must consider the business needs, budget, and future growth. Applications will continue to constantly change and adapt to the influx of data and changing business requirements. It's important to establish plans and priorities early on in order for your mission-critical systems to deliver service and value to the business.

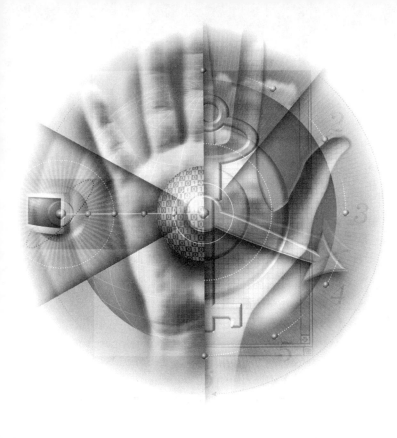

Chapter 6

ORACLE

This chapter is designed to prepare you for installing an Oracle database and implementing Oracle applications within a database. Installing an empty Oracle database is only one step that you will be asked to do, designing a specific application database structure to place into the database will be the other.

If you have already inherited an Oracle database or an Oracle application from others sources and are now in charge of maintenance, there are many things you can learn by taking a quick look under the hood. Developers might say their applications use an Oracle database, but what does that entail? Did the developers follow established guidelines for layout, maintenance, and performance? Did they just port to it? An experienced Oracle DBA can easily tell whether a developer integrated Oracle into their application or whether it was just an afterthought. Some of these afterthought signs include:

◆ Privileges must be granted for the application to run instead of the application having specific roles and correctly issued grants.

◆ The Oracle error "ORA-1631 max # of extents reached" is displayed during an installation or within a week after installation.

◆ There is no entity-relationship diagram (ERD), data dictionary, or other documentation for the application or database.

◆ All indexes and tables are in one large tablespace instead of being split up and organized for performance and optimization.

◆ All the tables were created with Oracle defaults (for example, using the initial 10KB and next 10KB table extent defaults, and default object names such as SYS_C061864 or SYS_C110464 instead of taking the time to make more descriptive primary key and foreign key names such as PKEY_JRCTBL or FKEY_JRCTBL_SMCTBL).

Beyond an application developer's choice of Oracle as the back-end for an application, other choices must be made that will have ramifications on the database. Therefore, it's important that the application developer work closely with an experienced DBA all through the project, or at a minimum, follow a set of guidelines such as the ones outlined in this chapter.

The purpose of this chapter is to show you, the Oracle DBA, a set of Oracle database design and development recommendations that you should employ at the start of the developmental cycle and well into production and maintenance.

Upon completion of this chapter, you should be familiar with the following:

- The Oracle Layout and Optimal Flexible Architectures
- Oracle database design and naming standards
- Database parameters
- Normalization

Oracle's Architecture using OFA

Oracle designers from the beginning have all agreed on having a standard architecture that should be used when installing and designing an Oracle database. This general architecture as developed by Oracle database designers was called the *Oracle Layout Architecture*. Today, Oracle has renamed this to OFA, or Oracle's Optimal Flexible Architecture. This section sets forth a general layout architecture that uses design and developmental standards that aid application developers who use Oracle databases as their back-end. The OLA or OFA standard uses guidelines that give you high-performing, reliable, and maintainable databases. It is used for developing consistent database designs with the highest accuracy and longevity. You should discuss deviations from the specified standards ahead of time with both the database administrator and the application programmer so as to reach an understanding and set goals for future production. Oracle's Optimal Flexible Architecture (OFA) is discussed in the next section.

Optimal Flexible Architecture (OFA)

Because the configuration of an Oracle database is complex, Oracle's Optimal Flexible Architecture (OFA) addresses design and structure issues. The OFA is a set of guidelines (requirements and rules) that will help in these areas:

- Giving you better database performance
- Establishing more reliable Oracle databases
- Lessening the time required for maintenance

Oracle has stated that the standard Oracle Optimal Flexible Architecture (OFA) should be used for all Oracle databases. Setting up an Oracle database to meet the OFA standard will yield maximum stability and minimum work. When a database is OFA-compliant, it is organized with an optimal environment. Database files are easier to find and maintain. Performance issues are easier to isolate and address.

The OFA consists of 13 requirements and 11 rules.

Oracle's 13 OFA Requirements

The OFA's 13 requirements are as follows:

1. The file system (devices and directory structures) should be organized in such a way that easy administration is possible.

2. Input/output (I/O) load should be distributed across different disks to help prevent performance bottlenecks.

3. Hardware costs should be minimized if at all possible.

4. The impact of a disk drive failure should be isolated.

5. Home directories should be distributed across multiple disk drives.

6. Home directories should be able to be added or moved without requiring the revision of other programs that refer to them.

7. Categories of database files should be separated into independent directory subdirectories.

8. Multiple versions of an application's software should be able to be executed simultaneously.

9. Each of your databases should have separate, distinct administrative information.

10. Database files should be named so that:

    ◆ They are easily distinguishable.

    ◆ Files from one database are easily distinguishable from files in another database.

    ◆ Different types of database files are easily distinguishable from each other.

    ◆ Tablespaces can be easily related to database files.

11. Tablespace contents should be separated to minimize fragmentation and I/O requests, and to maximize flexibility.

12. You should be able to tune disk I/O on all drives.

13. Administrative data should be stored in a central place; you should be able to relate administrative data about an instance by file name.

Oracle's 11 OFA Rules

Just like the 13 requirements, Oracle's 11 OFA rules (standards) are highly recommended by Oracle. Oracle encourages the use of this architecture so when you are talking to Oracle support over the phone, the architecture (placement of files) is understood. Note that these rules can, however, be modified by an experienced DBA.

 NOTE

The examples used in the following discussion of the 11 OFA rules are specific to the Unix operating system, but the same rules apply to all Oracle installations.

OFA Rule 1

Name all mount points that hold site-specific data so they match the pattern /*pm* where *p* is the string constant and *m* is a unique fixed-length key that distinguishes each mount point. The following are examples:

- ◆ /u01, /u02, /u03
- ◆ /disk01, /disk02
- ◆ c:\oracle, d:\oracle, f:\oracle

OFA Rule 2

Name home directories with the pattern /*pm*/*h*/*u*, where *pm* is the mount point name, *h* is selected from a small set of standard directory names, and *u* is the name of the owner of the directory.

OFA Rule 3

Refer to explicit path names only in files designed specifically to store them, such as /etc/passwd and /etc/oratab; refer to group memberships only in /etc/group.

OFA Rule 4

Store each version of the Oracle server distribution software in a directory named using the pattern $h/product/v$, where h is defined as the login home directory of the Oracle software owner, and v represents the version of the Oracle software.

OFA Rule 5

For each database named d, store the database administration files in the following subdirectories of h/admin/d (see Table 6.1), where h is the Oracle software owner's home directory.

Table 6.1: Database Installation Subdirectory Names

Admin Subdirectories	Description of the Directories
adhoc	Ad hoc SQL scripts for a given database
arch	Archived redo log files
adump	Audit files (set audit_file_dest in config<db_name>.ora to point here)
bdump	Background process trace files
cdump	Core dump files
create	Programs used to create the database
exp	Database export files
logbook	Files recording the status and history of the database
pfile	Instance parameter files
udump	User SQL trace files

OFA Rule 6

Name Oracle database files using the patterns in Table 6.2, where pm is a mount point name, q is a string that separates Oracle data from all other files, d is the database name, and *n* is a key that is fixed length for a given file type (usually 01, 02, 03, and so on).

Table 6.2: Patterns for Naming Specific Database Files

Name of File	Pattern of File
control files	*/pm/q/d/*control*n*.ctl
redo log files	*/pm/q/d/*redo*n*.log
data files	*/pm/q/d/t*n.dbf

OFA Rule 7

Separate groups of segments with different life spans, I/O request demands, and backup frequencies among different tablespaces. For each Oracle database, create the following special tablespaces in addition to those needed for application segments (see Table 6.3).

Table 6.3: Oracle Mandatory Tablespaces and Their Descriptions

Tablespace Name	Description of the Tablespace
SYSTEM	Data dictionary segments only
TEMP	Temporary segments only
RBS	Rollback segments only
TOOLS	General-purpose tools only
USERS	Miscellaneous user segments

OFA Rule 8

Generally, you should name tablespaces descriptively with eight or fewer characters. Descriptive names allow the administrator to easily associate the name of a datafile with the tablespace that uses it. For example, the tablespace OCSDATA stores data for the Okaloosa County School District, whereas the tablespace MCJ holds prisoner's photos for the Mobile County Jail.

OFA Rule 9

Choose a small set of standard sizes for all hardware devices that store Oracle database files. In general, standardizing on a single size is the way to go. If a single size is used, files can be safely moved from one partition to another. The size should be small enough so that a fairly large number of partitions can be created, but large enough to be convenient. For example, a 2GB drive can be divided into 10 partitions of 200MB each—a good balance between size and number. Any tablespace that uses hardware devices should replicate them across several disk drives.

OFA Rule 10

If you are using Oracle Parallel Server, select exactly one node to act as the Oracle administrative home. This cluster houses the administrative subtree defined in OFA rule 5. Create a directory for each instance that accesses the database within the bdump, cdump, logbook, pfile, and udump subdirectories of .../admin/*d*. Ensure that the admin directory of the administrative home is mounted as the admin directory of every instance.

OFA Rule 11 (for VLDBs)

If you can guarantee that each disk drive will contain database files from exactly one application, and you have enough drives for each database to ensure that there will be no I/O bottleneck, you can name mount points with the pattern /*qdm*, where *q* is a string denoting that Oracle data is to be stored there, *d* is the value of the db_name init<db_name>.ora or config<db_name>.ora parameter for the database, and *m* is a unique fixed-length key that distinguishes one mount point of a given database from another.

Oracle Object and Schema Naming Standards

The following sections describe in detail the naming standards that should be used when naming Oracle objects and schemas. The section also covers directory placement standards that suggest (according to the OLA and the OFA described previously) consistent locations for certain child directories and files.

Database Naming Standards

When determining how to name your database, it is a good idea to name it something meaningful that relates to what the database does. In other words, the database name should be a logical extension of the type of database or service it provides. The database or instance name should also not exceed eight characters. Because of the frequency of its use, more than eight characters typically introduces more human error.

Directory Naming Standards

When installing the Oracle server, tools, applications, and databases, you must make many decisions about where to place files and how to allocate data across disks. Oracle allows great flexibility in these installation decisions. If you follow the OFA guidelines, you'll have an appropriate mapping of the Oracle binary, control, administration, trace, and datafiles onto the file system. Because Oracle recommends that you divide your database into different tablespaces, Oracle's defined OFA directory structure helps you organize your files within this structure. Again, try to adhere to this directory structure as closely as possible.

Oracle Base Directory Standards

The Oracle base directory is the part of an Oracle directory structure from which all subdirectories originate. An example of an Oracle base directory is /*main disk drive*/*applications*/oracle.

Windows NT sample path	`c:\apps\oracle`
Unix sample path	`/usr1/apps/oracle`

Oracle Home Directory Standards

Oracle Home is the Oracle base directory, plus the initial Oracle product version information. An example of this is /*main disk drive*/*applications*/oracle/*Oracle products*/*Oracle version*.

Windows NT sample path	`c:\apps\oracle\ora_home\`
Unix sample path	`/usr1/apps/oracle/product/7.3.4`

Oracle Data Directory Standards

Most of Oracle's dictionary or database-related data should be kept under the oradata directory. This directory is located under the main drive designation. The following examples show where the oradata directory is located:

/*main disk drive* /oradata

Windows NT sample path   `c:\apps\oracle\oradata\`

Unix sample path   `/usr1/oradata`

Startup Files Naming and Directory Standards

Place the databases INIT*instance*.ORA and CONFIG*instance*.ORA in the DBS directory (under the Oracle Home directory).

Windows NT sample path   `c:\apps\oracle\ora_home\dbs`

Unix sample path   `/usr1/apps/oracle/product/7.3.4/dbs`

Figure 6.1 shows the header portion of a typical INIT*instance*.ORA file. The actual INIT*instance*.ORA file is longer and is the central point for most of the startup parameters for the database instance. The INIT*instance*.ORA file also calls the CONFIG*instance*.ORA file for more startup parameters.

Control Files Directory Naming Standards

You should have a minimum of three database control files, kept in separate areas or partitions. Oracle suggests that you keep the first control file in the first oradata directory of the first main disk drive or partition. Keep the remainder of the control files in other partitions under different oradata directories if possible. In addition, be sure to run a weekly Unix `cron` or MS Windows batch job to archive the latest control file structure.

Log Files Directory Standards

You should have a minimum of three database log files, kept in separate areas or partitions similar to the control files. Oracle suggests that the first log file be kept in the first oradata directory of the first main disk drive or partition. Keep the remainder of the log files in other partitions under different oradata directories if possible.

```
######################################################################
# Example INIT.ORA file
#
# This file is provided by Oracle Corporation to help you customize
# your RDBMS installation for your site.  Important system parameters
# are discussed, and example settings given.
#
# Some parameter settings are generic to any size installation.
# For parameters that require different values in different size
# installations, three scenarios have been provided: SMALL, MEDIUM
# and LARGE.  Any parameter that needs to be tuned according to
# installation size will have three settings, each one commented
# according to installation size.
#
# Use the following table to approximate the SGA size needed for the
# three scenarious provided in this file:
#
#                         -------Installation/Database Size------
#                         SMALL         MEDIUM         LARGE
# Block         2K        4500K         6800K          17000K
# Size          4K        5500K         8800K          21000K
#
# To set up a database that multiple instances will be using, place
# all instance-specific parameters in one file, and then have all
# of these files point to a master file using the IFILE command.
# This way, when you change a public
# parameter, it will automatically change on all instances.  This is
# necessary, since all instances must run with the same value for many
# parameters. For example, if you choose to use private rollback segments,
# these must be specified in different files, but since all gc_*
# parameters must be the same on all instances, they should be in one file.
#
# INSTRUCTIONS: Edit this file and the other INIT files it calls for
# your site, either by using the values provided here or by providing
# your own.  Then place an IFILE= line into each instance-specific
# INIT file that points at this file.
######################################################################

# replace "oracle" with your database name
db_name=oracle

db_files = 1024                                            # INITIAL
# db_files = 80                                            # SMALL
# db_files = 400                                           # MEDIUM
# db_files = 1000                                          # LARGE
```

FIGURE 6.1 *Sample INITinstance.ORA file.*

Datafile (DBF) Naming Conventions

Datafile names should be meaningful, yet should not exceed 25 characters. Also, be sure to use the extension .dbf to identify all datafiles. Add a number to the end of the datafile name to more easily identify it. This number also allows you to add datafiles more easily. The following examples include some of the more commonly seen datafiles:

◆ SYSTEM01.dbf

◆ USERS01.dbf

◆ TEMP01.dbf

- RBS01.dbf, RBD02.dbf, RBS03.dbf
- JOHN_PROD_DATA01.dbf
- SUSAN_DEV_DATA01.dbf, SUSAN_DEV_DATA02.dbf

Tablespace Naming Standards

Tablespace names should not exceed eight characters and should include the underscore character (_) to logically separate abbreviated names. Tablespace names should never be plural. Include a prefix that specifies the application that owns the table. Examples of prefixes include these:

- PAY for Payroll
- MON for Monthly
- TS for Tablespace

Table Naming Standards

Table names should not exceed 14 characters. Use the underscore character (_) to logically separate or break abbreviated names. Table names can and should be plural. During database design the entities should be singular like "INVEN-TORY", but the actual table name should be "INVENTORIES". The table name should accurately convey the use. Other table conventions include:

- Calculate proper PCTUSED and PCTFREE values according to their use in the database.
- Calculate proper INITIAL_EXTENT, NEXT_EXTENT, and PCTINCREASE values according to their use in the database.
- Include a prefix for table names to specify the application that owns or that created the table. Examples include
  - MST for Master Tables
  - TST for Testing Tables
  - ACCT for Accounting Tables

Column-Naming Standards

Column-naming conventions are similar to table-naming conventions, except that column names should not exceed 18 characters and should be listed in the order of importance (for example, primary key, mandatory, not mandatory). This convention groups all foreign keys together, as well as grouping the table's particular keys together. This will also allow not null columns to be first in the table and nullable columns to be last, which allows for better storage of data in the datafiles.

Index-Naming Standards

Index names should not exceed 14 characters. Use the underscore character (_) to logically separate the abbreviated names. Index names, just like the names mentioned previously, should never be plural and should accurately convey their use. Index names should conform to the pattern *table_name*_idx*n*, where *table_name* is the name of the table the index applies to, idx indicates that it is an index, and *n* is a sequential number that uniquely identifies multiple indexes on the same table. In addition, index names should have a prefix that specifies the application that owns the index. Examples of prefixes include these:

- ◆ EMP for Employee
- ◆ EMPNO for Employee Number

 NOTE

Be sure to check and edit index names generated by CASE tools or other products to ensure that they conform to these standards. Some case tools use different naming conventions for indexes than described above. PK is typically used to denote Primary Key, FK for Foreign Key, and IDX is used for a regular index.

 NOTE

Indexes should be used only when needed to maximize performance. This is an important rule and plays a major part in the tuning of the database. Chapter 12, "Analyzing, Tuning, and Reporting on Oracle," covers indexes and how to optimize them.

Database Parameters

There are many possible database parameters and, as mentioned earlier, most are defined in the INIT*instance*.ORA and CONFIG*instance*.ORA files. This chapter would go on for many more pages if it were to list in detail all the database parameters. Because there are other books written just for this purpose, this section covers only the installation-specific parameters.

INIT.ORA Conventions

The INIT.ORA file can contain a variety of documented and undocumented parameters, many of which are platform specific. A good rule of thumb is to start with the MEDIUM parameters uncommented. As you learn more about the database and production requirements, you can make additional changes. However, for any of the parameters, be sure to include a comment that reflects what the parameter affects, the date of the change, and what the parameter was changed from. (Refer to Figure 6.1 to see an example of the small, medium, and large conventions.)

Rollback Segments

In addition to the rollbacks Oracle creates upon installation (usually called System, R01, R02, R03, and R04), you should create a minimum of one additional RBS tablespace for the application RBS segments (for a medium-sized application, 100MB is a good first try). Within the RBS tablespace, you need to create additional RBS segments.

 NOTE

Rollback segments are a common source of errors when they fill up or are broken up into too many *extents* (pieces). Rollback segments should be one of the top 10 items you constantly monitor.

Normalization

Implementing your database so that it's fully relational is known as *normalization*. A *normalized database* eliminates functional dependencies in the data so that when it comes time to update the database, the task is efficient and trouble-free.

Data normalization is a particularly difficult concept for some folks, especially ones who have been using spreadsheets for their day-to-day work. For very simple applications with little data, a spreadsheet is probably all you need; however, for large data-based applications, you'll want to use a database rather than a spreadsheet because it's too difficult to manage the data properly on paper.

The fundamental advantage to using a database rather than a spreadsheet is that databases can be normalized. In other words, databases allow your data to grow over time without affecting your queries or reports. For example, Figure 6.2 shows a typical spreadsheet of a federal budget with no normalization. Notice how you need to add a field for each data year; this means your queries and reports must be restructured each time you do so. The other fields (rows going down the page) do not change over time.

Now look at Figure 6.3; it contains the same data as Figure 6.2, but notice how the normalized table lets you easily add more records (years) without having to restructure the table.

There are multiple degrees of normalization, referred to as *first normal form*, *second normal form*, and so on to the *fifth normal form*. Performance studies have shown that databases usually perform best when normalized to the third normal form, but to achieve third normal form, you must first achieve first and second normal form.

ID	Data Type	1990	1991	1992	1993	1994	1995	1996	1997
1	Receipt	$1,031,309.00	$1,054,264.00	$1,091,300.00	$1,154,400.00	$1,258,600.00	$1,351,800.00	$1,453,100.00	$1,505,400.
2	Outlay	$1,251,778.00	$1,323,011.00	$1,381,700.00	$1,409,400.00	$1,461,700.00	$1,515,700.00	$1,560,300.00	$1,631,000.
3	Deficit	$220,469.00	$268,747.00	$290,400.00	$255,000.00	$203,100.00	$163,900.00	$107,200.00	$125,600.
4	Human Resources	$619,327.00	$689,691.00	$772,440.00	$827,535.00	$869,414.00	$923,765.00	$958,254.00	$1,019,395.
5	Defense	$299,331.00	$273,292.00	$298,350.00	$291,086.00	$281,642.00	$272,066.00	$265,748.00	$267,176.
6	Other	$333,120.00	$360,028.00	$310,910.00	$290,779.00	$310,644.00	$319,869.00	$336,298.00	$344,429.

FIGURE 6.2 *Non-normalized table (spreadsheet view of data).*

Year	Receipt	Outlay	Deficit	Human Resources	Defense	Other
1990	$1,031,309	$1,251,778	$220,469	$619,327	$299,331	$333,120
1991	$1,054,264	$1,323,011	$268,747	$689,691	$273,292	$360,028
1992	$1,091,300	$1,381,700	$290,400	$772,440	$298,350	$310,910
1993	$1,154,400	$1,409,400	$255,000	$827,535	$291,086	$290,779
1994	$1,258,600	$1,461,700	$203,100	$869,414	$281,642	$310,644
1995	$1,351,800	$1,515,700	$163,900	$923,765	$272,066	$319,869
1996	$1,453,100	$1,560,300	$107,200	$958,254	$265,748	$336,298
1997	$1,505,400	$1,631,000	$125,600	$1,019,395	$267,176	$344,429

Federal Budget : Table

FIGURE 6.3 *Normalized table (Oracle relational database view of data).*

NOTE

As with everything in life, too much of a good thing can be bad. Overnormalizing your data design can create performance issues. A fully normalized database has many small tables, and each query requires many, many joins. True, these relations and joins make updating the data design easier, but also slow down most queries.

First Normal Form

To achieve first normal form, each field in a table must convey unique information. For example, if you have a STUDENT table with two columns for the postal ZIP code, your design would violate first normal form. Achieving first normal form is fairly easy, because few folks see a need for duplicating information in a table.

Second Normal Form

Achieving second normal form is a bit more difficult. To do so, the table must contain no fields with information that can be derived from another field in the table. For example, suppose that in the STUDENT table, you have a field called STUDENT_BIRTHDAY. As such, the table must not have a field called STUDENT_AGE because you can determine a student's age by knowing his or her birthday and the date. Fields that violate second normal form are not always obvious, so it is important that you closely examine your columns to make sure that any one column cannot be derived from any other column within the table.

Third Normal Form

For a table to meet the standards of third normal form, no duplicate information can exist throughout the *entire* database. For example, suppose your elementary school, Southside Elementary, has a database of all the students and all the books in its library. Specifically, the database has a STUDENT table and another table called BOOK_CHECKED_OUT; together, these tables track which student has checked out which library book.

A common mistake is to have the BOOK_CHECKED_OUT table store information about the student—such as name and address, which are already stored in the STUDENT table—instead of simply storing a key to refer to the student, such as STU_ID. To ensure third normal form, you need to have your BOOK_CHECKED_OUT table include only the STU_ID and perhaps the BOOK_ID for each book in Southside Elementary School's library.

Other Levels of Normalization

Although there are more normal forms, few developers or DBAs bother ensuring them because of the performance hit they experience. In fact, third normal form can sometimes be too normalized, especially with very large databases. The best approach is to normalize your database to third normal form, and then tinker with it to determine how to achieve the best performance. Using this approach is superior to starting with an un-normalized database and trying to normalize it to achieve certain performance levels.

Key In, Ignition On!
(Starting Up the Database)

Ready to start up the database? True, you haven't installed it yet, but this section gives you some environment-specific information and tips that you can refer to at a later time.

In the UNIX environment, Oracle instances are usually started from the Oracle Server Manager or using the dbstart script distributed with Oracle software. To start Oracle instances from the Server Manager, type **svrmgrl** at the command-line prompt and press Enter to enter into Server Manager. Once in the command-line mode, type **connect internal**. This allows you to enter commands for starting and stopping the database. The scripts for starting and stopping databases are $ORACLE_HOME/bin/dbstart and $ORACLE_HOME/bin/dbshut, respectively. SQL*Net is started with the lsnrctl command performed at the command-line prompt.

During Oracle startup, the shared memory segments for Oracle's SGA are allocated and the background processes are created.

 TIP

To start Oracle automatically when your server boots up, make sure the entry for your database SID in the **/etc/oratab** file ends in a capital Y.

Under Windows NT/2000, a process running independently of a login session must be configured as a service. Consequently, each Oracle instance is associated with one or more Windows NT services. The most significant services include these:

◆ **OracleServicesid.** This service must be defined for each Oracle instance on the NT server. The *sid* represents the instance identifier; in other words, OracleServiceABC1 represents the instance ABC1. Starting this service creates the Oracle process.

◆ **OracleStartsid.** Starting this service performs an automatic startup for the instance in question—equivalent to issuing a startup command from Server Manager.

◆ **OracleTNSListenerNN.** This service implements the SQL*Net listener. *NN* refers to the version of SQL*Net, typically 80 for Oracle8 and 23 for Oracle7.3.

Ignition Off, Key Out!
(Shutting Down the Database)

You can use the Oracle Instance Manager (oradim73.exe or oradim80.exe) in its command-line mode or from the Start menu within Windows to start or stop Oracle instances and services.

Starting Oracle Automatically within NT

To start an Oracle instance automatically, all you have to do is set the startup property to automatic for the respective services. You do this in the services applet or in the Oracle Instance Manager applet. To start an Oracle instance manually, either use the Start button on the services applet or issue the `net start` command to start the appropriate services. For example, the following commands start the TEST_DB instance and the SQL*Net listener service:

```
net start OracleServiceTEST_DB
net start OracleStartTEST_DB
net start OracleTNSListener80
```

In Windows NT/2000, terminating the OracleServicesid service will terminate the Oracle instance. However, simply terminating this service aborts the instance without performing any of the normal shutdown procedures. Thus, shutting down a Windows NT/2000 server will crash the Oracle instance. This is equivalent to performing a "shutdown abort" in the Unix environment. Although Oracle will almost always recover from such an abrupt shutdown, it is good practice to perform a cleaner shutdown of the database.

In Windows NT/2000, Oracle8 introduced a mechanism of performing a clean shutdown. If you set the value of the Registry parameter `ora_shutdown` or `ora_sid_shutdown` to True, Oracle will perform a shutdown immediately whenever the OracleServicesid service is stopped—including when Windows NT or Windows 2000 is shut down.

Oracle has three levels of shutting down the database.

- ◆ **Shutdown Normal.** This is the preferred method, but all users must be disconnected before the shutdown can occur. The next startup of the database will *not* require recovery procedures.

- ◆ **Shutdown Immediate.** This should be used when a power shutdown is going to occur soon or the database is behaving irregularly. This method terminates client SQL statements, rolls back any uncommitted transactions, and does *not* wait for users to disconnect. Also, recovery procedures might be needed upon the next startup of the database.

◆ **Shutdown Abort.** If all else fails and you need to shut down the database ASAP, use this method. All connections and transactions are terminated without rolling back data. Database recovery procedures are required upon the next startup of the database. Again, this method should not be your standard practice, but is available for emergencies such as during a power failure.

Summary

This chapter's intent was to steer you toward getting ready to either install your first database, migrate from an existing database, or to obtain tips and pointers for installing yet another Oracle database. Hopefully you discovered that in order to plan and execute a good database design, it is important to understand the different naming conventions, standards, and Oracle's OFA.

Overall, careful planning and design will ensure that your database installations run smoothly and efficiently for years to come.

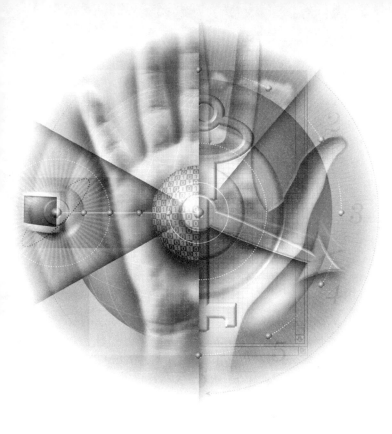

Chapter 7

Installing Oracle—Step by Step!

After reading the previous six chapters, you should now understand Oracle, its architecture, the problems and risks associated with it, and the amount of planning and preparation that must go into implementing it. This chapter changes gears, stepping you through two installations—one for the Oracle RDBMS software, and the other for installing an Oracle tool, specifically Oracle's Enterprise Manager.

Take note that the steps herein describe only one way to install your Oracle database. Depending on the choices you make during the installation, you might not see all the dialog boxes in this chapter. Note also that because of the many different platforms on which you can install Oracle, this book cannot cover in detail all possible installations. The installation of the Oracle RDBMS is outlined on a WindowsNT/2000 platform because this is one of the two more popular installation platforms.

TIP

Read through this chapter at least once before you sit down with Oracle in front of you. Familiarize yourself with the installation so that you are not surprised when you need additional information on hand.

NOTE

See Appendix A, "DBA Templates and Checklists," for checklists that list every possible option that you can choose when installing Oracle's RDBMS and the Enterprise Manager.

Installing Oracle RDBMS on WindowsNT/2000

To install Oracle RDBMS on a Windows NT/2000 system, do the following:

1. Insert the CD into your server and choose to install. You will see the Welcome screen shown in Figure 7.1; click on Next to continue.

 NOTE

Throughout these dialog boxes, notice the Help button in the bottom-left corner. The Oracle Help is very detailed—use it if you are unclear as to what some of the options or choices mean.

2. In the dialog box shown in Figure 7.2, choose the name for your Oracle Home variable, as well as the path where you want the Oracle software to be installed. Click on Next to continue.

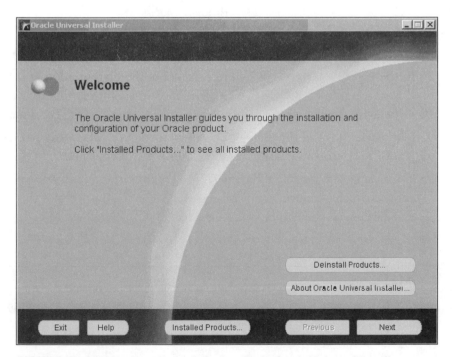

FIGURE 7.1 *This is the welcome dialog box for the Oracle Universal Installer.*

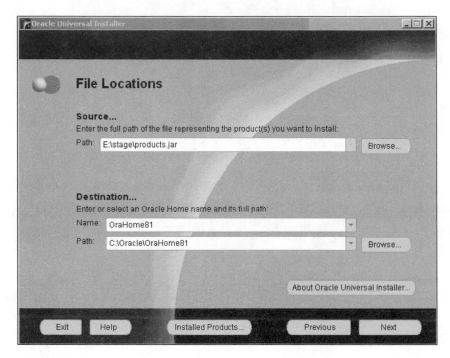

FIGURE 7.2 *These are the file location choices for your installation.*

3. In the dialog box shown in Figure 7.3, choose the first selection, Oracle8i Enterprise Edition 8.1.6.0.0. The other choices are for installing the client software or the management software only. Click on Next to continue.

4. Choose Custom in the dialog box shown in Figure 7.4. Doing so enables you to set your own parameters. Click on Next to continue.

5. The dialog box shown in Figure 7.5 is very important; it allows you to choose which products you want to install. For the purposes of this installation, all the components are selected. Click on Next to continue.

NOTE

Choose Typical to install a predefined database; choose Minimal to install a smaller, predefined database.

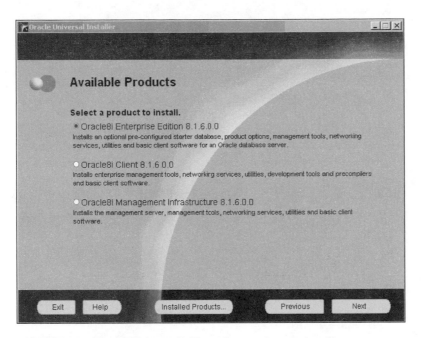

FIGURE 7.3 *These are the available products to choose to install.*

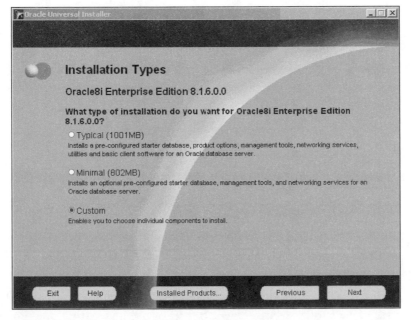

FIGURE 7.4 *These are the different types of installations.*

> **NOTE**
>
> Now is a good time to check your Oracle product sheet that you got when you purchased Oracle to determine what optional software you have licensed.

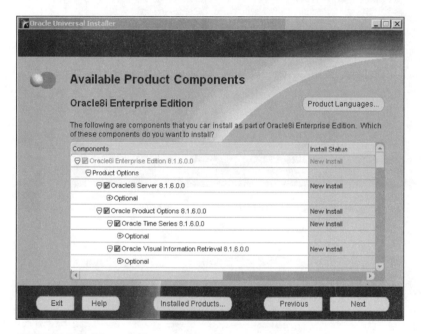

FIGURE 7.5 *These are the available product components.*

6. Although you can use the dialog box shown in Figure 7.6 to change the default locations of various components, it is best to leave these locations as the Oracle defaults. Click on Next to continue.

7. If you chose to install Oracle's Advanced Security, the dialog box shown in Figure 7.7 will appear. Depending on your operating system, you might not see the choices as they appear in this example. Click on Next to continue.

8. The dialog box shown in Figure 7.8 enables you to choose whether to install a new Oracle Management Server or use an existing one. For a new installation, create a new repository. Click on Next to continue.

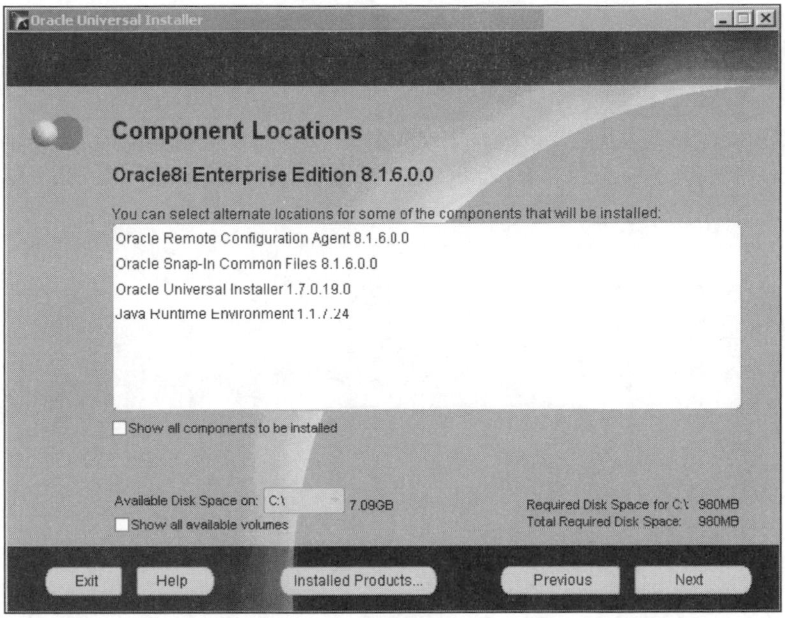

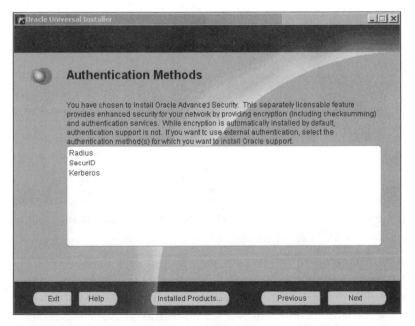

FIGURE 7.6 *These are the component locations for your installation.*

FIGURE 7.7 *These are the different authentication methods.*

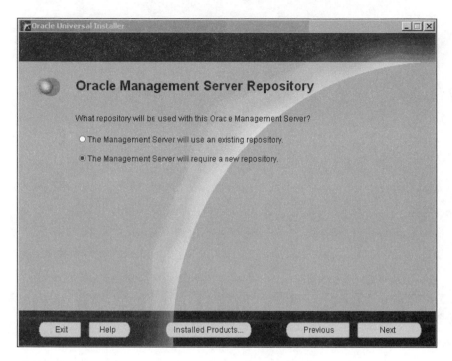

FIGURE 7.8 *This is the Oracle Management Server Repository dialog box.*

NOTE

The Oracle Management Server (OMS) is used with many of Oracle's Enterprise Manager tools. See your Oracle documentation for a more detailed explanation of the Oracle Management Server.

9. The dialog box shown in Figure 7.9 enables you to choose whether to use Oracle's Configuration Assistant to create the database. Choose Yes, and click on Next to continue.

10. Name your database in the dialog box shown in Figure 7.10. The Global Database Name is typically specific and usually contains a domain name. Oracle's System Identifier, or SID, is generally the first part of the Global Database Name and is used to identify your database. Select your database name, and click on Next to continue.

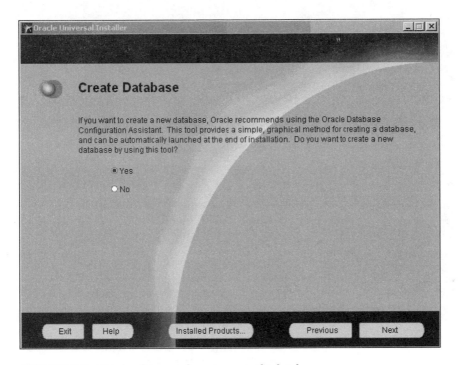

FIGURE 7.9 *This is where you choose to create the database.*

 NOTE

The Configuration Assistant is similar to a wizard, and aids in the creation of a database. If you choose not to use the Configuration Assistant, you have to create the database with your own scripts at the appropriate time.

11. The dialog box shown in Figure 7.11 summarizes the choices you have made this far; click on Install to continue.

12. After the installation starts, you have reached the point of no return (unless, of course, you click on Cancel). Time to refill your coffee, prop up your feet, and wait. You can view the progress of the installation in the dialog box shown in Figure 7.12.

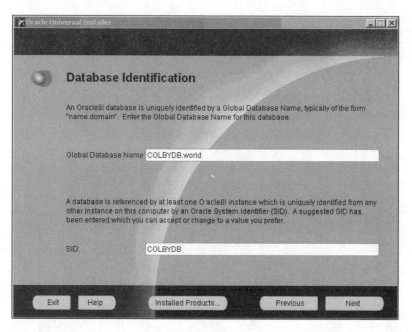

FIGURE 7.10 *This is the database identification.*

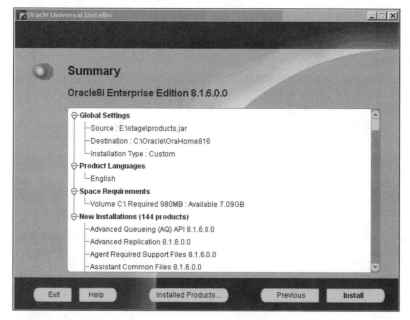

FIGURE 7.11 *This is the summarization of your choices for installation.*

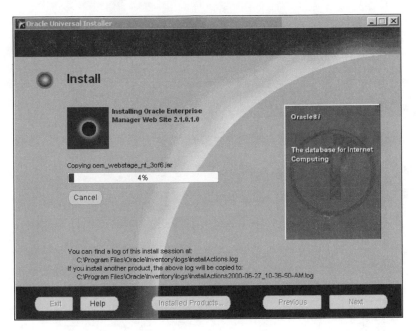

FIGURE 7.12 *This is the progress of the installation.*

13. After your Oracle software has been successfully installed, it is time to install Net8 (Oracle's networking software, which used to be called SQL*Net), the database itself, and any other software that you chose in step 5. The dialog box shown in Figure 7.13 indicates that the Net8 Configuration Assistant has started; no action is required on your part.

14. The dialog box shown in Figure 7.14 is the welcome screen for installing Net8 using the Net8 Configuration Assistant. If you so choose, you can manually set up Net8 with this wizard to custom install the Directory Service Access, the Listener, and the Naming Conventions. This will lead to a dialog box for each of the items just mentioned. Because Oracle's wizard for installing a typical Net8 configuration is pretty reliable, it's better to select the Perform Typical Configuration option. This will then bypass the intermediate screens and successfully install Net8. Click on Next to continue.

15. The dialog box shown in Figure 7.15 is the first of many that guides you through installing your Oracle database. Choose whether to install a database geared toward online transactions or data warehousing. If you

are not sure or know that your application can benefit from both, choose the Multipurpose option. Click on Next to continue.

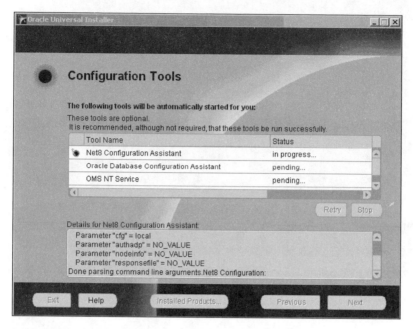

FIGURE 7.13 *These are the configuration tools to install.*

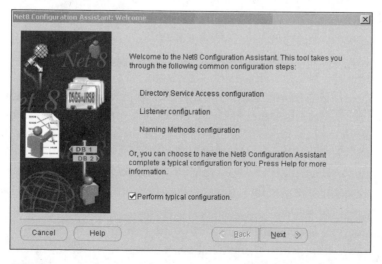

FIGURE 7.14 *This is the Net8 Configuration Assistant Welcome dialog box.*

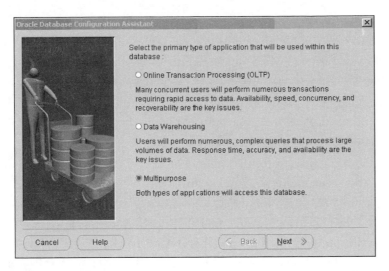

FIGURE 7.15 *This is the Database Configuration Assistant's type of application dialog box.*

16. Choose the number of concurrent users supported by your license agreement with Oracle in the dialog box shown in Figure 7.16 (this information can be found on the Oracle purchase agreement). For this sample installation, I used the default value of 15. Click on Next to continue.

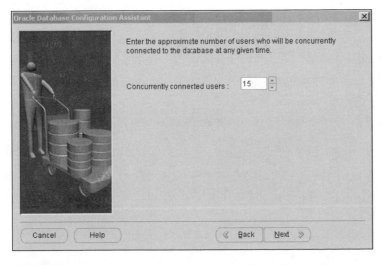

FIGURE 7.16 *This is the Database Configuration Assistant's Concurrent User dialog box.*

17. Specify whether your database will operate in Dedicated or Shared mode, and click on Next to continue. Shared mode enables Oracle's multithreaded server (MTS) feature. This mode shares a pool of resources whereby the database devotes one resource to one client.

18. Use the dialog box in Figure 7.18 to install specific options for which you are licensed. Again, check your Oracle purchasing agreement to see which database options you purchased. Click on Next to continue.

19. Review your database information and make any corrections in the dialog box shown in Figure 7.19. Click on Next to continue.

20. The Database Configuration Assistant will automatically assign names and paths for your three control files. It is a good idea to keep the default paths and names; however if you want to change them you can do so in the dialog box shown in Figure 7.20. This dialog box also presents the choices for the maximum datafiles, log files, and log members. After you've reviewed the information and made any appropriate changes, click on Next.

21. The dialog box shown in Figure 7.21 contains a lot of information about the default tablespaces that Oracle will install. Each tab on the top corresponds to the setting of parameters for different tablespaces. Be sure to click on each of the tabs across the top in order to ensure that your tablespaces will be installed to your preferences, and click on Next to continue.

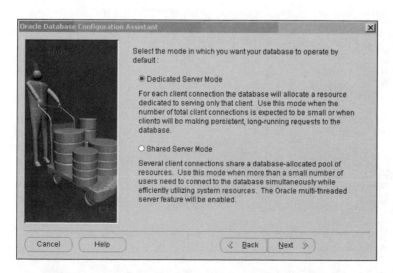

FIGURE 7.17 *This is the Database Configuration Assistant's Choice of Modes dialog box.*

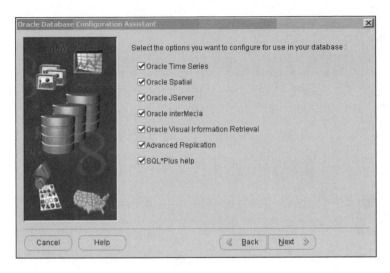

FIGURE 7.18 *This is the Database Configuration Assistant's Options dialog box.*

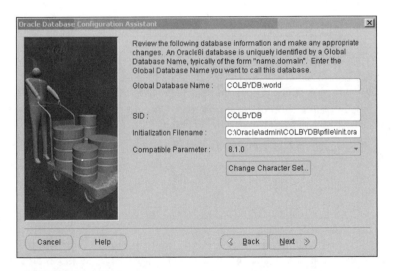

FIGURE 7.19 *This is the Database Configuration Assistant's Review of Database Information dialog box.*

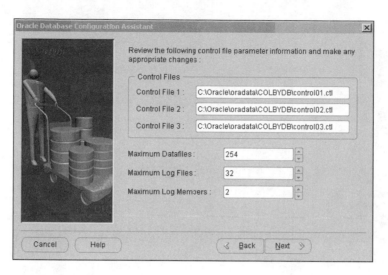

FIGURE 7.20 *This is the Database Configuration Assistant's Control File dialog box.*

 NOTE

It's usually a good idea to simply use Oracle's defaults for these parameters. Oracle determines the defaults by calculating your server hard drive space, the number of users you entered, and other information. Change this information only if, for instance, you think the rollback tablespace is going to fill up quickly because you have a lot of binary or long raw data in some or your tables.

 NOTE

Notice the interMedia tab in the dialog box shown in Figure 7.21. This tab is present only if you checked the Oracle interMedia option in step 18. Oracle interMedia is described in Chapter 5, "What's Oracle8i All About?"

22. The Database Configuration Assistant will automatically assign names and paths for your three redo log files. It is a good idea to keep the

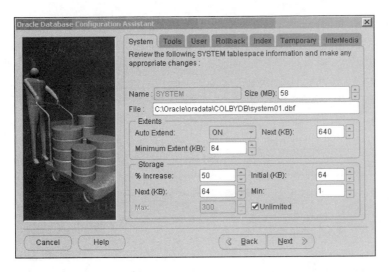

FIGURE 7.21 *This is the Database Configuration Assistant's Tablespace Configuration dialog box.*

default paths and names; if you want to change them, however, you can do so in the dialog box shown in Figure 7.22. Also presented in this dialog box are the choices for the sizes of these files. When the options in this dialog box are set to your preference, click on Next to continue.

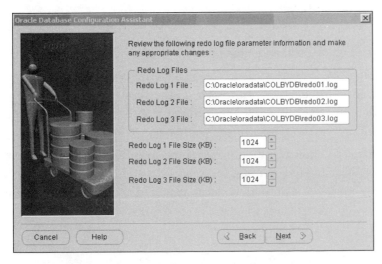

FIGURE 7.22 *This is the Database Configuration Assistant's Redo Log File dialog box.*

23. Either accept Oracle's default sizes (recommended) or change the values for the checkpoint intervals and checkpoint timeouts in the dialog box shown in Figure 7.23. This dialog box also allows you to choose whether you want to enable the archive log. When the options in this dialog box are set to your preference, click on Next to continue.

 NOTE

The archive log is a nice feature that tracks most database activity and stores it in log files. The advantages of using this feature are great if you need to know who does what in the database. The disadvantage is probably obvious: The added overhead bogs down the system and disrupts performance unless Oracle is running on a powerful platform. If you determined during the planning stages that your system needs a good audit trail, you'll need to boost your system's horsepower to handle this overhead.

24. Either accept Oracle's default sizes (recommended) or change the values of Oracle's System Global Area, or SGA, in the dialog box shown in Figure 7.24. In most cases, don't change these values without thoroughly understanding them; these values usually need to work together and should be adjusted accordingly. (See Chapter 12, "Analyzing, Tuning, and Reporting on Oracle," for more information.) For now, accept the default values and click on Next to continue.

25. If desired, adjust the directories for Oracle's trace files in the dialog box shown in Figure 7.25, and click on Next to continue.

26. The dialog box shown in Figure 7.26 enables you to create the database (the other option enables you to save all the choices you made into a batch file to be executed at a later time). Choose to create the database and click on Next.

27. The dialog box shown in Figure 7.27 shows you the database-creation progress. Within a few minutes (or longer, depending on the choices and your platform), you'll have an Oracle database that's ready to be populated.

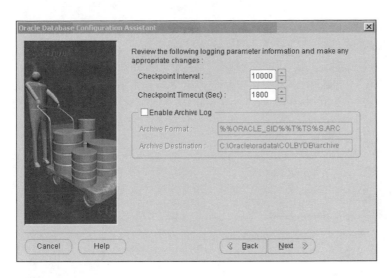

FIGURE 7.23 *This is the Database Configuration Assistant's Logging Parameter Information dialog box.*

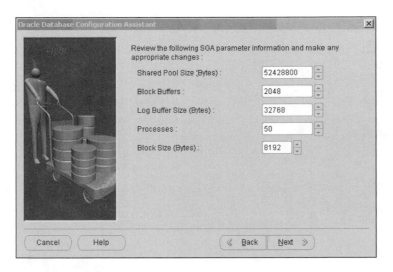

FIGURE 7.24 *This is the Database Configuration Assistant's SGA Parameter Information dialog box.*

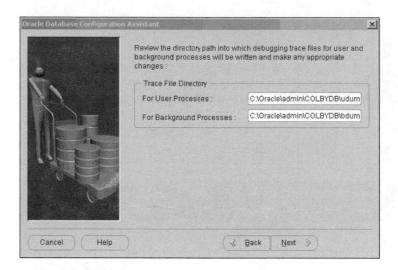

FIGURE 7.25 *This is the Database Configuration Assistant's Trace File dialog box.*

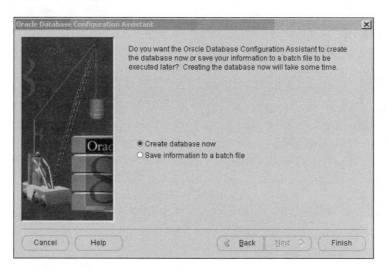

FIGURE 7.26 *This is the Database Configuration Assistant's dialog box for creating the database.*

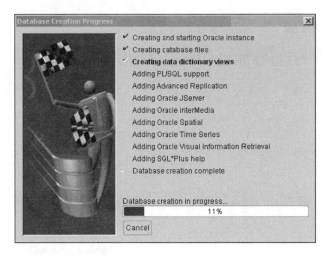

FIGURE 7.27 *This is the Database Configuration Assistant's Database Progress dialog box.*

What's Next?

You now have an Oracle database with all the tablespaces that Oracle needs to function correctly. Next, you must create or import your application-specific data. This usually involves creating application-specific tablespaces and then populating them with tables. There are many ways to do this, as described here:

◆ **By hand.** Go into SQL*Plus and start typing commands.

◆ **OEM.** Use Oracle's Enterprise Manager to create the needed schemas. The next section of this chapter discusses the installation of this tool.

◆ **Scripts.** Use predesigned scripts that contain the needed information.

◆ **Database design tool.** Use the scripts or the login sequences that these tools generate.

 NOTE

The easiest method is probably using a Database design tool. You design a conceptual model of your database and then let the tool create a physical model in the correct version of Oracle. After these scripts are created, the tool can either automatically generate the structures under the application owner, or generate the scripts so that you can run them at your leisure.

Installing Oracle's Enterprise Manager on Windows NT/2000

To install Oracle's Enterprise Manager on a Windows NT/2000 system, do the following:

1. Insert the CD into your server and choose to install. You will see a welcome screen, much like the one shown in the previous installation (Figure 7.1). Click on Install to view the dialog box shown in Figure 7.28. Here, you choose the name for your Oracle Home variable as well as the path where the Oracle software is installed. Make your choices and click on Next to continue.

TIP

Choose an Oracle Home that identifies the contents of the Home. In the example in Figure 7.28, EntMgr21 is selected, which specifies that Enterprise Manager version 2.1 is located there.

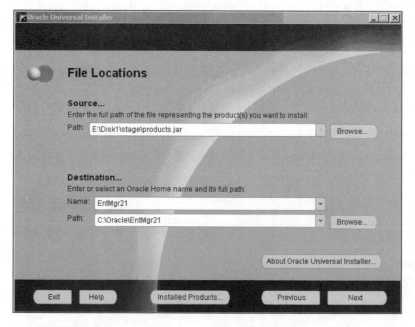

FIGURE 7.28 *These are the file location choices for your installation.*

2. In the dialog box shown in Figure 7.29, choose the first selection, Oracle Enterprise Manager Packs and Management Infrastructure (the other choice is for installing the Oracle Enterprise Manager Packs software only), and click on Next.

3. To ensure that all the tools you need are installed, choose the custom installation in the dialog box shown in Figure 7.30. Click on Next to continue.

4. The dialog box shown in Figure 7.31 is very important; it allows you to choose the products you want to install. For the purposes of this installation, all components are selected. Click on Next to continue.

TIP

Time to check your Oracle product sheet to determine what software you have licensed.

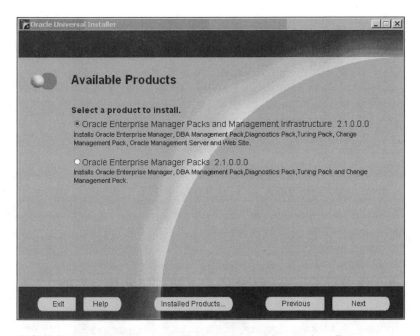

FIGURE 7.29 *These are the available products to choose to install.*

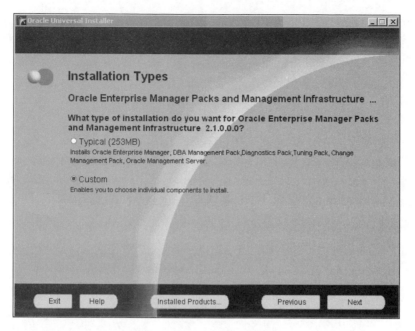

FIGURE 7.30 *These are the different types of installations.*

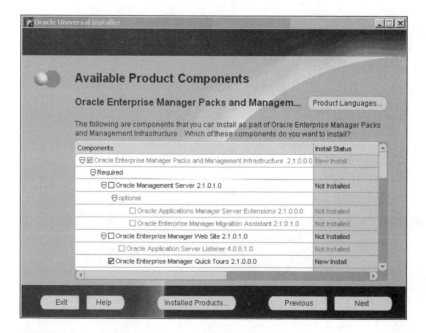

FIGURE 7.31 *These are the available product components.*

5. The dialog box shown in Figure 7.32 enables you to choose whether to install a new Oracle Management Server or use an existing one. Because you chose to create a new repository in step 8 of installing the Oracle RDBMS, use an existing repository here. Click on Next to continue.

6. The dialog box shown in Figure 7.33 summarizes the choices you have made thus far; click on Install to continue.

7. After the installation starts, you have reached the point of no return (unless, of course, you click on Cancel). Time to refill your coffee again, prop up your feet, and wait. You can view the progress of the installation in the dialog box shown in Figure 7.34.

TIP

The Oracle Management Server (OMS) is used with many of Oracle's Enterprise Manager tools. See your Oracle documentation for a more detailed explanation of the Oracle Management Server.

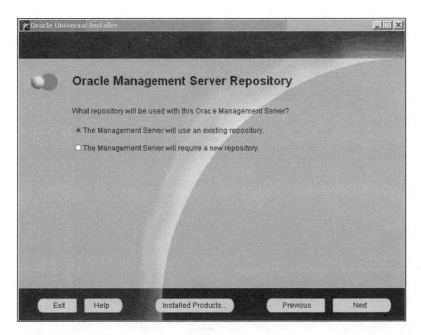

FIGURE 7.32 *This is the Oracle Management Server Repository dialog box.*

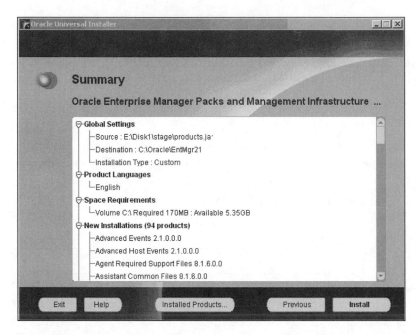

FIGURE 7.33 *This is the summary dialog box for your installation.*

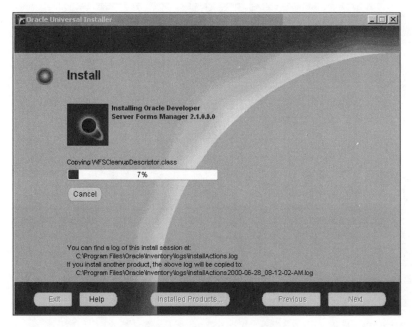

FIGURE 7.34 *This is the installation progress dialog box.*

8. After your Oracle software has been successfully installed, it is time to install Net8 (Oracle's networking software Net8, which used to be called SQL*Net), the database itself, and any other software that you chose in step 4. The dialog box shown in Figure 7.35 indicates that the Net8 Configuration Assistant has started; no action is required on your part.

9. The dialog box shown in Figure 7.36 is the first of several for the Net8 Configuration Assistant. If you choose, you can manually set up Net8 with this wizard to custom install the Directory Service Access and the Naming Conventions. Because Oracle's wizard for installing a typical Net8 configuration is pretty reliable, I recommend that you check the Perform Typical Configuration option. Click on Next to continue.

 NOTE

If you haven't noticed already, the installation steps for Oracle Enterprise Manager are very similar to those of the RDBMS. This is probably why they call it the "Oracle Universal Installer."

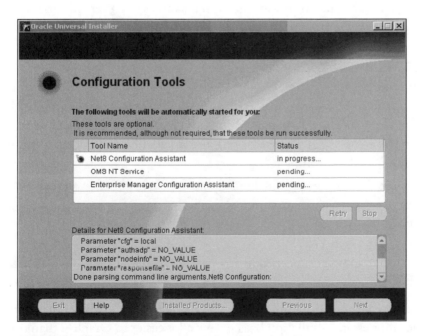

FIGURE 7.35 *These are the configuration tools to install.*

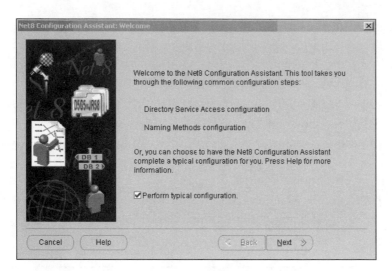

FIGURE 7.36 *This is the Net8 Configuration Assistant Welcome dialog box.*

10. The Configuration Assistant should finish installing Net8, and might ask you about the repository. It's a good idea to use the same repository as you had installed previously, as well as the same user/owner, for this repository. Figure 7.37 shows the second page of the Configuration Assistant for the repository, which displays a summary of the parameters. In the sample dialog box you can see that the repository owner is REPUSRCOLBY for the COLBYDB database. Click on Finish.

11. The dialog box shown in Figure 7.38 simply shows you the progress of the Configuration Assistant. Within a few minutes (or longer, depending on the choices and your platform), the installation of Oracle's Enterprise Manger will be complete.

12. Figure 7.39 shows the final dialog box of the installation process. Unless you want to install something else, click on Exit to end the installation process successfully.

Summary

Five or ten years ago, installing an Oracle database was a nightmare, with too much room for error. Installation has become a lot easier in Oracle8, thanks to the Java Universal Installer.

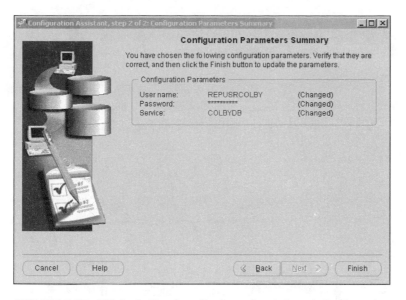

FIGURE 7.37 *This is the Database Configuration Assistant's Configuration Parameters summary.*

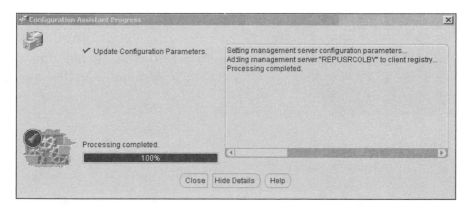

FIGURE 7.38 *This is the Database Configuration Assistant's progress dialog box.*

This chapter guided you through a complete database installation and Oracle's main database tool, Enterprise Manager. Each step is clearly illustrated with helpful wording on which choices to make. Hopefully this chapter helped you gain confidence in your ability to handle installing Oracle and its many tools.

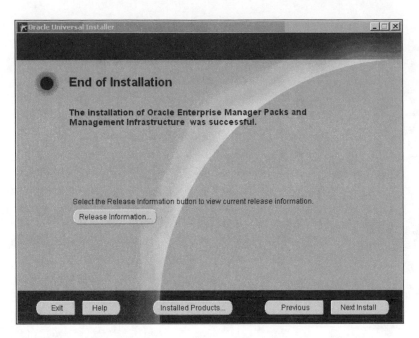

FIGURE 7.39 *This is the Oracle Universal Installer's End of Installation dialog box.*

The next chapter will take a break from the details of Oracle and introduce you to another area that is often overlooked when working with Oracle—specifically problems, risks, and errors.

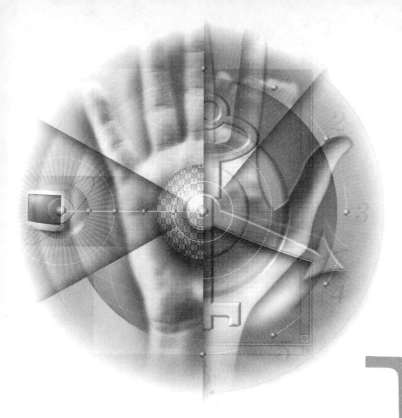

PART II

Maintaining Your Oracle Database

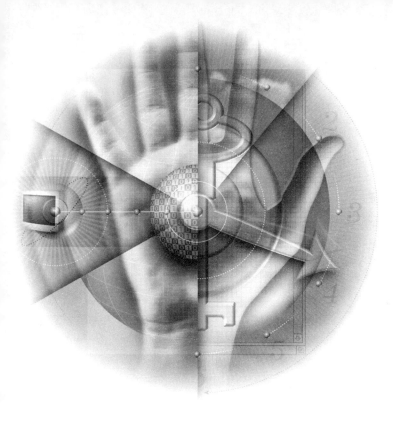

Chapter 8

**Understanding
Problems, Risks,
and Errors**

isk in the Oracle sense is the possibility of suffering data loss. For a given project, the loss can include situations in which the application cannot communicate with the database or the database is inaccessible during normal working hours. These losses can lead to missed deadlines or failure to achieve the mission and purpose of the project. In other words, a risk is a problem waiting to happen.

Unfortunately, risks are inherent in any project; indeed, risk-taking is essential to progress, and failure is often a key part of learning. Although some risks are inevitable, this does not mean that attempting to recognize and manage them will harm your opportunities for creativity.

Sources of Risk

Many, if not most, information technology projects fail, not for technology or project management reasons, but because of larger organizational pressures that are typically ignored. These organizational pressures come in many forms, such as competitive pressures, financial health, and organizational culture. Table 8.1 lists some of these risk sources and their possible consequences.

Table 8.1 Risk Sources and Possible Consequences

Risk Sources	Project Consequences
Mission and goals	Cost overruns
Decision drivers	Schedule slips
Management	Inadequate functionality
Customer/end user	Canceled projects
Budget/cost	Sudden personnel changes
Schedule	Customer dissatisfaction
Project characteristics	Loss of company image
Development process	Demoralized staff
Development environment	Poor product performance
Personnel	Legal proceedings

The elements of significant risk are not the same across all types of information-technology projects. Different types of projects pose different kinds of risks and must be addressed individually.

Managing Risks

Many Information Technology (IT) professionals have a misconception of risk management, considering it, at best, a necessary but boring task to be carried out at the beginning of a project before the *real* work of implementing or managing their Oracle database begins. Even worse, they might view risk management as yet another form of bureaucratic management that keeps the organization from achieving its objectives. Instead, risk management must be viewed as part of a dynamic, competitive process rather than as just an additional static project-management activity.

On many projects, risks are assessed only once—only during initial project planning. Major risks are identified and mitigated, but are never explicitly reviewed again. This is *not* an example of good risk management. An effective project team continuously assesses risks and uses the information for decision-making in all phases of the project.

 CAUTION

If the risk-management process is not integrated with the day-to-day project management of your Oracle database or application, the process will soon be become nothing more than a background activity.

Two inherently different approaches to risk management exist:

◆ **Reactive risk management.** The project team reacts to the consequences of risks (actual problems) as they occur.

◆ **Active risk management.** The project team has a visible process for managing risks that is measurable and repeatable.

Preventing risk is the transition point between reactive and active approaches. Prevention occurs in the planning stages of a project, when the team can take action to prevent problems. It is important to point out that prevention is still essentially a reactive strategy for managing risks; it is not a cure for the cause of risk, only a means to avoid its symptoms. To reach higher levels of active risk management, the team must be willing to take risks. This means not fearing risk, but rather viewing it as a means to create the right type of opportunity. To do so, the team must be able to unemotionally evaluate the risks (and opportunities) and then take actions that address the causes of these risks, not just their symptoms. No matter how good the risk assessment, the team's ability to manage risk and opportunity will be the determining success factor.

Active Risk Management

As mentioned previously, active risk management involves the constant assessment of risks, and the use of this information for decision-making in all phases of the project. The process of active risk management is illustrated in Figure 8.1.

As shown in Figure 8.1, active risk management involves five stages:

- ◆ Risk identification
- ◆ Risk analysis
- ◆ Risk action planning
- ◆ Risk tracking
- ◆ Risk control

Risk Identification

Risks must be identified before they can be managed; risk identification provides members of the project team with the opportunities, cues, and information needed to detect major risks before they adversely affect the Oracle development project.

Risk Factor Charts

After you identify risk factors through an open discussion among your team members and key project stakeholders, place these risks on a risk factor chart. You should group risk factors by focus area (such as custom software development, Oracle migrations, rapid infrastructure deployment, packaged software deployment, enterprise architecture planning, and platform-dependent database installation) and category (such as mission and goals factors, decision drivers, organizational management factors, and budget and cost factors).

Creating a Nurturing Environment

On some projects, reporting new risks might be viewed as a form of complaining (whining). In this situation, a person who reports risks is viewed as a troublemaker. People generally become wary of freely communicating risks under these circumstances. They select and soften the risk information they decide to share to ensure that it is not too negative. Effective risk management, however, requires an environment in which people who identify risks are safe from retribution. All must feel free to express tentative or controversial views.

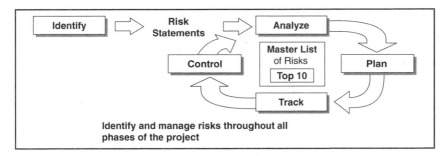

FIGURE 8.1 *The active risk-management process should be carried throughout all phases of the project.*

Each risk factor has one or more characteristic that describes whether the risk should be considered a high, medium, or low risk. Table 8.2 identifies various cues for certain risk factors.

 NOTE

The process that occurs between team members and stakeholders provides a powerful way to expose assumptions and differing viewpoints. Depending on experience, different team members will see the project differently. It is unlikely that a team will agree on the ranking of all risk factors. If, after discussion, you cannot reach an agreement, the best approach is a voting technique wherein the majority wins. If the votes are tied, use the worst-case scenario.

Table 8.2 Mission and Goals Risk Factors

Risk Factor	Low-Risk Cue	Medium-Risk Cue	High-Risk Cue
Project fit	Directly supports customer's mission and goals	Indirectly affects one or more goals	Does not support or relate to customer's mission or goals
Customer perception	Expects team to provide this product	Believes team is not working on the expected product	Believes the desired product is a mismatch with prior team products
Work flow	Causes little or no change to work flow	Changes some aspect or has small effect on work flow	Significantly changes work flow or method of organization

Risk Analysis

Risk analysis, the second step in the active risk-management process, involves the conversion of risk data into decision-making information. Thorough analysis ensures that the team is working on the right risks.

Risk analysis is composed of two factors:

◆ Risk probability
◆ Risk impact

Risk Probability

Risk probability is the likelihood that an event will actually occur. Using a numerical value for risk probability is desirable for ranking risks. Risk probability must be greater than zero or the risk does not pose a threat to the project. Likewise, the probability must be less than 100 percent or the risk is a certainty—in other words, it is a known problem.

Risk Impact

Risk impact measures the severity of adverse effects, or the magnitude of a loss, if the risk comes to pass. Deciding how to measure sustained loses is not a trivial matter. If the risk has a financial impact, a dollar value is the preferred way to quantify the magnitude of loss. The financial impact might be long-term costs in operations and support, loss of market share, short-term costs in additional work, or lost opportunity cost. With other risks, a subjective scale (such as from 1 to 5) is more appropriate. These rate the viability of project success. High values indicate serious loss to the project; medium values show loss to portions of the project or loss of effectiveness.

Risk Exposure

The overall threat of each risk needs to be clearly understood. Sometimes a high-probability risk has low impact, and can be safely ignored; likewise, you can usually ignore a high-impact risk that has low probability. The risks that have high exposure (high probability and high impact) are the ones worth managing. This means reducing either the risk probability or the risk impact.

NOTE

Although team members and key project stakeholders often perceive risk as negative, it is important that they not judge a project simply on the number and nature of the risks. They should remember that risk is the possibility, not the certainty, of loss. Team members who look at a project with a list of five or ten major risks might view the project with skepticism even though the total risk exposure might not be significant.

The Risk Statement

Before a risk can be managed, it must be expressed clearly. When stating a risk, the team must consider not only a symptom, but also a result. Hence, the statement of risk should include the cause of the situation (that is, the condition) and the expected result (that is, the consequence). Figure 8.2 shows the general structure of a risk statement.

Use this information when developing a risk statement form:

   ◆ **Risk identifier.** The name the team uses to uniquely identify a risk for reporting and tracking purposes.

   ◆ **Risk source.** The focus area (custom software development, packaged software deployment, infrastructure deployment, enterprise program management, or enterprise architecture planning), the risk factor category (mission and goals, decision drivers, organizational management, schedule, or budget/cost), and the risk factor (project fit, political influences, organization stability, or project size) used to identify the risk.

◆ **Risk condition.** A natural language statement, or a statement that is void of technical jargon, describing the existing condition that can possibly lead to a loss.

◆ **Risk consequence.** A natural language statement describing the loss that would occur to the project if the risk became certain.

◆ **Risk probability.** An expression of a percentage greater than zero and less than 100 that represents the likelihood that the condition will actually occur, resulting in a loss.

◆ **Risk impact classification.** Whether the impact of the risk is, for example, financial, strategic, technical, or legal.

◆ **Risk impact.** The magnitude of impact should the risk actually occur. This number can be a dollar value or simply a number between 1 and 10 that indicates relative magnitude. The result of multiplying risk impact by risk probability is often used to rank risks.

◆ **Risk exposure.** The overall threat of the risk to the project, balancing the likelihood of actual loss with the magnitude of the potential loss. The team uses risk exposure to rate and rank risks.

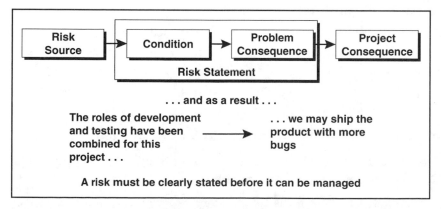

FIGURE 8.2 *The risk statement clearly identifies the condition and the possible consequences of the risk.*

NOTE

When ranking risk exposure, all the risk impact values must be in the same units of measurement, either dollars or levels of impact.

◆ **Risk context.** A paragraph containing additional background information that helps to clarify the risk situation.

◆ **Related risks.** A list of risk identifications the team uses to track interdependent risks.

Top 10 Risk List

Managing risk takes time and effort away from other parts of the project, so it is important for the team to do only what is absolutely necessary to manage them. A simple but effective technique for monitoring risk is to create a list of the major risk items in the project. The risk list is visible to all project stakeholders and can be included in the vision/scope document and the project plan.

Risk Action Planning

Risk action planning, the third step in the risk-management process, turns risk information into decisions and actions. Planning involves developing actions to address individual risks, prioritizing risk actions, and creating an integrated risk-management plan.

There are four key areas the team should address during risk action planning:

◆ **Research.** Do you know enough about this risk? Do you need to study the risk further to better determine its characteristics before you can decide what action to take?

◆ **Accept.** Can you live with the consequences if the risk were actually to occur? Can you accept the risk and take no further action?

◆ **Manage.** Can the team do anything to mitigate the impact of the risk should the risk occur?

◆ **Avoid.** Can you avoid the risk by changing the scope of the project?

Risk-Management Goals and Strategies

The three risk-management goals are to:

- ◆ Reduce the probability of occurrence
- ◆ Reduce the magnitude of loss
- ◆ Change the consequences of the risk

A number of strategies are possible to reduce risk:

- ◆ For those risks the project team can control, apply the resources needed to reduce the risk.
- ◆ For those risks outside the control of the project team, find workarounds.

It might be possible for the project team to transfer the risk by

- ◆ Moving to different hardware
- ◆ Moving a software feature to another part of the system that is better able to handle it
- ◆ Subcontracting the work to a more experienced player

The Risk Contingency Strategy

The idea behind a contingency strategy is to have a fallback plan in place that you can activate in case all efforts to manage the risk fail. For example, suppose a new release of the operating system is needed so that you can install Oracle on the new hardware that you ordered, but the arrival date for the new operating system is in jeopardy, therefore putting the installation at risk. The team might devise a plan to use an alternative operating system, a different version of Oracle, or a different platform altogether to lessen any impact on the overall schedule for the project.

Deciding when to start the second parallel effort is a matter of watching the trigger value for the contingency plan. Often, the team can establish trigger values for the contingency plan based on the type of risk or the type of project consequence that will be encountered.

The Risk Action Form

A risk action form is a paper that includes risks and possible actions. The following list contains information that your team might want to consider when developing a risk action form:

◆ **Risk identifier.** The name the team uses to uniquely identify the risk for reporting and tracking purposes.

◆ **Risk statement.** The natural language statement (explained earlier in this chapter) describing the condition that exists that might possibly lead to a loss. It also describes the impact of the loss.

◆ **Risk-management strategy.** A description of the team strategy for managing the risk, including any assumptions.

◆ **Risk-management strategy metrics.** The metrics the team uses to determine whether the risk-management actions are working.

◆ **Action items.** A list of actions the team will take to manage the risk. They will log these action items in the project tracking system.

◆ **Due dates.** The date when the team will complete each planned action item.

◆ **Personnel assignments.** The people assigned to perform the action items.

◆ **Risk contingency strategy.** A description of the team strategy in the event that the actions planned to manage the risk don't work. The team executes the risk contingency strategy if the risk contingency strategy trigger were reached (see next bullet).

◆ **Risk contingency strategy metrics and trigger values.** The metrics and triggers the team uses to determine when the risk contingency strategy should be put into effect and whether the contingency strategy is working.

Risk Tracking

Risk tracking is the fourth step in the risk-management process. Here, the team monitors the status of risks and the actions taken to mitigate them. Risk tracking is essential to effectively implementing the plan, and entails devising the risk metrics and triggering events needed to ensure that the planned risk actions are working. Triggering events are similar to follow on procedures if a certain path is taken. Risk metrics is the raw data involved with the measurement of how well the risks are managed. Tracking is the watchdog function of the risk action plan.

Risk Status Reporting

It is a good idea to include a risk review during regular project reviews and debriefings. This review should include an assessment of the progress of resolving the project's top 10 risks. For project reviews, the team should show the major risks for the project and the status of risk-management actions. If project reviews are regularly scheduled, showing the previous ranking of risks is useful, as is the number of times a risk was in the top 10 risk list.

Risk status reporting can identify four possible risk-management situations:

◆ A risk is resolved, completing the risk action plan.

◆ Risk actions are tracked in the risk-management plan, where they continue as planned.

◆ Some risk actions are not tracked in the risk-management plan, in which case corrective measures should be determined and implemented.

◆ The situation has changed significantly with respect to one or more risks (this usually involves reassessing the risks or re-planning an activity).

As the project team takes actions to manage risks, the project's total risk exposure should begin to approach acceptable levels.

Risk Control

Risk control is the last step in the active risk-management process. After the team has chosen the risk metrics and the triggering events, there is nothing unique about risk management. Rather, risk management melds into project-management processes to control the risk action plans, correct for variations from the plans, respond to triggering events, and improve the risk-management process.

Risk management relies on the project-management processes to:

◆ Control risk action plans

◆ Correct for variations from plans

◆ Respond to triggering events

◆ Improve the risk-management process

Knowledge Discovery for Problem Solving

Today, virtually all companies find themselves part of a fast moving and competitive world market. Customer preferences change quickly, and competitors are always looking for better and faster applications, new niches, and other ways to improve their market share. One crucial weapon in this ever-changing world is knowledge. Knowing more about the outside world, and being able to detect early trends and to better predict customers' behavior, are critical for survival.

One of the ways to learn about the outside world is to analyze the wealth of data that is already available. Many companies collect (or have access to) voluminous data about their customers, the products they buy, and how they pay for these products. Successful organizations have learned to analyze the data available to them, to turn this data into knowledge, and to take actions based on this knowledge. The process of applying automated pattern-detection software tools to gather this type of knowledge for use in decision-making is referred to as *data mining*.

Data mining is not carried out in isolation from the rest of the world; successful data-mining projects are driven by business needs such as these:

◆ Discovering business problems

◆ Defining solutions to those problems

◆ Using appropriate data

◆ Building useful models

Addressing these needs requires an integrated process. The *knowledge discovery* process provides the necessary framework to ensure a successful outcome, if one is possible.

Data Mining: Looking at the Components

Knowledge discovery works well for identifying problems and the solutions to those problems. The data-mining part of the process focuses on the three key activities:

◆ **Data preparation.** This is the most important part of mining. Data mining requires that missing and empty variables, categorical ordering, and many more problems be fixed.

◆ **Data surveying.** This involves looking at the whole data set by building a map of the territory before expending the time and effort required to create models. The survey helps you determine whether the solution you seek is in the data you have.

◆ **The data model.** This is the small-scale map of some particular part of the territory. The nature of the data and the purpose of the model determine which tools are appropriate. The model will be one of two types:

◆ **Explanatory.** Explanatory models explain the relationships that exist in data. They can indicate the driving factors for stock market movements, or show failure factors in printed circuit board production. Regardless of purpose, these models help explain relationships.

◆ **Predictive.** Predictive models might not explain relationships. Primarily, they make output predictions given a set of input conditions.

Whether explanatory or predictive, the data-mining model must provide information that you and your group can act upon.

Summary

This chapter has attempted to help you realize that there are problems and risks associated with any project—not just Oracle developments. This chapter discussed how to manage risks associated with your task. You also read about a method of solving problems using the knowledge discovery process. As your knowledge and skill set become more and more tuned to managing and implementing your Oracle database, the risks and number of problems will diminish.

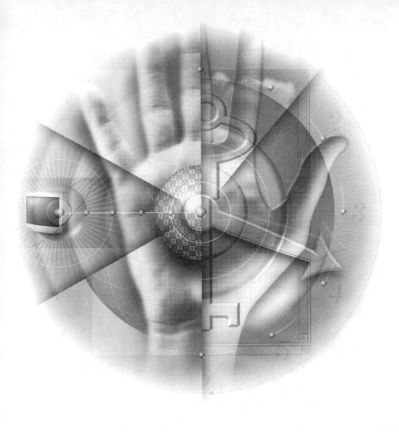

Chapter 9

**Choosing Manual
or Automatic
Database
Management**

In the old days, DBAs had only one database, platform, or vendor to manage. Today, however, managing database systems has become more complex as companies grow and go global. Instead of using a single database server, a company might have several scattered throughout the company and across the world. With this growth comes a significant rise in the complexity of database maintenance. More and more database administrators are faced with the challenge of keeping databases constantly online and operational to meet business needs. With increased application use, coupled with new functionality such as Web enablement, the number of people needed for maintenance tasks and the amount of time devoted to those tasks have increased. And unlike DBAs of old, today's DBA must design, deploy, and maintain multiplatform, multivendor databases across various network mediums. Not only do you need database skills, but you also need skills in networking, applications, SQL tuning, and server technologies. Adding to this plight is the fact that most DBAs are forced to operate defensively, taking action as problems are discovered or only after major issues have already occurred. DBAs are so occupied with reacting to current problems that small, smoldering database problems become raging fires before they can be identified.

In response to these issues, a variety of database tools have been developed to enable you to more productively manage the network of database systems. Through the use of tools, you can take a more active approach in managing the database. Instead of having to constantly fight fires, you can architect a strategy ahead of time to prevent problems. By working with thresholds, for example, you can preset alert points, monitor the database for potential problems, and remedy them before they erupt. With more advanced tools, events can be correlated to trigger preventive or corrective actions.

This chapter discusses how to determine which tools assist in these efforts, and how to justify the cost of acquiring database-management tools.

The Many Available Database Tools

Database administration tools help DBAs to collaborate on problem solving, manage distributed resources, automate critical management processes, actively monitor system health, and isolate and resolve problems before they become critical and impact system availability. Most database tools can be grouped in one of these seven categories:

◆ Database modeling, repositories, and documentation

◆ Database object creation, including security issues

◆ Reorganization and maintenance

◆ Database monitoring, thresholds, and alerting

◆ Event management and correlation

◆ Application design, tuning, and capacity planning

◆ Backup, recovery, and loading

 NOTE

Given that most companies utilize a diverse Web of platforms, environments, databases, and networks, database administration tools should lead you straight to a problem across heterogeneous, highly distributed environments.

Options for Database Monitoring

There are several approaches to administering databases. When deciding which approach to use, consider the following:

◆ What type of items do you need to maintain and monitor?

◆ How often should the database be monitored?

◆ Are there any tradeoffs? Will monitoring affect performance?

◆ How many database environments need to be maintained?

◆ What sizes, versions, and types of databases are needed?

◆ Do you have any other job responsibilities?

◆ Do you have a backup or additional help from other resources?

◆ What are the windows for reorganization?

◆ Should you write your own tools, use host tools, or buy third-party packages?

To make a decision, you need to be aware of differences in the available tools:

◆ **Manual monitoring.** In manual monitoring, you execute manual queries in SQLPLUS or SQLDBA, or use Oracle Server Manager to monitor the database.

◆ **Automated scripts.** At this level, you automate these queries into daily or weekly scheduled jobs using cron, batch queues, or other methods.

◆ **Host operating system tools.** Most host systems have a set of operating system tools. For VMS, this can be Monitor or Polycenter. For Unix, this can be IOSTAT, SAR, VMSTAT, or GLANCE. For Microsoft NT, there are the system monitor, resource monitor, and the task and process managers. These tools help identify problems at a system level, but do not address internal database problems.

◆ **Host-based monitoring tools.** You might decide to purchase a third-party tool instead of reinventing the wheel. Host-based tools reside on the machine running the database, and connect to the instances on that machine.

◆ **Client/server-based monitoring tools.** These allow you to maintain a console that can maintain multiple databases on many machines across a network.

 NOTE

Client/server-based tools are reliant upon a robust network. If the network is not reliable, a host-based tool might be the better choice.

◆ **Event or sampling monitoring tools.** Many third-party-monitoring tools are currently available. Some are event-based, whereas others are samplers. Event monitoring tools send messages to counters when events occur. If a table or index update occurs, an event is triggered. SNMP is a simple event-monitoring tool. Sampling tools perform sampling queries over a time-based interval. These samples determine the performance of the database over time. Both of these methods can have an impact on the database's performance if not properly configured.

In-House Development Tools

Many DBAs write their own manual scripts, and run them each morning to check the status of their databases. Managing in-house tools, however, can be difficult and costly. After all, you can spend a lot of time writing, testing, and maintaining these scripts. Although the use of predefined scripts can help simplify this process (Appendix A, "DBA Templates and Checklists," contains many such scripts that you can copy and use in your day-to-day activities), the following issues should be addressed:

◆ What resource will you use to write, maintain, and update scripts or various utilities in order to perform end-to-end management functions?

◆ What resource will you use to modify and test existing scripts or utilities so that they support the latest releases of your O/S, databases, applications, and networks?

◆ What resource will you use to perform development and integration into existing technologies such as OpenView, Tivoli, or tools?

◆ Do custom scripts or utilities have any common components or architecture?

◆ After the person who wrote the scripts has left the company, what then?

Third-Party COTS Tools

This section briefly describes some of the more popular and effective tools that can help you automate and manage your Oracle database using commercial off-the-shelf (COTS) tools. Most of these tools were chosen because they are tried and true. For the most part, the descriptions of the products are summarized from the sales literature of the products. To get more information about a product, visit its Web site.

Oracle Enterprise Manager

`www.oracle.com/take_control/oem.html`

You cannot list Oracle's database tools with out mentioning Oracle's Enterprise Manager. This is Oracle's recommended choice for managing Oracle databases, and is also a favorite among professional Oracle DBAs.

Oracle Enterprise Manager is the comprehensive management framework that provides a user-friendly console, a rich set of tools, and the extensibility to detect, solve, and simplify the problems of any managed environment. This product includes many well-documented features.

Tool for Oracle Application Developers (TOAD)

`www.toadsoft.com/index.htm`

Another top choice for Oracle database tools has to be TOAD. There are many reasons it's a good choice, including the fact that its freeware version has some commercial-quality features on par with Oracle's Enterprise Manager. This is a great way to try the product without having to front the dough. If you decide to advance to the commercial version of the software, you should have plenty of justifications for the return on investment!

TOAD is a powerful tool built around an advanced PL/SQL editor. TOAD's GUI object browsers give users quick access to database objects and make PL/SQL editing and testing quicker and easier. TOAD's object browser allows you to quickly

---

Computer Associates' ManageIT

A Winter Corporation survey of 120 VLDB (very large database) installations found that database monitoring was the top-rated technical practice critical to a database project's success. In most instances, a single database is small enough to be maintained under manual control with simple scripts. Once the number of database instances or database size grows, however, a third-party solution is necessary to avoid strapping the DBA to the console 10 hours a day.

Many systems and network-management products monitor events within a database, CPU, and network subsystems, providing a system administrator's perspective, as opposed to a DBA view of the world. Computer Associates' ManageIT, on the other hand, has an agent/console technology that enables database management as well as database performance monitoring. ManageIT's console architecture enables you to monitor heterogeneous DBMS environments from a single console. This tool helps address accessibility problems by sending events not only to their proprietary consoles, but also to system management frameworks (HP Operations Center, TIVOLI, SUN Net Manager, and others).

view the data dictionary, as well as tables, indexes, and stored procedures—all through a simple, multitabbed browser.

ManageIT Performance

`www.cai.com/products/manageit_perf.htm`

ManageIT Performance is designed for hands-free monitoring and is suitable for comprehensive application and database performance management. Through the collection and analysis of detailed metrics—and the capability to predict and prevent potential problems before they occur—ManageIT Performance gives you active management capabilities. ManageIT Performance provides 24×7 real-time monitoring and management of many Oracle-related applications, middleware, databases, and operating systems.

DBA Assist

`www.dba-assist.com/`

DBA Assist is another popular tool that has many features. The main menu has lots of buttons that quickly report on many areas of your database. DBA Assist is a simple application that uses the DSN, or data source name, that you configure to connect to your remote Oracle databases. This allows you to produce reports and graphs.

I/Watch

`www.quest.com/i_watch/index.html`

I/Watch is an unattended database application and system-monitoring tool for the Enterprise version of Oracle. I/Watch has a built-in alarming and alerting system that notifies you of impending problems. It also includes historical and statistical data collection for further analysis, and recommendations for tuning improvements.

Oracle Monitor

`www.softtreetech.com/monitor/monitor.htm`

Oracle Monitor is a set of advanced database management, tuning, measuring, and monitoring tools. Some of the more impressive features of this tool include customizable monitors, recent-past and real-time graphs, and historical trends.

PLATINUM DBVision

`www.platinum.com/products/provis/po/dbv_pv.htm`

PLATINUM DBVision offers a comprehensive performance monitoring and management tool for distributed relational Oracle databases. DBVision provides 24×7 real-time continuous monitoring and management of both small and large Oracle RDBMS environments. DBVision can be configured to take automated corrective actions if certain events occur. It also provides multithreshold alarming that notifies specific personnel using e-mail or a pager and escalates the alarm if it is not resolved.

Avoiding "Analysis Paralysis" by Justifying the Purchase of Database Tools

Selecting database tools can be as simple as a credit card purchase, or as complex as an RFP (request for proposal) and year evaluation. Many companies get locked into an endless cycle of tool evaluations, or *analysis paralysis*; in most cases, the cost of any tool could have been reclaimed within that initial evaluation period.

When making a tool decision, it is often best to look at the Return on Investment (ROI); you'll want to consider the following:

◆ Reduced downtime

◆ Increased performance

◆ Labor savings

◆ Training time spent to train on the tool

◆ Elimination of time spent on manual methods

Compare the costs of downtime, personnel (database, server, network, and Internet personnel), and other costs over a one-year period to the software tool investment to determine the ROI. Consider all factors that might affect the company, including:

◆ Defaults on contracts or penalties based on not meeting service levels

◆ Delayed transactional costs or missed delivery date costs

Estimating Your Downtime

Ever wondered how much downtime costs your company? Wonder no more. Use the following to calculate approximate downtime losses.

Costs

1. Hours of operation
   (24-hr. operation enter 8736, 8-hr. enter **2080**)   _____

2. Number of employees   _____

3. Average employee hourly wage   _____

4. Annual company gross income   _____

Loss Variables

5. Cost per hour (Line 1/Line 4)   _____

6. Lost wages (Line 6 × Line 2 × Line 3)   _____

7. Total number of hours the systems are down   _____

Total Downtime Costs = (Line 8 × Line 6) + (Line 8 × Line 7)   _____

According to the Contingency Planning Research, other attributed losses that some companies experience along with the primary financial impact of downtime include:

◆ Lost productivity (88.9%)

◆ End-user/management dissatisfaction (87.1%)

◆ Customer dissatisfaction (66.9%)

◆ Overtime (59.3%)

◆ Lost revenues (41.8%)

◆ Lost transactions (34.4%)

◆ Lost customers (23.1%)

◆ Penalties or fines (7.6%)

◆ Lost business or loss of customer contracts because of delays

◆ Other business costs (trucking, shipments) for contracted work not completed within the required time

There can be several specific sources of savings:

◆ Active monitoring and administration reduces the amount of time you must spend at a console.

◆ Multiserver monitoring from a central console eliminates additional hardware and personnel dedicated to monitoring individual databases.

◆ Automated reporting eliminates the need to manually check and generate database health and statistical reports.

◆ Centralized GUI analytical tools reduce time spent hunting for scripts and troubleshooting the problems.

Also, a reduction in non-integratable point-management tools, or stand-alone tools that cannot interact with other tools, can provide a savings. If a new product or integrated suite performs the functions of many existing disparate products, the savings might justify the ROI. Other financial benefits can provide the core of such justification:

◆ Reduction in software/hardware licensing costs

◆ Reduction in software/hardware maintenance costs

◆ Reduction in staff training costs

◆ Ability to use the same staff on different problems because they can use the same tool without additional training

◆ Reduction in costs of supporting the management technology

 NOTE

Many tools help improve levels of efficiency in an organization, but the administrative overhead of some such tools can introduce additional work in the form of updates, infrastructure changes, and configuration management. In some cases, that cost is greater than the savings originally forecast.

Areas of ROI

In calculating ROI, you'll want to take the following into account:

◆ **Cost savings.** The amount of money saved when comparing the cost of investment in tools minus the total amount of estimated costs if these tools were not purchased.

◆ **Payback period.** The time in weeks, months, or years required to return the value of the investment made in purchasing the performance tools.

◆ **Opportunity cost saved.** The costs avoided or deferred as a result of investment in performance tools.

◆ **Return on investment.** The percent of effective interest rate return on the software investment over a given period, typically one year. In other words, for every dollar spent, how much more of a dollar is returned. This comparison is typically done when a company has limited capital to invest and wants to select in the most attractive business solution.

◆ **Value-added savings.** "Soft" or less quantifiable savings gained (or costs avoided) as the result of purchasing these tools.

You'll also want to do the following when calculating ROI:

◆ Anticipate the need to perform different, and often more sophisticated, analyses, forecasts, and reports.

◆ Understand and develop requirements, required functionality, alternatives, anticipated benefits and costs, shortcomings of existing systems, and current anticipated timelines.

◆ Determine whether the current solution complies with organizational policies, requirements, and procedures.

◆ Determine whether the current solution meets user requirements.

◆ Evaluate risks, benefits, and costs, comparing the in-house option to commercial alternatives.

◆ Determine whether the current solution is consistent with overall strategic direction and business objectives.

◆ Determine whether the current solution is cost-effective.

◆ Objectively evaluate the build versus buy alternatives.

NOTE

In-house effort invested in tool building often duplicates existing third-party tool functionality, but the savings in dollars are likely to be offset by the actual cost of the labor needed to create and maintain the custom tool solution. Additionally, in most cases, custom code is not documented or maintained as rigorously as third-party products are. Also, the custom code is probably not regression tested, meaning not all the software code was retested even though only a small part was changed, to verify that a software fix in one area, didn't break functionality in another. Compounding this problem is the fact that when the person who developed the code leaves the company, so goes the knowledge about the code. In the case of a third-party tool, however, other personnel can be quickly brought up to speed by way of vendor training or consulting services. Although custom code might appear to be an immediately cost efficient third-party tool, vendors usually add value with support and training solutions.

◆ Perform the analysis—refine the requirements, thoroughly evaluate the commercial products, and estimate comparable in-house development requirements.

◆ Determine how quickly the solution needs to be in full production.

One of the most important steps in calculating ROI is knowing which assumptions are being made about the tool. Following are some typical assumptions made about database-administration tools. They:

◆ Allow IS personnel to become more active

◆ Automate repetitive tasks

◆ Reduce human error and overtime costs

◆ Reduce cost of system downtime

◆ Create faster problem resolution

◆ Centralize event management and correlation to provide faster problem determination and correction

◆ Compare analysis of schema versions

◆ Increase potential hours saved because of reduced failures

◆ Increase potential hours saved on the recovery process

◆ Debug scripts for every database and environment change

- Delay upgrade costs because of improved performance and tuning
- Determine differences between databases
- Determine when and how often a database needs to be reorganized
- Save disk space because of optimization
- Identify the root cause of a failure
- Identify which archive logs to recover
- Impact analysis of change requests
- Improve user productivity because of faster response times
- Improve security, reducing the threat of accidental or deliberate sabotage
- Increase user confidence and satisfaction
- Create labor savings in administrating additions or by making changes more quickly
- Decrease weekly employee hours spent writing reorganization scripts
- Decrease manual initiation of reorganizing jobs
- Migrate data between Oracle servers or between Oracle and other databases
- Decrease manual monitoring backup process
- Decrease manual monitoring reorganization jobs for completion
- Create active management to improve performance and reduce downtime
- Decrease productivity loss because of application availability
- Decrease productivity loss because of poor application response times
- Reduce time to create DDL scripts and propagate database changes
- Reduce training costs
- Reduce manual efforts and CPU costs because of improved SQL performance
- Reduce manual monitoring requirements
- Restore files and archiving
- Create cost savings from reduced human error because of standardization of the backup and recovery processes
- Provide a single vendor solution combined with standards, policies, and best practices to improve serviceability software or hardware upgrades
- Synchronize database instances

◆ Create a wall clock of CPU hours of application unavailability during reorganizations

◆ Create Web response time/EDI (electronic data interchange) applications

An ROI Example

Suppose you are working in a Unix environment, and need a robust production-scheduling tool. You decide to evaluate the Unix tool called *cron*.

Although this tool offers many advantages, there are also some problems that companies commonly face when utilizing cron:

◆ **Shell scripts must be developed in-house.** This is problematic because shell scripts are not easily maintained, and often do not provide for straightforward error-detection when processing problems occur.

◆ **cron offers no inherent fault tolerance.** Processing is tied to specific hardware devices.

◆ **cron lacks reliability and centralization.** It must be set up on each machine specifically for that machine. Processing is therefore hard-coded to a specific resource.

◆ **cron lacks an easily reviewed processing audit trail.** It's often difficult to determine where things actually went wrong when processing errors occur.

◆ **Problems in processing typically require manual intervention.** There is no automatic restart, rerouting, or recovery in error conditions.

Before you decide against using cron, however, you'll want to evaluate the cost of IT activities and of lost CPU cycles. When evaluating the cost of IT activities, you need to determine the following:

◆ Time required to use cron to manually perform job scheduling

◆ Time savings resulting from reduced manual effort

◆ Time savings from reduced errors occurring during production

◆ Reduced human errors resulting in costs

◆ Cost when production jobs fail

When evaluating the cost of lost CPU cycles, you need to determine the following:

◆ Cost of production downtime because of failures in the existing job management system

◆ Cost associated with job management system shutdown

◆ Jobs run out of sequence

◆ Jobs run with wrong or incomplete data

◆ Jobs re-run because of operator error

◆ Unutilized CPU time between manually submitted jobs

The goals of ROI are as follows:

◆ Elimination of production downtime

◆ Increase of productivity, job optimization, and workload balancing

◆ Automation-exception only processing

◆ Increase of CPU processing time savings

◆ Decrease of lost business opportunity when production jobs fail

As you can see from this ROI for a simple tool such as Unix's cron, you should discuss and consider many issues in order to determine whether a tool is worth the investment.

Summary

In the old days, DBAs relied on manual scripts, which they wrote and ran each day, to check the status of their databases. With current tool offerings, manual processes are no longer the only alternative. You can now be active instead of reactive, thereby allowing time for root causes analysis and prevention planning. Tools assist in the identification of problems and in alerting you to thresholds met. They help you take corrective action and help correlate events. Database tools also assist in data reorganizations and migrations. Determining which tool is best for your circumstances and justifying cash allocation for those tools is a detailed process.

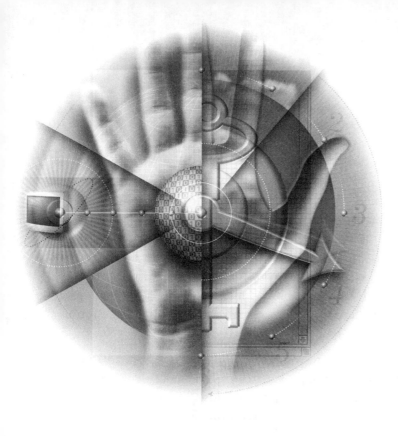

Chapter 10

Maintaining Your Oracle Database with 5-Nines

ORACLE

In today's competitive business landscape, 24×7 operations are the standard, especially for those areas driven by e-commerce, intranet, and the Web. Downtime on applications, systems, or networks can translate into a significant loss of revenue. Industry experts and analysts agree that in order to support e-commerce applications, typical network availability must provide a minimum of 99.999 percent availability, also called "5-Nines" availability. This level of availability requires careful planning and a comprehensive, end-to-end strategy, with business availability as the goal.

If 5-Nines availability seems extreme to you, consider this: If you have a 97 percent availability rating, you will incur approximately 263 hours of downtime per year, or 6.6 days. With 99 percent availability, you will lose 88 hours, or 2.2 days. Table 10.1 illustrates the hit you'll take with various other availability ratings.

Table 10.1 Downtime measurements at various availability ratings.

Availability Percentage	Year Downtime
99	2.2 Days
99.5	44.0 Hours
99.9	8.8 Hours
99.95	4.0 Hours
99.99	53.0 Minutes
99.999	5.3 Minutes
99.9999	32.0 Seconds
99.99999	3.2 Seconds

The 5-Nines initiative, promoted by Hewlett Packard and other vendors, is setting industry standards, but what does it take in terms of technical capability to achieve it? This chapter helps you answer these questions and more. You will learn the steps you can take to foster maximum data availability, including how to effectively monitor and maintain enterprise systems.

The High-Availability Environment

Availability, which is usually measured on an annual basis, refers to the percentage of time that an application is available to the users. The definition covers mission-critical applications, including distributed applications, networking applications, e-mail, scheduling services, and other business solutions on which companies rely for day-to-day operations.

High availability arises thanks to a combination of environmental, process, software, and development strategies; computing hardware; and an investment in terms of dollars and human capital. It cannot be achieved simply by implementing a service level or purchasing a hardware solution.

There are three levels of availability:

- **High availability.** A system or application designed to prevent a total loss of service by reducing or managing failures. The major goal of a highly available system is to provide a higher level of availability than a standard system. Preventing single points of failure (SPOF) through component redundancy is a way of providing hardware high availability. Common hardware SPOFs include the CPU, disks, host adapters, network adapters, hubs, and routers.

- **Fault tolerance.** More expensive than a highly available system (by as much as five times), a fault-tolerant system contains multiple hardware components that function concurrently, duplicating all the computation and I/O. This type of system protects against hardware failures by incorporating redundant hardware components in a single system. Keep in mind, however, that even a fault-tolerant system can fail when the system or application software fails.

- **Continuous availability.** As the name suggests, these systems are designed to provide continuous availability, which equates to non-stop service, no planned or unplanned outages. Hardware and software failures can occur; however, the intent is to insulate the users from the failure and to reduce the time needed to recover from that failure to several minutes or fewer. In a continuously available system, environment patches and upgrades can be performed with no impact to the users.

Downtime

Downtime is the amount of time that a system is inaccessible to users. Outages can be caused by environmental factors such as loss of electricity, fires, floods, and earthquakes; hardware failures; application failures; software failures; or human error. Although hardware failures are traditionally the major cause of downtime, software failures and user error are growing.

 NOTE

Uptime is the opposite of downtime; it is usually a measurement of availability. It refers to the time that users can access the application.

There are two types of downtime:

◆ **Planned downtime.** Planned downtime is scheduled time for patches, upgrades, and maintenance activities such as database reorganizations, adding disk storage, performing offline backups, and installing patches, upgrades, or new application or system operating software. It usually occurs during off-peak processing times, such as off-hours or holidays.

 NOTE

Because today's applications run in a global 7×24×365 environment, many IT organizations are eliminating planned downtime.

◆ **Unplanned downtime.** Unplanned downtime is associated with unexpected events such as network, hardware, and software failures. A typical distributed application usually consists of a Web browser front-end and an application reliant upon servers, networks, and databases. Because a problem with any of these components can cause the application to become unavailable, all components need to be monitored equally.

Achieving 5-Nines Availability

A 5-Nine implementation has its foundation in these principles:

◆ **Mitigation of risks.** Risk mitigation depends on monitoring (real-time and historical), trends, rules, and models to predict the occurrence of failures and to prevent them. Common risk mitigation techniques are

◆ **Fault avoidance.** Use of processes and tools to minimize the introduction of faults.

◆ **Fault minimization.** In spite of efforts to prevent or eliminate them, there will be faults in any system. Proper risk assessment and fault minimization can ensure uptime.

◆ **Fault recognition and removal.** Monitoring and recognition can actively locate faults and assist with remediation of their root cause.

◆ **Resiliency.** The capability of a system to prevent degradation or failure as well as minimize the damage or loss from a failure or malfunction. Resiliency is affected by quality, design, and stability.

◆ **Redundancy.** The use of multiple redundant critical components, such as CPUs, network cards, electrical transmission, power supplies, disk drives, switches, routers, cooling systems, and other equipment used to support operations. Redundancy is not limited to hardware; it can also include mirrored applications, setup, and configuration files.

◆ **Inclusion.** Including high availability through the entire application stack, including the client, middleware, and hardware.

◆ **Serviceability.** The ability of the system to detect and rapidly correct problems, and reconfigure itself online.

◆ **Manageability.** The ease and ability to evaluate and tune for maintenance and availability; to identify critical resources, traffic patterns, and performance levels; and to configure business-critical applications.

◆ **Methods and skills.** To achieve a 5-Nines environment, the administration, monitoring, and control of the high availability IT environment must be simple. Otherwise, installation issues, upgrades, human error, and customization will affect availability. Because user error is a growing cause of outages, you need to apply techniques to reduce the chance of user and or administrator errors.

Other keys to achieving 5-Nines availability include system scalability and system architecture.

Scalability

Scalability of the system, network, databases, and applications is key to availability. An available, well-defined, and properly configured scalable platform is one that has enough capacity to handle the estimated or measured application's workload, with no bottlenecks in the hardware.

Because companies are so dependent on data and systems, proper analysis is crucial in the selection of reliable and scalable servers. To jump-start the analysis process, research such sources as industry-standard benchmarks and reviews, network with peers in other companies, and conduct in-house benchmarks. When gathering scalability information, consider these important decision drivers:

◆ Query complexity

◆ Expected response time

◆ Number of concurrent users

◆ Backup and recovery

◆ Security

◆ Integration with other applications or systems

◆ Skillsets of users

 NOTE

Achieving the goal of scalability—and therefore dependability and availability—requires effort at all phases of development: design time, implementation time, execution time, and during maintenance.

 TIP

Performing an environmental audit and system overview prior to installation is critical to a successful implementation, and can help you reduce downtime during the installation process.

System Architecture

Poor planning, architecture, or operational support can foster poor performance, impeded functionality, high cost of ownership, complex administration, lack of capacity and scalability, and poor reliability and availability. A properly developed system, on the other hand, is one that's high-quality, high-performance, and highly available, with a capacity for growth. Properly architecting your system requires that you understand the business requirements, and design the system to meet those requirements. Consider these important points when planning your system architecture:

◆ Processor technology

◆ Storage and I/O subsystems

◆ Ability to support change

◆ Ability to support growth

◆ Well-defined use and capacity planning

◆ Elimination of data redundancy

◆ Elimination of process redundancy

◆ Price/performance

◆ Implementation and integration planning

◆ Administration automation

◆ Server, client/server, N-Tier, and Web-based architecture

 NOTE

A common pitfall is employing "bleeding edge" technologies in expectation of meeting or overcompensating for existing requirements. Only after you gather and understand the business requirements should you purchase technologies to meet them.

Maintaining Uptime and Availability

Maintaining uptime and availability involves the following issues:

◆ Data protection

◆ Disaster recovery

- ◆ Application protection and recoverability
- ◆ Network management
- ◆ System management monitoring and measurement
- ◆ Automating processes
- ◆ Service level agreements
- ◆ Training and support
- ◆ Standards and documentation

Data Protection

Any data critical to business needs to be protected; backups are the easiest way to protect such data. Even if you perform frequent backups, you should still employ data protection safeguards through the use of hardware, replication, or software, to bridge backup periods.

Disaster Recovery

The capability to recover from a natural disaster, such as a fire, a flood, an earthquake, or a tornado, is as important as being able to recover from a hardware or software failure. Results of these disasters usually include physical damage or complete loss of systems, data, and even the workplace. Recovery time is directly related to how much up-front planning occurred and what procedures were established to restore the business locally. The impact and likelihood of a disaster and its cost to the business must be weighed against the cost of preventing the damage that results from such a disaster.

Application Protection and Recoverability

Web servers are an excellent example of why application recoverability is a critical issue. Most companies with e-commerce servers cannot afford the business impact of unplanned downtime. Give careful consideration to the design and use of an application in a high-availability situation, with the primary goal being to insulate the users from outages or system failures. Methods include employing client reconnects to an alternative server if a connection is lost, using error-handling, automating tasks, and setting up recoverable transactions.

Network Management

The network has become so ubiquitous in the computing environment that people now take it for granted. Proper network architecture, planning, maintenance, and monitoring are just as important as with any of the other system components or applications. Be sure to consider redundancy and network switching, as well as the capacities of your networks, when planning.

System Management Monitoring and Measurement

DBAs often overlook the planning and selection of the architecture, procedures, and system-management processes. A vast majority of installations occur on an existing platform because of available space. Then, after the application is in production, performance and administration problems, as well as bottlenecks, appear. To combat this cycle, systems must be properly planned, architected, and refined through a set of methods and processes. It's not enough to slap in a set of monitoring tools and expect it take care of all deficiencies.

True system management involves monitoring, measuring, altering, and reporting on the levels of availability, performance, and service. System-management tools can also provide real-time business application for the many operational components. System management usually begins with taking measurements, setting baselines for uptime, and establishing performance metrics.

Automating Processes

Human error is a leading cause of downtime; any effort to reduce human interaction with the system therefore reduces the risk of human error. Consequently, anything that can be automated should be. You should employ any tools that perform the automation, control it, or monitor it in order to eliminate downtime. You can reduce risk through the use of automation in the following areas:

◆ Backups and recovery

◆ Upgrades

◆ Operations and administration

◆ Maintenance

◆ Usage

◆ Performance

 ◆ Capacity planning
 ◆ Security and control
 ◆ Testing, upgrading, and implementation

Service Level Agreements

You need to derive service level agreements (SLAs) from the business requirements that list availability goals, response time, planned downtime periods, and specific performance requirements. An SLA typically specifies user response times and expectations for key business applications, networks, and servers. In addition, the SLA provides a valuable baseline that the MIS department and system managers can use to justify the need for additional resources.

Training and Support

Training and support are critical to sustaining and maintaining availability, and can make or break the business. With technology and product updates leapfrogging every six months, personnel must be able to quickly judge which features and upgrades map to existing business requirements. Annual training, as well as participation in user groups, can help users keep abreast of issues, features, and technologies.

Standards and Documentation

The standards and procedures you write provide the foundation for implementation. Without a serious effort to consistent standards and procedures, a project will decline into an indecipherable hodgepodge of unsupportable variations and techniques. Documentation is also important for employees new to the department or database. Standards, procedures, and documentation for the 5-Nines environment should include the following:

 ◆ **OS standards and procedures.** These include file system layouts, kernel parameters, system backup/recovery, security, performance monitoring, installation, and upgrades of the operating system.

 ◆ **Database standards and procedures.** These include instance parameters, object sizing, storage and naming conventions, procedures for installation and upgrades, security guidelines, and backup/recovery plans.

◆ **Applications development standards.** These include techniques for managing change procedures, detailed coding standards including source code control, change control, naming conventions, and table/index creation.

◆ **Network standards and procedures.** These define network addressing and protocols supported for database and application communication.

Summary

With the explosion of e-commerce and the increased focus on Web-enabled data, users and customers expect to have 24×7 accessibility. A 5-Nines approach helps companies that cannot survive downtime, avoid it, or survive when it happens.

A successful strategy incorporates procedures and components that work together to ensure that failure situations are handled appropriately. For 5-Nines to succeed, you must identify and prioritize all components and dependencies in terms of availability and service levels. Your comprehensive service levels should address availability (in the form of planned and unplanned downtime), performance, and recoverability. One key to keeping your applications available all the time is the ability to rapidly identify issues and redirect application connectivity. When your systems identify a computing resource failure, applications and their data need to quickly move to an alternative server with minimal impact to users.

Availability and scalability cannot be an afterthought. It is impossible to scale an application or system that was not designed to handle the anticipated load. All components must be tightly integrated, from the hardware and operating system to the database software, the application layer, the network, and the interfaces. In addition, the need for tighter integration between applications—such as Enterprise Resource Planning—and the systems they support becomes more apparent with increases in data volumes and the number of transactions performed.

Selecting products that support high availability and ensure success are the only ways to maximize the computing power investment and see a viable return-on-your investment. A highly available system provides substantial benefits, but can require a significant investment in terms of money and resources. Like any investment, ensuring that the proper strategy and tools are in place is the foundation to successfully managing and maintaining the environment.

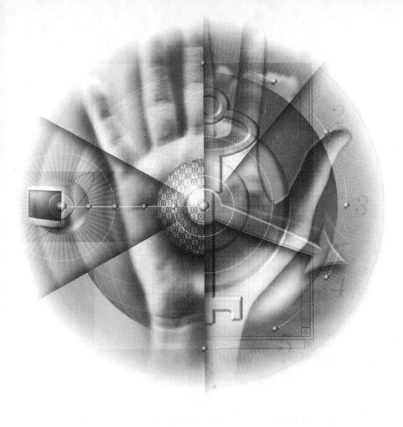

Chapter 11

**Monitoring Your
Oracle Database**

DBAs are more frequently facing the challenge of getting databases online, operational, and on-schedule. But what happens after installation? Will databases continue to run without additional interaction? With lack of attention, unidentified smoldering problems can become major crises. For this reason, monitoring your Oracle database is critical. You should implement monitoring procedures to ensure stability. Answering the following questions is a good place to start:

◆ What types of database objects do you need to monitor?

◆ What is the database monitoring frequency?

◆ Are there any tradeoffs between performance and the quality of monitoring data?

◆ Should you write your own monitoring scripts, use database tools, system tools, or buy third-party monitoring packages?

What to Monitor, and How Often

What should you monitor? This is a very good question! The obvious answer is, monitor the things that can go awry! Of course, the next question is, "What can possibly go awry with *my* database?!"

Some of the things you should monitor include:

◆ **Available space.** Check the amount of disk space available in the file system that contains items such as the archive logs. Look for segments that have more extents than you want. Make sure that no segment has a next extent larger than the largest chunk of contiguous free space. Monitor the rapid growth of tables to make sure that you can accommodate for the current rate of growth.

◆ **Memory.** Monitor the redo log space requests to ensure that they are near zero. Check the buffer cache hit ratio periodically to ensure it is around 95 percent.

◆ **The internals of the machine.** Be sure to check on areas such as memory, hard disk space, and the power supply.

◆ **Disk and file I/O.** Periodically monitor v$FILESTAT to identify problem data files, which appear to be taking more I/O than other datafiles.

◆ **Miscellaneous general items.** Ensure that security is not compromised by old user IDs or obvious passwords on DBA accounts. Ensure that you can recreate all objects from current scripts. Ensure that you are backing up your data regularly and that your backups are correct. Periodically rebuild indexes on large tables with a high insert/update/delete activity on indexed columns.

Monitoring should occur on a daily, weekly, or monthly basis, depending on the task. Items that should be checked daily include these:

◆ **Whether the application is running.** Either you or the application manager should perform a daily check on the health of all applications. Users can also perform this activity if they are using the application on a daily basis.

◆ **The ORACLE ALERT file.** You should perform daily checks of the ORACLE ALERT file to identify any errors or unusual events.

◆ **System resources.** You should perform daily checks of system resources such as disk, memory, and CPU utilization. This includes maintaining an open dialog with the system administrator when any new applications are loaded or when changes are made to the system.

◆ **Whether backups are occurring.** You should check daily to ensure backups are continuing without error.

◆ **Archive logs.** If archive-logging is enabled on the database, you should check daily to ensure the archive logs are copied to the correct location.

Monitor and maintain the FREESPACE on a weekly basis; include tablespaces, tables, indexes, and clusters in your weekly audits. Your monthly audits for fragmentation and extents should include indexes, tables, and clusters.

 TIP

Within a stable database environment, the previously mentioned time intervals are good recommendations. However, in an unstable or ever-changing system, you might consider performing these monitoring routines more frequently.

Other items that should be monitored include these:

◆ **The network.** For client/server systems, you should have an open dialog with the network administrator regarding changes that might impact the load on the network.

◆ **SQL statement performance.** Application tuning can yield the most performance benefit. Through the joint efforts of the DBA and application developer, SQL statement tuning can yield 60-percent performance increases. Monitoring the SQL can help locate the bottlenecks.

TIP

Use this list as a starting point to help you identify and establish your own methodology. Once you establish a monitoring method, your next job is to analyze the information you've collected.

Figures 11.1 and 11.2 show some of the more common Oracle monitoring tools. Oracle Storage Manager monitors the storage of various components including tablespaces, datafiles, rollback segments, and so on. Oracle Instance Manager allows you to monitor different aspects of each Oracle instance.

Monitoring Technologies

If you don't perform database maintenance or monitoring, an ORA-*xxxx* message —such as ORA-1547 Failed to allocate extent or ORA-00059 Maximum number of DB_Files exceeded—is sure to show up at the most inopportune moment. Although monitoring your database can't prevent you from getting ORA-*xxxx* messages, it will prevent such errors from being a complete surprise. With early detection, you can take care of issues before they become crises.

The next section will show a very common and general script that if run each day will help in your day-to-day Oracle monitoring process.

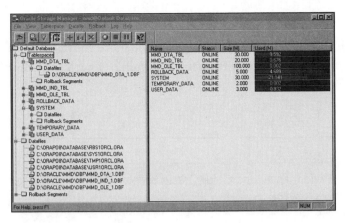

FIGURE 11.1 *Oracle Storage Manager showing tablespaces and their usage percentage.*

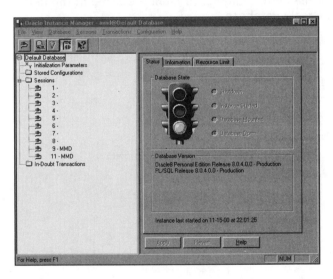

FIGURE 11.2 *Oracle Instance Manager showing general status of the database.*

 NOTE

No single monitoring technology can magically solve your problems. You must work closely with developers, applications managers, network administrators, and system administrators to establish guidelines, baselines, and performance expectations prior to releasing the application into production.

A Sample Monitoring Script

The script shown in Listing 11.1 monitors some of the more common areas of an Oracle database (note that the numbers at the beginning of each line have been added for your reference; they are not part of the script).

NOTE

Appendix B, "Usage, Performance, and Other Oracle Scripts," is full of scripts to help you with the monitoring process.

Listing 11.1: This data file monitoring script monitors some of the more common areas of an Oracle database.

```
1.  rem =====================================================
2.  rem == Data File Monitoring Script
3.  rem == Originally Created by David Kennedy, Oracle DBA
4.  rem == Modified by John Colby, Oracle DBA
5.  rem ==
6.  rem == This script dumps information about the Data Files,
7.  rem == Size Allocations, Free Space, Tablespace Configuration,
8.  rem == Rollback Segments, and Status.
9.  rem =====================================================
10. set feed off
11. set lines 80
12. set pages 60
13. set echo off
14. column segment_name jus cen hea 'Segment Name '
15. column segment_id jus cen hea 'ID' for 999
16. column status jus cen hea 'Status'
17. column next_extent jus cen hea 'Next' for 9,999,999,999
18. column max_extents jus cen hea 'Max|Extents' for 9,999,999,999
19. column min_extents jus cen hea 'Min|Extents' for 999
20. column mb jus cen hea 'Largest|Extent' for 9,999,999,999
21. column pct_increase jus cen hea '%|Incr' for 999
22. column initial_extent jus cen hea 'Initial' for 9,999,999,999
```

```
23. column total jus cen hea `Total Amount|Remaining' for 9,999,999,999
24. column tablespace_name jus cen hea `TableSpace|Name ' for a11
25. column Pieces jus cen hea `Pieces'
26. column d_file jus cen hea "Data File" form a50
27. spool Data_File.lis
28. rem ====================================================
29. ttitle `Data Files and Size Allocations'
30. select substr(file_name,1,50) d_file, tablespace_name,
31.             round((bytes/1024)/1024) MEG
32. from sys.dba_data_files
33. order by tablespace_name
34. /
35. rem ====================================================
36. select tablespace_name,
37.             round(sum((bytes/1024)/1024)) MEG
38. from sys.dba_data_files
39. group by tablespace_name
40. /
41. rem ====================================================
42. ttitle `Free Space'
43. select tablespace_name,count(*) Pieces,sum(bytes) total,max(bytes) mb
44. from sys.dba_free_space
45. group by tablespace_name
46. /
47. rem ====================================================
48. ttitle `Tablespace Configuration'
49. select tablespace_name,initial_extent,next_extent,
50.             min_extents,max_extents,pct_increase,status
51. from sys.dba_tablespaces
52. order by tablespace_name
53. /
54. rem ====================================================
55. ttitle `Rollback Segments and Status'
56. select substr(segment_name,1,15) segment_name,
57.             tablespace_name,
58.             segment_id,
59.             next_extent,initial_extent,pct_increase,
60.             substr(status,1,7) status
```

```
61. from sys.dba_rollback_segs
62. order  by tablespace_name, segment_name/
63. /
64. spool off
65. exit
66. rem =======================================================
67. rem == End of Data File Script
68. rem =======================================================
```

Analysis

Lines 1–9 of the script identify the script and its authors, and describe what the script does. The set section (lines 10–14) sets certain attributes of the system.

For example, set pages 60 sets a page length to 60 lines of text before repeating header information. The column commands (lines 14–27) set up the script's reporting features for column headings and formatting.

The spool command spools or writes the results into a file called Data_File.lis.

Lines 28–34 list the data files and their size allocations. The script selects d_file and tablespace_name from sys.dba_data_files and then organizes the data by tablespace_name. Lines 35–40 simply list the tablespace names. This select command also selects the tablespace names from the sys.dba_data_files table and groups them by the tablespace_name.

Lines 41–46 show you how much free space is available. The select statement selects the tablespace_name, the number of pieces, and the total available space from sys.dba_free_space and groups the information by tablespace_name. Lines 47–53 describe the tablespace configuration. The script selects the tablespace_name, initial_extent, next_extent, min_extents, max_extents, pct_increase, and status from the sys.dba_tablespaces table and then organizes this information by the tablespace_name. Lines 54–63 show the users the status of the rollback segments.

Output

To see the output of this script, type the script into a script file on your database and run it. You can also set up a cron or batch job that runs periodically so that you can automate your monitoring process.

Dynamic Performance Tables

Oracle stores its system statistics in its dynamic performance tables. These are key tables that include vital statistics on how your Oracle database is running. Normally, these views are accessed solely using Oracle's Server Manager. The V$TABLEs continually change from version to version of Oracle. Find a list of the current views on your system by selecting the information in the V$FIXED_VIEW_DEFINITION view. Table 11.1 lists some of the common views located in the V$TABLEs.

Table 11.1   V$TABLE Contents

System-Wide Information
V$PARAMETER
V$SGA
V$SGASTAT
V$SORT_SEGMENT
V$SQL
V$SQLAREA
V$SQLTEXT
V$SQLTEXT_WITH_NEWLINES
V$STATNAME
V$SYSSTAT
V$SYSTEM_CURSOR_CACHE
V$SYSTEM_EVENT

Transaction Information
V$DBLINK
V$SESSION
V$LOCKED_OBJECT
V$SQLTEXT
V$SQLSAREA
V$TRANSACTION
V$SQLTEXT_WITH_NEWLINES

(continued...)

Parallel Query Information

V$PQ_SLAVE

V$PQ_SYSSTAT

V$PQ_TQSTAT

CPU Information

V$SESSTAT

V$SQL

V$SQLAREA

V$SYSSTAT

V$TRANSACTION

Session Information

V$ACCESS

V$LATCHHOLDER

V$LOCK

V$LOCKED_OBJECT

V$OPEN_CURSOR

V$SESSION

V$SESSION_CONNECT_INFO

V$SESSION_WAIT

V$SESSTAT

V$SESS_IO

Multithreaded Server Information

V$CIRCUIT

V$QUEUE

V$DISPATCHER

V$SESSION

V$SHARED_SERVER

(continued...)

Packages, Procedures, and Trigger Information

V$DB_OBJECT_CACHE

V$LIBRARYCACHE

V$SHARED_POOL_RESERVED

V$SQL

V$SQLAREA

Disk I/O Information

V$DATAFILE

V$FILESTAT

V$ROLLSTAT

V$SESSTAT

V$SESS_IO

V$SORT_SEGMENT

V$SQL

V$SQLAREA

V$SYSSTAT

V$TRANSACTION

Memory Information

V$BH

V$SYSTEM_CURSOR_CACHE

V$LIBRARYCACHE

V$DB_OBJECT_CACHE

V$ROWCACHE

V$SESSTAT

V$SGA

V$SHARED_POOL_RESERVED

V$SQL

V$SQLAREA

V$SYSSTAT

(continued...)

Locking and Contention Information
V$LATCH
V$LATCHHOLDER
V$LATCHNAME
V$LATCH_CHILDREN
V$LATCH_MISSES
V$LATCHPARENT
V$LOCK
V$LIBRARY_CACHE
V$DB_OBJECT_CACHE
V$PROCESS
V$ROLLSTAT
V$SESSION
V$SESSION_EVENT
V$SESSION_WAIT
V$SHARED_POOL_RESERVED
V$SYSTEM_EVENT
V$WAITSTAT

When your database is first created, only the user SYS has access to the V$TABLEs. To allow other users to run products that require the V$TABLES, you must run the script UTLMONTR.sql, which is located in the $Oracle_HOME/rdbms/admin directory. This script creates a role called MONITORER and then grants that role privileges on the tables. These privileges can in turn be granted to other users.

Reporting/Trending

Monitoring tools collect volumes of data. You can then generate reports (analyses of collected data) and trend information (analyses of report information over time) from that data. Using historical data, you can determine known operating ranges or baselines from which the database should operate. Deviation from this baseline becomes an immediate red flag. By using the data collected over a period of time, you can create a variety of trend charts. Trending can reveal database use, growth, and where potential problems exist. Much like monitoring, you can perform reporting by manual or automated means. For example, you can run BATCH and CRON jobs daily, weekly, or monthly to perform the reporting.

Monitoring and trending database and system usage patterns can also improve database productivity, because collected data can be extremely useful in capacity planning, forecasting, and budgeting. Additionally, reporting and trending information can help you make accurate estimates of system resources and space requirements. When you extrapolate this data and combine it with estimates of future production requirements, you have a good baseline for database design. Alternatively, this information can yield usage patterns, which can help you deploy under-utilized servers and postpone acquisition of new, unnecessary hardware. These steps help reduce the cost of software licenses, which are often priced according to the number of peak or concurrent users.

Monitoring Security

In addition to monitoring system performance to eliminate downtime, you must also monitor system security. Depending on your environment, security can range from a little thing the boss wants you to look into to a mission-critical issue. You cannot protect all your data all the time, but once you've established a solid foundation for your security practices, you'll greatly improve your data protection and security procedures. This foundation involves the following:

◆ Changing passwords regularly

◆ Safeguarding database backups

◆ Mapping the names and locations of all your databases

◆ Managing access to sensitive databases

◆ Protecting production data

Changing Passwords Regularly

No doubt about it, changing passwords is an inconvenience. Even so, you should require users to change their passwords frequently (the frequency usually depends on the project's security policies). In Oracle8, you can force passwords to expire on a regular basis and prevent users from reusing old passwords.

If you force users to change their passwords regularly, try to make the process as simple and painless as possible. The tool of choice for changing user accounts is Oracle's Security Manager (see Figure 11.3).

In addition to ensuring that your users frequently change their passwords, you should make sure that no database accounts on your system are set to their default passwords. Upon installation, Oracle creates as many as 12 database accounts, including the ones listed here (the default passwords are listed alongside the account names):

- ◆ **SYSTEM/MANAGER.** One of the basic Oracle accounts used to gain access to the Oracle system. SYSTEM owns the views created on the base system.

- ◆ **SYS/CHANGE_ON_INSTALL.** This is the other basic Oracle account that is created when Oracle is installed. This account owns most of the data dictionary tables.

- ◆ **SCOTT/TIGER** and **DEMO.** If you have been anywhere around Oracle, you know this user and password. SCOTT has limited privileges and owns a few demo tables. These are demo accounts that you should delete from any production environment.

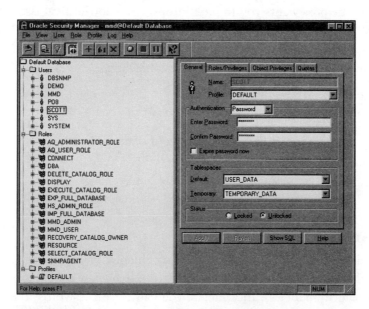

FIGURE 11.3 *Oracle Security Manager showing general information about the DBADMIN account.*

Safeguarding Database Backups

A backup of your production database enables you to easily restore the database in the event of a failure. The downside? It can also enable nefarious persons to copy your database. And if someone can obtain a copy of your backup, that someone can recreate your database on other servers! To prevent such a disaster, you must control access to each copy of your production data.

Backup production data is typically located in one of three places:

◆ **Disk backups.** When using disk-to-disk backups, you must protect the backup disk locations from unauthorized personnel.

◆ **Tape backups.** When backing up to tape, ensure that you store them in a secure location.

◆ **Development databases.** Here is one that you might not have thought of. Usually it is common practice to periodically dump your production data to your development database in order to test it. You should protect this data as you do your actual production data.

 NOTE

If you must use production data during development and testing, edit the data in the development and test databases so that confidential and proprietary data is concealed. Unless you must use production data, it's better to generate test data that accurately tests the system's functionality without compromising private company data.

Mapping Your Databases

With Oracle8 came the replacement of SQL*Net, called Net8. Net8 enables you to use service names and aliases to map the physical location and name of all your databases. This aliasing means that there is no need for anyone to know the name of any of the databases within your realm.

Managing Access to Database Services

Another security concern is Oracle's tnsnames.ora file, which is used to manage access to database services and might contain valuable information about sensitive databases. This file, which is in the Oracle directory structure under …/Network/

Admin, is accessible to every user who has a copy of the file on their machine. Instead of maintaining one grand tnsnames.ora file, consider maintaining multiple copies of the tnsnames.ora file, each corresponding to a particular group of users. Give the members of each group only the particular tnsnames.ora file they need. This means some extra management on your side, but does provide tighter security.

Protecting Production Data

Protecting your production database and data is probably the most important of these issues. The more you can isolate your production database from the rest of the world, the better you can protect it. To isolate your production database, you should incorporate these practices:

◆ Forbid anyone from using the production database for any purpose other than that of production. In other words, absolutely no development or testing is allowed on the production database.

◆ Revoke operating-system–level access from developers and testers on the production machine.

◆ Implement a standardized change-control process with built-in software configuration management.

◆ Never publicize the name of the database and server supporting the production application. Allow only necessary personnel access to the name of the server.

Summary

A database needs attention after installation. Do you have the time to monitor it? Do you hire another resource to monitor it? Do you create or buy tools? The choice is yours. If you decide to buy tools, you must first determine what monitoring method is best for your site. To select the right monitoring strategy for your company, you must consider the company's business needs, budget, and growth potential. For mission-critical applications, monitoring tools can be cheap insurance.

Take the ideas in this chapter and incorporate them into your methodology or routine. The tools or scripts alone cannot magically take care of the your database problems. You must also work closely with developers, applications managers, network administrators, and system administrators to establish guidelines, baselines, and performance expectations prior to releasing the application into production.

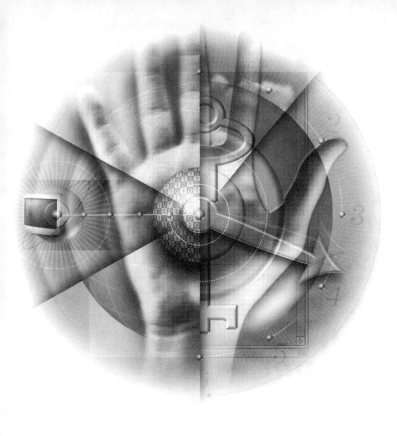

Chapter 12

**Analyzing, Tuning,
and Reporting
on Oracle**

Suppose your company is growing and just acquired some more work, which, coincidentally, involves some legacy Oracle databases. Because you've done such a great job maintaining the company's current Oracle database, your boss wants you to take on the responsibilities of maintaining the newly acquired ones. Of course you say yes, but what does this actually entail?

Generating an Analysis and Tuning Report (ATR)

This chapter guides you, in the form of a sample report, through the process of analyzing a system and making recommendations about correcting problems and tuning the databases for better performance. The sample report in this chapter covers a sample database about which you can assume the following:

◆ Your newly acquired database is a legacy system that has recently been upgraded to Oracle version 7.3.4.

◆ The name of the database is COLBYDB.

◆ The owner of the user tables is Colby_Owner.

◆ An application does access the database, but as far as analyzing and tuning goes, you are only concerned with the database.

◆ The findings and observations documented in the sample report were prepared over a four-week period as observed by you, the company's Oracle DBA.

◆ The intent of the sample report is to report major and minor recommendations (*major recommendations* are problems with the data or database; *minor recommendations* are changes or modifications that would increase performance or efficiency).

◆ You have access to tools such as SQL*Plus (to run your scripts), Oracle's Performance Monitor (to monitor different areas while users are accessing the database), and a third-party tool (such as Oracle's Enterprise Manager) that helps in listing schema and object information.

Introduction

The first part of your analysis and tuning report (ATR) is its introduction. It should provide all the introductory information for your report, such as the who, what, when, where, why, and by whom (you in this case). Be descriptive, but don't let the cat out of the bag until the next section, the executive summary.

Executive Summary

The second section of your ATR is the executive summary. This section lists your recommendations, both general and specific, as well as a summary of the report. The recommendations should be brief but descriptive, and should include page references that detail your findings. The report should categorize the recommendations into major and minor issues.

General Recommendations

Include general recommendations in this section. Include items that are found throughout the database. Following are some sample general recommendations.

- ◆ **Recommendation: Review and Make Changes.** Review and discuss this document and make any changes to the recommendations.

- ◆ **Recommendation: Plan and Schedule.** Once this document has been reviewed and discussed with supervisors, other DBAs, and the application developers, you should recommend putting together a plan and a schedule to implement the major recommendations. The plan and schedule should also define the time and resources needed to correct or modify the areas identified in the minor recommendations.

Specific Recommendations

You place your specific findings here, backing them up later in the sample report by presenting specific tests and recordings. The following are sample findings for the COLBYDB database.

 NOTE

You should, of course, replace all instances of "page *x*" with the correct page number in your report.

Recommendation #1: Tables with No Primary Key Names

(MINOR) All tables should have a primary key. Review these tables and determine whether a primary key is needed in order for the application that accesses the COLBYDB database to function properly.

Recommendation #2: Tablespace Usage and Percentage of Free Space

(MAJOR) It is recommended that more space be allocated to the tablespaces that have less than 10 percent free space. Some of these tablespaces are turned offline or are read-only—these don't need to have more space allocated to them. Only the tables that are online and have less than 10 percent free space, need additional space.

Recommendation #3: Next Possible Extent Failures

(MAJOR) Allocate more memory to the tablespaces that were discovered by running this script.

Recommendation #4: DB Links

(MINOR) If possible, cut down on the number of database links to and from the production database. As a matter of security, check development machines listed here and their links and ensure that the links are necessary. Also ensure that only people with a need to know can link to production.

Recommendation #5: Profiles

(MINOR) Set up another profile so that the resource_name SESSIONS_PER_USER is not unlimited and assign this profile to your users. Users could potentially start up sessions, one by one, until the MAX_NUMBER_SESSIONS parameter for the instance is met, although this is unlikely.

Recommendation #6: Fragmentation

(MAJOR) The goal is to have tablespaces broken into as few as possible pieces. The first few tablespaces in this list are much higher than expected. Recommend coalescing the tables.

Recommendation #7: DB Buffer Ratio

(MAJOR) Increase the DB_BLOCK_BUFFERS so that this value is closer to 95 percent or greater.

Recommendation #8: Number of Users in Database

(MINOR) Because there are many more unique users with accounts than there are users who actually use the system, it would be a good idea to delete users who no longer exist.

Recommendation #9: Number of Users Logged on COLBYDB

(MINOR) If possible, start the backup process later than 18:00 hours because most users seem to be logging into the system in the afternoon and some are still on the system at 18:00 hours.

Recommendation #10: Number of Active Users

(MINOR) The number of active users does not correspond to the number of Oracle licenses. You do not need to purchase licenses for 200 plus users when you have 200 active users using your database applications. Check with Oracle licensing to verify this.

Recommendation #11: Table Records

(MINOR) For tables with over one million records, develop a plan to reduce those records. On the other hand, check to ensure that tables with no records are still needed.

Recommendation #12: Invalid Objects

(MAJOR) The objects were found to be invalid and a description of why they are invalid is included. Recommend looking into these procedures and triggers to verify that they should indeed be invalid.

Recommendation #13: Compilation Errors

(MINOR) Determine whether these stored procedures and triggers are still being used and correct them if they are.

Summary

In the summary, offer your assessment of the data and database. See the following example:

> Overall, the newly acquired COLBYDB database and its data are in average-to-good condition. Upon correction of the major recommendations, the database would be in very good condition. Upon correction of all the recommendations (including minor ones), the database would be in excellent condition.
>
> Although it is recommended that we look into correcting or modifying everything dictated by the minor recommendations in this study, it might not be beneficial to follow through on some of the minor recommendations. Some of these minor recommendations might not result in any noticeable performance gain.

Current COLBYDB Database System

This section is the heart of your study and details the tests you conducted to determine the condition of the database. The next paragraph is a sample introduction for this section.

> The following section is divided into different areas that make up the COLBYDB database. In each area covered under the current configuration of the database, performance monitoring and tuning scripts were used to deduce key information for each of the sections. Included in each of the subsections are a brief description, the script used, and the results. If the script used to retrieve the results is lengthy, it is included in the appendix for reference.

The next sections reflect an overall study of a sample database to give readers a complete picture of the database. There are numerous ways to organize these sections; take these sections and the areas that were tested as examples only. You might find that you want to concentrate on other areas. Alternatively, you might want to include only a few areas, either because you are limited in your tool set or on time. Whatever the case, tailor these next sections to fit your report.

Database Objects

COLBYDB Database Duplicate Records

Description

The purpose of this script is to find duplicate records within the tables.

Script

```
set pagesize 80
set verify off
set echo off
select Person_ID, last_name, first_name, birth_date, rowid from
    person a where rowid >
(select min(rowid) from person b where b.last_name=a.last_name and
    b.first_name=a.first_name and b.birth_date=a.birth_date)
order by 1,2,3
/
```

Results

This script was run to obtain a sample of the COLBYDB tables. For each of the tables run, no duplicate records were found. This was expected because of the data integrity on the tables.

Recommendation

None.

Note in this example that you have to substitute the key fields in your table for the fields listed in this script. For example, substitute `first_name`, `last_name`, and `birth_date` for the key fields in your tables.

Also, this is the first of many scripts that are easily run from within SQL*Plus. Figure 12.1 shows this script being loaded into SQL*Plus. Either type this script in by hand or obtain an electronic copy of the script and copy and paste it into SQL*Plus.

COLBYDB Tables with No Primary Key Names
Description
The intention of this test is to find COLBYDB tables without primary keys.

Script
This test was done using a third-party tool called ER/Win; therefore, there is no script for this test.

Results
The tool found that the following COLBYDB tables don't have primary keys:

```
CUSTOMERS
CERTIFICATES
ACCOUNTING
COMPUTERS
```

Recommendation
(MINOR) All tables should have a primary key. Review these tables and determine whether a primary key is needed. If the application that accesses the COLBYDB database functions properly, the primary key might not be necessary.

Database Views
Description
This is a listing of the views for informational purposes only.

```
± Oracle SQL*Plus                                                    _ □ ×
File  Edit  Search  Options  Help

SQL*Plus: Release 8.0.5.0.0 - Production on Wed Nov 15 22:46:52 2000

(c) Copyright 1998 Oracle Corporation.  All rights reserved.


Connected to:
Oracle8 Personal Edition Release 8.0.4.0.0 - Production
PL/SQL Release 8.0.4.0.0 - Production

SQL> set pagesize 80
SQL> set verify off
SQL> set echo off
SQL> select Person_ID, last_name, first_name, birth_date, rowid from person a where rowid >
  2  (select min(rowid) from person b where b.last_name=a.last_name and
  3  b.first_name=a.first_name and b.birth_date=a.birth_date)
  4  order by 1,2,3
  5
SQL>
```

FIGURE 12.1 *Oracle's SQL*Plus with a Duplicate Records script loaded into the buffer.*

Script

```
select owner, view_name, text_length, text from dba_views;
```

NOTE

To select data in views and tables such as the dba_views above requires that that user has dba privileges.

NOTE

Note that some of the scripts in this chapter end with a "/" as the very last line. This symbol is short for the command RUN. Also note that the character ";" at the end of the script acts the same as the "/" or the RUN command.

Result

Owner	VIEW_NAME	Length	Text
COLBY_OWNER	V_CBG_ACCOUNT_DETAIL	8246	SELECT account_detail.account_detail_id,
COLBY_OWNER	V_MILTON_INVOICING	793	SELECT MAIN.MILTON_NUM, SUB.title_name, MAIN
COLBY_OWNER	V_CURRENT_MEMBERSHIP	683	Select person_id, reported_plan_code, report
COLBY_OWNER	V_CBG_FUNDS_AVAILABLE	709	SELECT To_Date(FUND_DATE. Log_Entry_Date),
COLBY_OWNER	V_TYBRIN_INVOICE_RECS	3884	SELECT INVOICE_NUM FROM COLBYDB.INVOICE_
COLBY_OWNER	V_TRUELOVE_RECORDS	2445	SELECT MB_TRUELOVE_NUM FROM COLBYDB.
COLBY_OWNER	V_TQDBS_RECORDS	72500	SELECT HARR_LEAD FROM COLBYDB.FDOT
COLBY_OWNER	V_CSL_PROJECT	72525	SELECT KENNEDY_RECS FROM COLBYDB
COLBY_OWNER	V_CURRENT_ADDRESS	789	Select "PERSON_ID","BEGIN_DATE", "MAIL_TO_NA

Recommendation

None.

Synonyms

Description

There are 1,268 synonyms, most of which are public. Some of the synonyms are owned by system and sys; the remaining synonyms are documented in the "Results" section.

Script

```
Select owner,synonym_name,table_owner,table_name from dba_synonyms
```

Results

Owner	SYNONYM_NAME	TABLE_OWNER	TABLE_NAME
JOEL_OWNER	DBA_TABLESPACES	SYS	DBA_TABLESPACES
DBADMIN	DBA_FREE_SPACE	SYS	DBA_FREE_SPACE
DBADMIN	DBA_SEGMENTS	SYS	DBA_SEGMENTS
COLBY_DBA	JOB_EVENTLIST	COLBY_DBA	JOB_EVENTLIST_
COLBY_DBA	JOB_ID	COLBY_DBA	JOB_ID_
SUSAN_OWNER	READING_MASTER	COLBY_OWNER	READING_SPEC_MASTER
CLEANUP	JOB_EVENTLIST	CLEANUP	JOB_EVENTLIST_
CLEANUP	JOB_ID	CLEANUP	JOB_ID_
COLBY_OWNER	MILTON_RECS	MILTON_OWNER	MILTON_RECORDS

Recommendation

None.

Database Storage

Tablespace Usage and Percentage of Free Space

Description

This table was developed to show the percentage of free space in the tablespaces.

Script

```
rem Tablespace Usage
set pagesize 66
set line 132
clear breaks
clear computes
column "Total Bytes" format 9,999,999,999
```

```
column "Bytes Free" format 9,999,999,999
column "% Free" format 999.99
select substr(fs.FILE_ID,1,3) "ID#", fs.tablespace_name, df.bytes
   "Total Bytes",
sum(fs.bytes) "Bytes Free", (100*((sum(fs.bytes))/df.bytes)) "% Free"
from sys.dba_data_files df, sys.dba_free_space fs
where df.file_id(+) = fs.file_id
group by fs.FILE_ID, fs.tablespace_name, df.bytes
order by "% Free"
/
```

Results

This table shows, in order, the amount of free space left in the tablespaces. The first few tablespaces are italicized because they show tablespaces with less than 10 percent free space.

ID#	TABLESPACE_NAME	Total Bytes	Bytes Free	% Free
24	STATIC_INDEX	419430400	1900544	0.45
63	ACCOUNT_DETAIL_INDEX	210763776	1040384	0.49
40	PAYROLL_DATA	524288000	3473408	0.66
62	ACCOUNT_DETAIL_INDEX	209715200	2121728	1.01
3	RBS	1048576000	20676608	1.97
19	PERSON_DATA	576716800	16293888	2.82
41	PAYROLL_INDEX	419430400	33333248	7.95
1	SYSTEM	104857600	28647424	27.32
4	JRC_DATA	11041964	82493424	69.68
15	SMC_DATA	6181964	5932416	71.90
26	ZJC_DATA	4281994	3224362	72.87
55	TEMP	629145600	402915328	74.04
7	JAC_DATA	8071996	3162336	75.25
21	TEC_DATA	2211999	982393	86.34
6	USERS	209715200	175562752	89.71
5	TOOLS	52428800	51068928	97.40

Recommendation

(MAJOR) More space should be allocated to the tablespaces that contain less than 10 percent free space. Some of these tablespaces can be turned offline or are read-only—these don't need to have more space allocated to them. The remainders that are online need more space.

Next Possible Extent Failures

Description

This script detects the next possible extent failures of your database. Certain objects on your database will grab the next allocated extent (chuck of memory). However, when doing so, they will have trouble because the next available size of memory is less than that of the next allocated extent.

Script

```
select
substr(sg.tablespace_name,1,30) Tablespace,
substr(sg.segment_name,1,30) Object,
sg.extents extents,
sg.next_extent next,
max(sp.bytes) available
from dba_free_space sp, dba_segments sg
where sp.tablespace_name = sg.tablespace_name
having max(sp.bytes) < sg.next_extent
group by sg.tablespace_name, sg.segment_name,sg.extents,sg.next_extent
order by 1,2
/
```

Results

Tablespace	Object	Extents	Next extent	Available memory
RBS	R01	35	29360128	20676608
STATIC_INDEX	ADDR_PER_FK	12	2097152	1900544
COLBY_TBS_01	CUSTOMER_TABLE	1	2097152	1900544
COLBY_TBS_01	PAYROLL	22	8388608	1900544
STATIC_INDEX	PAYEE_CUST_FK	1	2097152	1900544

Recommendation

(MAJOR) Allocate more memory to the tablespaces in question.

Database Security

DB Links

Description

These are the database links, or DB links, and are listed here for information purposes only.

Script

```
Select owner, db_link, username, host from sys.dba_db_links
/
```

Results

Owner	DB_LINK	User Name	Host
PUBLIC	CBG.WORLD	SYS	CBG
COLBY_OWNER	DB1.WORLD	COLBYDB	DB1
COLBY_OWNER	DB1.WORLD	COLBYDB	DB1
JOEL_OWNER	PROD.WORLD	JOEL_C	PROD
JOEL_OWNER	PROD.WORLD	JOEL_C	PROD
CONVERSION	DEV.WORLD	SYS	DEV
CONVERSION	TYB.WORLD	SYS	TYB

Recommendation

(MINOR) If possible, cut down on the number of database links to and from the production database. As a matter of security, check development machines listed here and their links and ensure that the links are necessary. Also ensure that the only people with a need to know can link to production. This suggestion will increase security by not allowing as many connections to the production database.

Profiles

Description

This script lists the profiles on the COLBYDB sample database.

Script

```
select profile, resource_name, limit from dba_profiles
/
```

Results

Profile	RESOURCE_NAME	Limit
DEFAULT	COMPOSITE_LIMIT	UNLIMITED
DEFAULT	SESSIONS_PER_USER	UNLIMITED
DEFAULT	CPU_PER_SESSION	UNLIMITED
DEFAULT	CPU_PER_CALL	UNLIMITED
DEFAULT	LOGICAL_READS_PER_SESSION	UNLIMITED
DEFAULT	LOGICAL_READS_PER_CALL	UNLIMITED
DEFAULT	IDLE_TIME	UNLIMITED
DEFAULT	CONNECT_TIME	UNLIMITED
DEFAULT	PRIVATE_SGA	UNLIMITED

Recommendation

(MINOR) Set up another profile so that the resource_name SESSIONS_PER_USER is not unlimited and assign this profile to your users. Users could potentially start up sessions, one by one, until the MAX_NUMBER_SESSIONS parameter for the instance is met, although this is unlikely.

Database Performance

Fragmentation

Description

The following table shows the tablespaces in order of the number of extents or fragmented pieces.

Script

```
select    substr(de.owner,1,8) "Owner", substr(de.segment_type,1,8) "Seg Type",
          substr(de.segment_name,1,35) "Table Name (Segment)",
          substr(de.tablespace_name,1,20) "Tablespace Name",
count(*) "Frag NEED", substr(df.name,1,40) "DataFile Name"
from sys.dba_extents de, v$datafile df
where de.owner <> 'SYS' and de.file_id = df.file# and de.segment_type = 'TABLE'
group by de.owner, de.segment_name, de.segment_type, de.tablespace_name,
    df.name
having count(*) > 1
order by count(*) desc
/
```

Results

Owner	Tablespace Name	Fragmented Pieces	Data File Name
SYSTEM	TEMP	8710	/sioux/oradata/COLBYDB/temp01.dbf
SYSTEM	RBS	612	/sioux/oradata/COLBYDB/rbs01.dbf
SYSTEM	USERS	263	/sioux/oradata/COLBYDB/users01.dbf
COLBY_OWNER	ACCOUNT_DATA	254	/durango/oradata/COLBYDB/accounts01.dbf
COLBY_OWNER	SAVE_DATA	130	/zachary/oradata/COLBYDB/data01.dbf
COLBY_OWNER	PAYROLL_INDEX	39	/zachary/oradata/COLBYDB/data01.dbf
COLBY_OWNER	PERSON_INDEX	5	/zachary/oradata/COLBYDB/data01.dbf
COLBY_OWNER	PERSON_DATA	3	/zachary/oradata/COLBYDB/data01.dbf
SYSTEM	SYSTEM	1	/sioux/oradata/COLBYDB/system01.dbf
SYSTEM	TOOLS	1	/sioux/oradata/COLBYDB/system01.dbf

Recommendation

(MAJOR) The goal is to have tablespaces broken into as few as possible pieces. The first few tablespaces in this list are much higher than expected. Recommend coalescing the tables.

Database System

Control Files, Datafiles, and Redo Logs
Description
The following script displays the control files, datafiles, and redo logs for the COLBYDB database.

Script

```
set pagesize 80
set heading off
set feedback off
set verify off
column file_name format a40
column bytes format 999,999,999,999
set echo off
select 'Physical information for database : ', name from v$database;
set heading on
break on report on tablespace_name
compute sum of bytes on report
select 'online redo log group number :' tablespace_name, b.group# file_id,
    b.member file_name, a.bytes
from v$log a, v$logfile b where a.group# = b.group#
union
select 'controlfile number : ' tablespace_name, rownum file_id, name
    file_name, 1048576
from v$controlfile
union
select tablespace_name, file_id, file_name, bytes from dba_data_files
order by tablespace_name
/
```

Results

Datafiles

TABLESPACE_NAME	FILE_ID	FILE_NAME
ACCOUNT_DETAIL_DATA	7	/sioux/oradata/COLBYDB/account_detail_data_01.dbf
ACCOUNT_DETAIL_INDEX	8	/sioux/oradata/COLBYDB/account_detail_index_01.dbf
CONVERSION_DATA	11	/shell/oradata/COLBYDB/conversion_data_01.dbf
GROWING_DATA	13	/durango/oradata/COLBYDB/growing_data_01.dbf
PAYROLL_DATA	40	/durango/oradata/COLBYDB/payroll_data_01.dbf
PAYROLL_DATA	56	/sioux/oradata/COLBYDB/payroll_data_02.dbf
PERSON_DATA	19	/bethal/oradata/COLBYDB/person_data_01.dbf
RBS	2	/shell/oradata/COLBYDB/rbs_data_01.dbf
SAVE_DATA	23	/shell/oradata/COLBYDB/save_data_01.dbf
SYSTEM	1	/kiowa/oradata/COLBYDB/system_data_01.dbf
TEMP	4	/kiowa/oradata/COLBYDB/temp_data_01.dbf
TOOLS	5	/thurston/oradata/COLBYDB/tools_data_01.dbf
USERS	6	/thurston/oradata/COLBYDB/users_data_01.dbf

Control Files

TABLESPACE_NAME	FILE_ID	FILE_NAME
controlfile number :	1	/sioux/oradata/COLBYDB/controlCOLBYDB01.ctl
controlfile number :	2	/kiowa/oradata/COLBYDB/controlCOLBYDB02.ctl
controlfile number :	3	/thurston/oradata/COLBYDB/controlCOLBYDB03.ctl

Redo Logs

TABLESPACE_NAME	FILE_ID	FILE_NAME
online redo log group number :	1	/sioux/oradata/COLBYDB/redoCOLBYDB01b.log
online redo log group number :	1	/kiowa/oradata/COLBYDB/redoCOLBYDB01a.log
online redo log group number :	2	/sioux/oradata/COLBYDB/redoCOLBYDB02a.log
online redo log group number :	2	/kiowa/oradata/COLBYDB/redoCOLBYDB02b.log
online redo log group number :	3	/sioux/oradata/COLBYDB/redoCOLBYDB03a.log
online redo log group number :	3	/kiowa/oradata/COLBYDB/redoCOLBYDB03b.log

Recommendation

None.

Database Hit/Ratios

DB Buffer Ratio

Description

The init.ora parameter DB_BLOCK_BUFFERS, one of the more important ratios to determine for performance, controls the amount of memory allocated to the data cache. When an application requests data, Oracle first attempts to find it in the data cache. Anytime Oracle finds requested data in memory, a physical I/O is avoided, and thus overall performance is better. Under normal circumstances, this ratio should be greater than or equal to 95 percent. Initially set the DB_BLOCK_BUFFERS size to be 20–50 percent of the size of the SGA.

Script

```
select round((1-(pr.value/(bg.value+cg.value)))*100,2) "Buffer Cache Hit"
from v$sysstat pr, v$sysstat bg, v$sysstat cg
where pr.name = 'physical reads'
and bg.name = 'db block gets'
and cg.name = 'consistent gets'
/
```

Results

DB buffer ratio is 83.33 percent.

Recommendation

(MAJOR) Increase the DB_BLOCK_BUFFERS so that this value is 95 percent or greater.

Dictionary Cache Efficiency

Description

The init.ora parameter SHARED_POOL_SIZE controls the amount of memory allocated to the shared buffer pool. The shared buffer pool contains SQL and PL/SQL statements (library cache), the data dictionary cache, and information about database sessions. This percentage will never equal 100 because the cache must perform an initial load when Oracle first starts up. The percentage, therefore, should continually get closer to 100 as the system stays up.

Ideally, the entire data dictionary would be cached in memory. Initially set the SHARED_POOL_SIZE to be 50–100 percent of the size of the init.ora parameter DB_BLOCK_BUFFERS and then fine-tune the parameter.

Script

```
select round(sum(gets)/(sum(gets)+sum(getmisses)) * 100,2) from v$rowcache
/
```

Results

Dictionary cache efficiency is 96.50 percent.

Recommendation

None. The results are within the expected range for optimal performance.

Library Cache Efficiency

Description

This is the percentage at which a SQL statement does not need to be reloaded because it was already in the library cache. The init.ora parameter SHARED_POOL_SIZE controls the amount of memory allocated to the shared buffer pool. The shared buffer pool contains SQL and PL/SQL statements (library cache), the data dictionary cache, and information about database sessions. The percentage should be close to 100. For maximum efficiency, no SQL statement should be reloaded and reparsed. Initially set the SHARED_POOL_SIZE to be 50–100 percent of the size of the init.ora parameter DB_BLOCK_BUFFERS and then fine-tune the parameter.

Script

```
select round(sum(pinhits)/sum(pins) * 100,2) from v$librarycache
/
```

Results

Library cache efficiency is 97.26 percent.

Recommendation

None. The results are within the expected range for optimal performance.

Sort Area Efficiency

Description

Sort area efficiency refers to the percentage of sorts performed in memory as opposed to sorts performed in temporary segments on-disk. This should be greater than 95 percent.

Script

```
select round((sum(decode(name, 'sorts (memory)', value, 0))
   / (sum(decode(name, 'sorts (memory)', value, 0))
  + sum(decode(name, 'sorts (disk)', value, 0)))) * 100,2)
from v$sysstat
/
```

Results

Sort area efficiency is 97.7 percent.

Recommendation

None. The results are within the expected range for optimal performance.

Database Usage

Number of Users in Database

Description

The following script determined the maximum number of unique users who have access to the production system.

Script

```
select count(*) from dba_users where default_tablespace = 'USERS'
and username not like 'TRAIN%'
and username not like '%_DBA'
and username not like 'SEC_%'
order by username
/
```

Result

There are 337 unique users in the database. Also, the database survey observed over a four-week period that no more than 256 users were logged into the system at one time.

Recommendation

(MINOR) Because there are many more unique users with accounts than there are users who actually use the system, it would be a good idea to delete users who no longer exist.

Number of Users Logged on COLBYDB

Description

The Number of Users Logged On chart displays the number of concurrent user sessions logged on to the database instance, whether or not activity is being generated. This was observed by turning on Oracle's performance monitor each day for a month and noting the maximum number of users logged on to the system.

Script

None were used; the Oracle Performance Monitor determined the values.

Result

Of the four weeks of observations, the fewest number of users logged on one day was 207, whereas the highest number of users logged on one day was 256. The maximum number of users was normally recorded after lunch (13:00 hours). At 18:00 hours, the database shuts down for backup and other purposes. However, 25 users on average are still logged into the system at this time.

Recommendation

(MINOR) If possible, start the backup process later than 18:00 hours because most users seem to be logging into the system in the afternoon and some are still on the system at 18:00 hours.

Number of Active Users

Description

The following result was obtained by monitoring the database for four weeks using Oracle's Performance Monitor software. The Number of Users Active chart in the software displays the number of users actively using the database. Most likely, the users were running transactions on the database.

Script

None were used; the Oracle Performance Monitor determined these values.

Results

The Oracle Performance Monitor was set to record the activity on the database and refresh every 10 seconds throughout the day. During the days monitored, no more than 17 users tried to use the database at the same time. The number of users concurrently using the database ranged from 9 to 17. For a production database that has an average of 200-plus users logged in, only an average of 13 users hit the database at the same time.

Recommendation

(MINOR) We might need to adjust the current Oracle licenses to match the actual load on the database. Check with Oracle licensing. We do not need to purchase licenses for 200-plus users when only a maximum of 17 use the database at the same time.

Table Records

Description

The following tables show how many records are in each table.

Script

```
SELECT TABLE_NAME, NUM_ROWS
FROM ALL_TABLES
WHERE OWNER = 'COLBY_OWNER'
order by NUM_ROWS
```

Results

The following active COLBY_OWNER tables have over one million records. Determine how to reduce the number of records if possible.

TABLE_NAME	NUM_ROWS
ACCOUNT_DETAIL	11491474
PAYMENT_HISTORY	7296557
CURRENT_MEMBERSHIP	2974403
SMC_READ_TRANS	2029402
AUDIT_LOG_DETAIL	1256886

The following tables have fewer than one million records but more than 100,000, and are probably okay.

TABLE_NAME	NUM_ROWS
PERSON	957378
PERSON_JOURNAL	693857
PAYEE_BENEFIT	393915
PAYEE	209887
PAYEE_CALENDAR_YEAR	187587
PAYEE_DEDUCTION	117123

The following tables contain between 100,000 and 1,000 records.

TABLE_NAME	NUM_ROWS
DEPARTMENT	37273
ANNUITY	21880
RETIREE_LETTER_HISTORY	19285
SUPPLEMENTAL_BENEFIT	18802
BENEFICIARY	16469
DEDUCTIONS	12122
AGENCY	4629
AGENCY_POSITION	2826
PAYEE_DEDUCTION_HISTORY_ADJ	2688
DISABILITY ANALYSIS	1333
MESSAGE_CODE	1194

The following tables have fewer than 1,000, but at least one, record.

TABLE_NAME	NUM_ROWS
AGENCY2	874
SCHEDULE	865
DEPOSIT	765
PLAN_TABLE	654
PAYROLL_SCHEDULE	611
SALARY	455
PAST_SERVICE	344
RANK	233
INTEREST_RATE	122
PROCESS	111
COVERED_GROUPS	68
DOCUMENT_TYPES	49
RELATIONSHIP_CODE	32
TEMP_PERIOD	7

The following tables have no records. You will need to verify that these records are still necessary.

TABLE_NAME	NUM_ROWS
EARLY_RETIREMENT	0
SOCIAL_SECURITY	0
CHANGE_LOG	0
AUDITOR_LOG	0

Recommendation

(MINOR) For tables with over one million records, develop a plan to reduce those records. On the other hand, check to ensure that tables with no records are still needed.

Miscellaneous

Invalid objects

Description

This script lists the COLBY_OWNER objects that are invalid and a possible explanation of why.

Script

```
column invalid_object format A30
column likely_reason format A35 word_wrapped
set recsep off
break on type on invalid_object
select owner || '.' || object_name invalid_object, '-- ' || object_type ||
    ' --' likely_reason
from dba_objects where status = 'INVALID'
union
select d.owner || '.' || d.name, 'Non-existent referenced db link ' ||
    d.referenced_link_name
from dba_dependencies d
```

(continued...)

```
where not exists (select 'x' from dba_db_links where owner in ('PUBLIC', d.owner)
        and db_link = d.referenced_link_name)
        and d.referenced_link_name is not null
        and (d.owner, d.name, d.type) in (select owner, object_name, object_type
        from dba_objects where status = 'INVALID')
union
select d.owner || '.' || d.name, 'Depends on invalid ' || d.referenced_type || ' '
        || d.referenced_owner || '.' || d.referenced_name
from dba_objects ro, dba_dependencies d
where ro.status = 'INVALID' and ro.owner = d.referenced_owner
        and ro.object_name = d.referenced_name and ro.object_type =
d.referenced_type
        and d.referenced_link_name is null
        and (d.owner, d.name, d.type) in (select owner, object_name, object_type
        from dba_objects where status = 'INVALID')
union
select d.owner || '.' || d.name, 'Depends on newer ' || d.referenced_type || ' '
        || d.referenced_owner || '.' || d.referenced_name
from dba_objects ro, dba_dependencies d, dba_objects o
where nvl(ro.last_ddl_time, ro.created) > nvl(o.last_ddl_time, o.created)
        and ro.owner = d.referenced_owner and ro.object_name = d.referenced_name
        and ro.object_type = d.referenced_type and d.referenced_link_name is null
        and d.owner = o.owner and d.name = o.object_name
        and d.type = o.object_type and o.status = 'INVALID'
union
select d.owner || '.' || d.name, 'Depends on ' || d.referenced_type || ' '
        || d.referenced_owner || '.' || d.referenced_name
        || decode(d.referenced_link_name, NULL, '', '@' || d.referenced_link_name)
from dba_dependencies d
where d.referenced_owner != 'PUBLIC' — Public synonyms generate noise
        and d.referenced_type = 'NON-EXISTENT'
        and (d.owner, d.name, d.type) in (select owner, object_name, object_type
        from dba_objects where status = 'INVALID')
union
select d.owner || '.' || d.name invalid_object,
        'No privilege on referenced ' || d.referenced_type || ' '
        || d.referenced_owner || '.' || d.referenced_name
from dba_objects ro, dba_dependencies d
```

(continued...)

```
where not exists (select 'x' from dba_tab_privs p
        where p.owner = d.referenced_owner
        and p.table_name = d.referenced_name
        and p.grantee in ('PUBLIC', d.owner))
        and ro.status = 'VALID' and ro.owner = d.referenced_owner
        and ro.object_name = d.referenced_name
        and d.referenced_link_name is not null
        and (d.owner, d.name, d.type) in (select owner, object_name, object_type
        from dba_objects where status = 'INVALID')
union
select o.owner || '.' || o.object_name, e.text from dba_errors e, dba_objects o
where e.text like 'PLS-%' and e.owner = o.owner
        and e.name = o.object_name and e.type = o.object_type
        and o.status = 'INVALID'
/
```

Results

Invalid Object	Reason for Its Being Invalid
COLBY_OWNER.SP_COPY_FILES	—- PROCEDURE —-
COLBY_OWNER.SP_DBMS_CALC	Depends on NON-EXISTENT COLBY_OWNER.DBMS_OUTPUT
COLBY_OWNER.SP_CALC_ACCOUNT	Depends on newer TABLE COLBY_OWNER.ACCOUNT_DETAIL
COLBY_OWNER.TR_PLAN_TABLE	—- TRIGGER —-
COLBY_OWNER.TR_PLAN_TABLE	Depends on newer TABLE COLBY_OWNER.PLAN_TABLE
COLBY_OWNER.TR_PLAN_TABLE	PLS-00049: bad bind variable 'NEW.ACTIVITY_USER_ID'

Recommendation

(MAJOR) These objects were found to be invalid; a description of why they are
invalid is included. Recommend looking into these procedures and triggers to verify that they should indeed be invalid.

Compilation Errors

Description

The following table contains errors associated with the most recent compilation attempt for the procedural object.

Script

```
set heading off
spool cinv.sql
select 'alter '||decode(object_type,'PACKAGE BODY','PACKAGE',object_type)
|| ' '||owner||'.'|| object_name ||' compile' ||
decode(object_type, 'PACKAGE BODY', ' body;', ';')
from dba_objects
where status = 'INVALID';
spool off;
@cinv.sql
```

Results

OWNER	NAME	TYPE	TEXT
COLBY_COMPILE	SP_CALC_DATE_NEW	PROCEDURE	PL/SQL: SQL Statement ignored
COLBY_COMPILE	SP_CALC_BENEFIC	PROCEDURE	PLS-00904: insufficient privilege to access object BENEFICIARY
COLBY_COMPILE	SP_CALC_SALARY	PROCEDURE	PLS-00904: insufficient privilege to access object SALARY
COLBY_COMPILE	SP_CALC	PROCEDURE	PL/SQL: SQL Statement ignored
COLBY_OWNER	TR_PLAN_TABLE	TRIGGER	PLS-00049: bad bind variable 'NEW.ACTIVITY_DATETIME'
COLBY_OWNER	TR_PLAN_TABLE	TRIGGER	PLS-00049: bad bind variable 'NEW.ACTIVITY_USER_ID'
COLBY_OWNER	TR_PLAN_TABLE	TRIGGER	PLS-00049: bad bind variable 'NEW.ACTIVITY_DATETIME'
COLBY_OWNER	TR_PLAN_TABLE	TRIGGER	PLS-00049: bad bind variable 'NEW.ACTIVITY_USER_ID'

Recommendation

(MINOR) Determine whether these stored procedures and triggers are still being used and correct them if they are.

There are many more areas, scripts, tuning tools, and performance analysis tests that you can add to this section of your report, including areas such as indexes, functions, and normalization. Hopefully these examples have helped you develop areas that you can cover in your own analysis and tuning report.

Data Dictionary

One last item to include in your ATR is the Oracle data dictionary. The data dictionary, sometimes referred to as the database dictionary, is a printed listing of all the objects in the database, including the table structures, views, functions, procedures, and all the common objects that you and your application developers reference each day. The data dictionary should also include a diagram of all the tables and how they relate to one another. This information is usually included in the appendix of the ATR.

Summary

If you are very good at your job (and of course you are!), you will likely be asked to analyze a database created by a different department or a customer. No matter how it happens, the task of analyzing someone else's database—or tuning your own—is going to be laid at your feet. This chapter has presented an approach to planning and documenting such a task. Intertwined in this sample report are several good scripts that will become part of your arsenal in the future. Be sure to check Appendix B, "Usage, Performance, and Other Oracle Scripts," for more useful scripts.

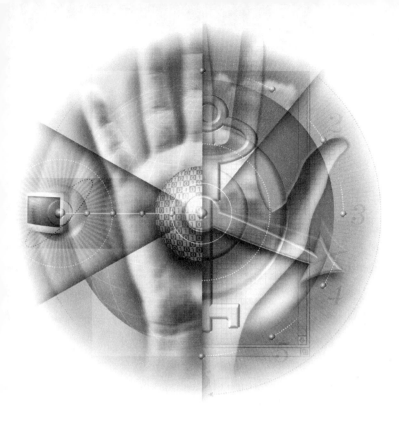

Chapter 13

Planning for Disaster Recovery

According to *SunExpert Magazine*, the top five causes of data loss and downtime are

◆ Hardware or system malfunction (44%)
◆ Human error (33%)
◆ Software program error (14%)
◆ Viruses (6%)
◆ Natural disasters (3%)

The financial impact of downtime can be staggering. The average hourly impact of downtime per industry as reported by Contingency Planning Research is detailed in Table 13.1.

Table 13.1 The Average Hourly Impact of Downtime

Hourly Impact	Industry
$6,450,000	Retail Brokerage
$2,600,000	Credit Card Sales Authorization
$113,750	Home Shopping Channels
$90,000	Catalog Sales Centers
$89,500	Airline Reservation Centers
$41,000	Cellular Service Activation
$28,250	Package Shipping Service
$25,250	Online Network Connect Fees
$14,500	ATM Service Fees

Coupled with the primary financial impact of downtime are other attributed losses experienced by a percentage of companies, as reported by *HP Professional* magazine:

◆ Lost productivity (88.9%)

◆ End-user/management dissatisfaction (87.1%)

◆ Customer dissatisfaction (66.9%)

◆ Overtime (59.3%)

◆ Lost revenues (41.8%)

◆ Lost transactions (34.4%)

◆ Lost customers (23.1%)

◆ Penalties or fines (7.6%)

The purpose of this chapter is to enable you to contain downtime and data loss by helping you prepare a *disaster-recovery plan* (DRP). A DRP performs two functions:

◆ Aides in recovery in the event of a disaster

◆ Helps prevent disasters from happening

A DRP includes procedures to be followed in the event of a disaster situation, such as a fire, tornado, or any unanticipated event that makes the computers or networks unusable or compromises the integrity of the hardware, data, or software on the systems for any extended period of time. The disaster-recovery plan, sometimes called a business resumption or contingency plan, consists of a series of steps that guide you through the process of recovering a system, data center, or business in the event of a major hardware or site outage. The plan (and all the materials required to execute it) is stored off-site at a safe location—one that would not be affected in the event of a disaster.

The first half of this chapter discusses the different areas and ideas that you need to implement in a plan, along with the format of the plan. The second half of the chapter walks you through Oracle's Technical Assistance Requests (TAR) process, and what you can expect from Oracle when you need help.

 TIP

Put together your DRP using the disaster plan template included in Appendix A, "DBA Templates and Checklists."

Disaster Plan Issues

To increase the effectiveness of the DRP, consider the following issues prior to a disaster:

◆ **Facilities.** Determine which facilities will be used in the event of a disaster. You'll need a prearranged recovery location. Each department should consider what resources it needs in the event of a disaster. Be sure to investigate and document requirements such as square footage, number of desks, and hardware well in advance.

◆ **Project priority directives.** Although situation-specific priorities will emerge during a crisis, management should be involved in determining priorities for a disaster situation. You must consider and document the critical business functions ahead of time so that the highest priority items will be addressed appropriately. If you cannot make such priorities, your organization must do what it can to resume business functions in proper order, depending on the state of emergency.

◆ **Security.** The security of disaster and recovery areas should be handled by corporate security, unless directed otherwise. Those involved with recovery must work with any directives issued by corporate security throughout the disaster.

◆ **Human resources (HR).** HR needs to act as necessary to aid in locating temporary or permanent replacement personnel, providing assistance to current employees, and ensuring employees' personal safety. It is also assumed that the majority of personnel will survive the disaster.

◆ **Legal consultation.** The company should obtain adequate legal consultation and counseling if required. The staff needs to work as closely to the guidelines as possible to avoid possible legal conflict.

◆ **Vendor disaster-recovery commitments.** Suppliers are responsible for providing disaster-recovery plans for their equipment.

The Makeup of the DRP

A disaster-recovery plan is comprised of four basic parts:

◆ Business continuity planning

◆ Risk management

- Project/department impact assessment
- Disaster-recovery procedures

The following sections cover those parts in detail, starting with the business planning aspect.

Part 1: Business Continuity Planning

Proper prevention efforts can help minimize the effect of a disaster on financial assets, customer satisfaction, legal obligations, and corporate image. During the design of computing systems, be sure to consider protection against various failure scenarios. Don't overlook fire prevention techniques, local ordnance codes, and company insurance requirements for data centers. In addition, it is important to have a solid backup and recovery strategy. Data recovery is key to effective business resumption.

Part 2: Risk Management

For a disaster-recovery plan to be feasible, all risks need to be identified and categorized. In the event of a disaster, the DRP helps minimize or eliminate those risks that hinder the goal of complete recovery. Additionally, risk management can minimize the likelihood of preventable disaster by deploying appropriate safeguards such as education, security, backups, recovery strategies, fire suppression, water detection, and detection of power fluctuations or failures.

Risk management takes these issues into account:

- **Minimization of the effect of a disaster because of risk assessment.** By assessing all the risk that is involved with a disaster, it is possible to discover ways to reduce or minimize the effect of a true disaster.
- **Testing of the DRP.** The DRP is no good if it is written and placed on a shelf somewhere. The DRP needs to be tested and updated at regular intervals.
- **Cross-training of personnel.** This goes hand in hand with testing the DRP. By cross-training the personnel so they know what to do in the case of a disaster, you can minimize the time involved in recovering from a disaster.
- **Outside assistance.** When a disaster occurs, usually you are not the only one involved. Stay abreast of your surroundings. You never know what kind of outside assistance you'll need when a disaster strikes.

Part 3: Project/Department Impact Assessment

Recovery strategies have changed with the evolution of distributed computing. With the advent of distributed computing, the network has become an integral part of disaster recovery. In the past, recovering the data center and reconnecting users to terminals were the primary goals. With the new decentralized client/ server organization, however, even more planning must be done to identify critical networks and applications. This might involve an extensive multi-department site plan, including the following issues:

◆ **Power influences.** When evaluating power, identify all disturbances, including external ones, such as outages and weather disturbances. In addition, identify internal sources, such as microwave ovens, radio equipment, wiring, welders, and large electrical motors.

◆ **Replacement of equipment.** The plan should address the replacement of inoperable equipment. One approach is to replace damaged machines with units acquired off the shelf. Another approach is to replace damaged machines from a designated vendor within a contracted period of time.

Part 4: The Disaster Recovery Procedure

You need to document the procedures for implementing the disaster-recovery plan, train the personnel, and then test the process. Rehearsing the actual plan to identify potential pitfalls is key to proper disaster planning. During such a rehearsal, be sure to carefully document the results and integrate the lessons learned into the planning guide. The planning guide should include the following sections:

◆ **Incident notification.** Using concise, one-line action statements, this section walks through the various steps to follow when an incident occurs. A plan should be created for both minor-loss and major-loss situations.

◆ **Recovery facilities.** This section documents the locations, phone numbers, available hardware and software, and activation procedures of the recovery locations. The type of facility needed is usually dictated by how critical the business function is. If required, you can set up a *hot site* (a temporary physical location). This hot site can range from backup tapes to new systems to a duplicate of a company's data center. Several vendors offer data duplication, including COMDISCO, Wang, HP, and SunGard.

◆ **System recovery plans.** This section contains the step-by-step procedures to be performed at the recovery site in order to restore the systems and applications.

◆ **LAN environment recovery plans.** This section contains the step-by-step procedures to be performed at the recovery site in order to restore the LAN and its applications.

◆ **System backup/restore procedures.** The backed-up data should be stored at an off-site facility. This section contains the procedures for recalling the off-site tapes and restoring the backed-up data.

◆ **Special forms and supplies lists.** The lists contained in this section are used to gather any special forms, manuals, and supplies that are kept at off-site locations for transport to the recovery site.

◆ **Software recovery and installation.** This section lists all software needed for recovery.

◆ **Vendor lists.** This section lists all vendors—hardware, software, and network—that might need to be contacted in the event of a disaster.

◆ **Inventory and required information.** This section contains miscellaneous documentation, including detailed hardware, network infrastructure, and backbone configurations; inventory lists; and warranty information.

◆ **Master phone lists.** This section lists the business, home, and pager numbers of all personnel who might need to be contacted in the event of a disaster.

Calling Oracle: The TAR Process

If something does go terribly wrong, one of the steps in your disaster plan might be to make an emergency phone call to Oracle and use Oracle's Technical Assistance Requests (TAR) process. Figure 13.1 illustrates Oracle's TAR process.

Oracle's TAR process is divided into four levels of severity:

◆ **Severity Level Four.** Severity Level Four TARs are the least disastrous, causing no loss of service. The result is usually a minor error, erroneous behavior, or an error in the documentation that in no way impedes the operation of your Oracle system.

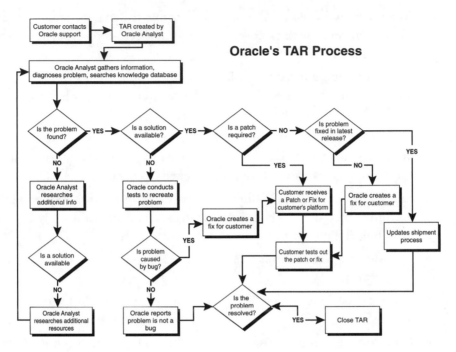

FIGURE 13.1 *Oracle's TAR process shows the flow of how Oracle corrects a problem.*

◆ **Severity Level Three.** Severity Level Three problems or defects cause a minimal loss of operation. The defect, error, or problem has only a minor impact on your Oracle operation. Examples of Level Three Severity TARs include problems for which you have incorporated a workaround but would prefer that the system to work as advertised, occasional errors that occur that merely inconvenience the system, and performance issues that arise because of an error or problem.

◆ **Severity Level Two.** A Severity Level Two TAR is a problem that regularly causes the system or software to issue an error or an incorrect action that then causes a severe loss of service. No workarounds are available for Severity Level Two TARs. With Severity Level Two TARs, operations can continue, but in a restricted manner. Examples of Level Two Severity TARs include the following situations:

  • The application does not run because of an internal software error

  • The system fails, but a restart or reboot is possible

Backup and Recovery Considerations: Databases

In a database backup, it's important that the names and locations of all the files that comprise the database tables, as well as the master control files, be tracked so that the appropriate files will be backed up. As the database grows and changes, you need to track the additions and maintain and manage the scripts. Because of availability requirements, backups must be performed quickly.

There are several backup methods available:

◆ **Full system backup using file system tools.** Full offline backups are the traditional method for database backup; they work well for small databases and databases that are not governed by high availability. You can combine full physical backups with incremental backups to reduce backup time. An alternative is to combine full physical backups with regular archive logs to accomplish recovery until a given point in time.

◆ **Online backup using scripts.** Backing up online using scripts enables you to back up larger databases while ensuring availability. These types of backups involve interacting with the database to extract data and transaction log information while the database is online. Unfortunately, online backups involving custom scripts require a higher level of administrator expertise as well as management of the scripts.

◆ **Online backups using third-party tools.** This method makes possible increased reliability and faster recovery by reducing manual intervention and automating tape volume management.

- Most of the functionality is gone, but some areas do perform correctly.
- Performance is very slow.

◆ **Severity Level One.** A Severity Level One problem causes a complete loss of service. Your system is down completely and you cannot work. Examples of Level One Severity TARs include the following situations:

- The system is down and you cannot reboot or restart.
- Data is lost or corrupt and cannot be restored to your system.
- The system crashes and hangs and nothing will bring it back.

NOTE

Oracle gives Level One Severity TARs first priority, which is why Oracle support might seem to take forever when your TAR is a lower level of severity.

When you call Oracle with a problem, the following occurs:

◆ The TAR is logged.

◆ The problem is diagnosed.

◆ The error is recreated.

◆ The problem is resolved.

Step One: The TAR Is Logged

When you call Oracle and register your problem, the TAR is logged into the system. At that time, Oracle assigns your TAR to a technical analyst, who performs a preliminary investigation. The technical analyst's role is to work on your request until the problem has been resolved. Your role is to provide whatever information you can at each stage of the process. In most cases, a solution already exists, and the analyst can provide an answer immediately.

TAR Ownership

The support center where the TAR is handled is considered the owner of the TAR. Depending on what time the TAR is called in or the length of time the TAR takes to complete, ownership of the TAR can be transferred to another support center, where it will be handled within normal business hours in its time zone. For example, if you call Oracle at 5a.m. EST, you might get Oracle support in Europe, because it is within their normal working hours. If your problem continues for several hours, you probably will be transferred to Oracle support in the United States when its support service centers open. Oracle will consult you before changing the owner of your TAR.

Step Two: The Problem Is Diagnosed

If the technical analyst's preliminary investigation does not reveal a solution, the analyst will attempt to diagnose the problem or error. This step involves a detailed exchange of information between you and the analyst. After reaching a diagnosis, the technical analyst will search for a resolution in Oracle's Knowledge Base. If the problem is a common one, chances are that the solution is just a search away.

 NOTE

The solution to your problem might involve installing a patch to your existing software. If that is the case, Oracle will send you a patch, or direct you to their FTP site, and instructions on how to install and use it. Usually the TAR is kept open at this point until you have applied the patch and tested it thoroughly.

Step Three: The Problem Is Recreated

If a patch or solution is not available, the analyst's next step is to reproduce the error or problem at an Oracle site. If this is not possible, the technical analyst might have to connect to your system and run these tests at your location. After the analyst has reproduced the problem (either on your machine or a local one) and determined that there is no existing solution, he or she will write up a problem description and send the necessary information to Oracle's Development department. The Development department will then determine whether you have discovered a bug in the Oracle software. If so, a patch will be created and shipped to you for testing.

Step Four: The Problem Is Resolved

A TAR remains active until you have tested the solution and determined that it has resolved the problem or eliminated the error. After the TAR is satisfied, it is assigned one of the following statuses:

- ◆ **Inactive.** Inactive status allows you time to thoroughly test the solution within your environment.
- ◆ **Soft-closed.** If a TAR is soft-closed, you can call Oracle support to reopen it.

◆ **Hard-closed.** If after successful testing you and the analyst agree to close the TAR, it will be assigned this status. At this point, an Oracle analyst is the only one who can update the TAR.

 NOTE

If you haven't contacted Oracle Support Services about your TAR for more than two weeks, it is automatically hard-closed.

Summary

This chapter has focused on planning for disaster recovery and has given you Oracle's process for helping with this and other areas of support. Review Oracle's process and call them for support a few times just to get the feel for what you need to do and know in order to receive help. Once you've used Oracle's TAR process a few times, you will feel much more comfortable if you need to use them in a real disaster.

By no means is this the definitive list for disaster recovery and planning. Each site needs to access its business needs and requirements and plan accordingly. At a minimum, use this information as a template to help start that process. These procedures ensure the continuity of business and engineering operations by providing access to pertinent data, minimum system configurations with respect to hardware, software, and data, and personnel to aid in defining priorities necessary to allow for restoration of critical computing needs in a timely and orderly fashion.

Appendix A, "DBA Templates and Checklists," has a detailed plan for disaster recovery. Modify this plan to meet your business's needs. Once you have a plan and a set of procedures, take the time to practice a disaster and go through the steps. This might sound like a waste of time and resources, but it can save time and resources if a disaster occurs somewhere down the line.

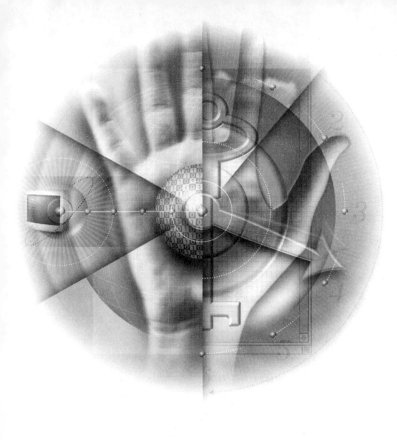

Chapter 14

ORACLE

Most companies do not operate from a single room, building, or even continent. Most likely, their users require access to data from points both far and near. Providing up-to-date and accurate information from data stored in a variety of systems poses a challenge. Whether one needs to consolidate information in a data warehouse or distribute information into decentralized servers, information must flow from one system to another with the utmost transparency and accuracy.

Replication enables the placement of shared data at geographically disparate locations throughout an organization, thus providing corporate-wide availability of current enterprise data and applications. Organizations can use replication to provide fast local access by eliminating long-distance distributed links between users and database servers. You can schedule large data transfers for set times in order to minimize telecommunications costs and disruption of application processing. Replication can also ensure high availability of business-critical database applications, making them resistant to single-system failures.

Developers and DBAs must thoroughly understand and plan for replication before it is implemented; this is difficult, however, because replication multiplies single-system challenges by the number of locations participating in the replicated environment. The purpose of this chapter is to provide a basic overview of the configurations and capabilities of replication and discuss the choices you have when implementing it.

Devising a Replication Strategy

Before diving into the process of replicating your Oracle databases, you should devise a strategy that spells out which databases you are going to replicate, how you are going to replicate them, and when you plan on implementing your replication. The following sections outline the strategy involved when replicating your databases.

Replication Models

When devising a replication strategy, it's often helpful to consider the various replication models available:

- **Distribution.** Distributing information from a master site to remote sites as read-only information. An example of this is a company's parts list.

- **Consolidation.** Gathering information from remote sites. This can be a consolidation of sales information from remote offices to coordinate inventory.

- **Data off-loading.** Removing heavy reporting from an On-Line Transaction Processing (OLTP) system. This can occur with a catalog sales database replicating the data to another server for read-only reporting.

- **Multisite data sharing.** The previous models assume exclusive ownership of data; some applications, however, can benefit from some kind of shared-ownership, update-anywhere model.

- **Disaster recovery/maintenance.** With full data replication, it becomes possible to maintain a backup site for database operations. The backup site is fully accessible, and you can use it to test read-only functions or provide extra processing to deal with sporadic user demands.

- **Dynamic ownership.** Provides the capability (or right) to update replicated data moves from site to site while ensuring that at any given point, only one site can update data. Sophisticated centralized systems allow the application modules that perform these steps to act on the same data contained in one integrated database. Each application module acts on an order (each module performs updates to the order data) when the state of the order indicates that the previous processing steps are complete.

- **Shared ownership.** Allows symmetric replication to be employed where primary site ownership and dynamic ownership methodologies would be too restrictive. In those cases where temporary inconsistencies are permissible and conflict resolution routines have been devised, it can offer greater flexibility.

Synchronous versus Asynchronous Delivery

For each kind of activity you want to replicate, you can choose one of two methods to deliver it to remote locations:

- ◆ **Synchronous.** Synchronous distributed database technology provides real-time remote data access and real-time propagation of replicated data updates.

- ◆ **Asynchronous.** Asynchronous distributed database technology provides deferred remote data access and deferred propagation of replicated data updates.

The tradeoffs between synchronous and asynchronous delivery involve application integrity, complexity, performance, and availability. Synchronous technology ensures application integrity and minimizes complexity, but availability suffers if the systems and networks are not reliable. Also, poor response time can occur if network access between systems is slow. Asynchronous technology maximizes availability and response time, but can be more complex and requires careful planning and design to ensure application integrity.

Synchronous Replication

Also referred to as *real-time replication*, synchronous replication immediately makes changes to all locations at the same time. Synchronous technology ensures application integrity, but requires that communication between systems be available in order to complete a transaction. This method ensures that all updates are made before a transaction completes. Thus, all copies are synchronized at a single point in time.

When determining whether to use synchronous replication, you need to consider the following points:

- ◆ Modifications at other sites are immediately reflected at your local site.

- ◆ Conflict resolution takes care of common data updated from multiple sites.

- ◆ Data propagation cannot take place during network downtimes.

- ◆ Updates can be slower because responses must come from all sites before a transaction is completed or rolled back.

- ◆ Synchronous replication is appropriate where absolute consistency between replicated data is a requirement.

If you determine that your database requires synchronous replication, you must decide whether you need to distribute or replicate your data. A distributed system consists of multiple servers, each responsible for its own data. In a replicated system, each site contains a copy of all necessary data for that site, with multiple sites potentially having multiple updateable copies of the same data.

 NOTE

Synchronous technology ensures application integrity and minimizes complexity, but can introduce poor performance and lower availability when the systems and networks involved are unreliable and slow.

Asynchronous Replication

Also referred to as *store-and-forward replication*, asynchronous replication immediately records information about replicated activities in a deferred queue to be delivered at a later time. Asynchronous technology allows applications to complete transactions without requiring access to the replicated copies of the data. Updates made to the source are committed, and the updates to replicated targets are deferred. If a system is not available, the operation is delayed until the system becomes available. Eventually, all copies will be identical, but discrepancies will always exist between the various copies of the data at any single point in time.

When determining whether to use asynchronous replication, you need to consider the following points:

◆ Remote network or site failures do not block local querying and/or updating of local data.

◆ For maximum fault tolerance, a dedicated fail-over site can support mission-critical operations.

◆ Data propagation can be set to convenient intervals.

◆ Inconsistencies will result because data updates are not immediately committed.

◆ Conflicting changes can be made at other sites. These conflicts are not detected until the changes are propagated. Built-in mechanisms do exist for detecting and resolving these conflicts.

NOTE

Asynchronous technology maximizes database availability and performance, especially as transactions operate against local data. The technology can initiate deferred operations that need to be propagated to other systems. If these other systems are not available, the propagation will be deferred until the systems are back online.

Replication Architectures

When devising a replication plan, it's important to decide exactly what type of replication architecture is appropriate. For simplicity, replication options are classified into four groups:

◆ **Copy.** Operating system can copy, back up software, import/export, and utilize SQL*Loader and SQL*Plus. These methods all constitute an asynchronous copy of data.

◆ **Third-party.** Tools such as log-sniffing products and other replicators.

◆ **Simple read-only replication.** Read-only table snapshots that support primary-ownership replication, an architecture in which one site in the system owns (can read and update) the master table and other sites subscribe to the data of the master table (and can only read it).

◆ **Advanced update-anywhere symmetric replication.** These are updateable table snapshots and multimaster replication that supports several replication models, including dynamic-ownership and shared-ownership replication. The primary reason for using a symmetric-replication system is to provide multiple points of update access to replicates of the same table. Symmetric-replication environments can also include read-only snapshots.

Replication Technology

In devising a replication strategy, it is important that you have a thorough understanding of the replication technology available, that you understand the business problems you are attempting to solve, and that you understand the tradeoffs of each technology. Following is a list of available replication technologies, and points to consider about each one:

◆ **File transfer**
  ● Complete operating system/backup copies of the database.
  ● Asynchronous.

◆ **SQL*Plus copy**
  ● Requires an external scheduling mechanism.
  ● Complexity escalates as selectivity increases.
  ● Feedback is misleading.
  ● Asynchronous.

◆ **Create Table As Select**
  ● Table cannot exist in order for command to succeed.
  ● Asynchronous.

◆ **Import/export**
  ● Requires external file space and scheduling.
  ● Whole tables only.
  ● Must manually re-export in order for replica to see changes.
  ● Asynchronous.

◆ **SQL*Loader**
  ● Reads data from a flat file into a table or set of tables.
  ● Direct path can improve performance.
  ● Requires additional temporary tablespace.
  ● Asynchronous.

◆ **Third-party tools**
  ● Log sniffers (SQL*Trax).
  ● Replicators (Prism, Platinum Infopump, Praxis, and EMC).
  ● Build your own. The scheduler can initiate dynamic PL/SQL jobs. This allows you to create a self-contained manual method of replication data in lieu of using snapshots (discussed in the next section).
  ● External replication server-based methods process each row change written into the log file to determine whether the change needs to be replicated. Contention for log access can jam systems even when only a relatively small amount of data is being replicated.

◆ **Triggers and remote procedure calls**

- Database and network must be available.

- It is possible to write custom triggers on every table to replicate changes to remote locations.

- Triggers can be written to handle table changes (inserts, updates and deletes) for every row change.

- Synchronous, real-time.

- For asynchronous replication you can select the method that best suits your needs. This includes basic replication (uses read-only snapshots to enforce a form of primary site replication) and advanced replication (supports a symmetric, update-anywhere replication model).

Creating Snapshots

A *table snapshot* is an asynchronous copy of some master data that reflects a past moment in time. A *snapshot* is a read-only table that points to some table, view, other snapshot, or any combination of these objects. This configuration is called *primary site replication*, where the master site "owns" the data, and is the only site that can update that data. Other sites "subscribe" to the data, meaning that they have access to read-only copies of the replicated data.

You can create two types of snapshots:

◆ **Simple.** A snapshot in which each row corresponds to exactly one row in a single master table.

◆ **Complex.** Created as the result of a complex query involving several tables or grouping functions.

The type of snapshots you decide to implement can significantly affect the performance of the queries your applications use. Complex snapshots are well suited for

◆ De-normalizing data
◆ Reporting
◆ Data warehousing

Simple snapshots are well suited for

◆ Single tables

◆ Databases that include simple and complex subqueries with the `where` clause

◆ Replication of base table data

◆ Databases that use a fast refresh

◆ Database that horizontally or vertically partition data

Snapshots that are not reliant on versions are well suited for

◆ Same system, different databases

◆ Summarized information

◆ Online backup databases

Read-Only Snapshots

Read-only snapshots are objects that implement a master-slave architecture in which the slave location is periodically refreshed with the most recent changes from the master location. At a remote location, a `CREATE SNAPSHOT` command is issued, which creates a table filled with the desired rows from the master location. A view is placed on top of this table to hide the details of the master-slave row correspondence from the users. Applications can query this view just as they do the table at the master location. You can place extra indexes (non-unique) on the base table at the slave location to improve the performance of specific queries.

The snapshot log is a table that lists recently changed ROWIDs and the action that occurred against them (`INSERT`, `UPDATE`, or `DELETE`). When a read-only snapshot is refreshed, the snapshot log determines which rows to replace at the snapshot site.

Read-only snapshots cannot be modified at the slave location, because a refresh might overwrite any changed rows. Additionally, constraints and unique indexes are not allowed on them (they cannot be enforced during a refresh operation). At the end of a successful refresh, the snapshot looks exactly like its master table. Groups of snapshots can be refreshed together (a "refresh group") in order to ensure consistency between them.

Refreshing Snapshots

To keep a snapshot's data current with a master's data, which is constantly changing, the server that manages the snapshot must periodically refresh it. Depending on the type of snapshot, two types of refreshes are available:

◆ **Complete.** Updates the entire snapshot. A complete refresh truncates the snapshot table, leaves the unique index on the ROWID column, and then inserts a new set of records into the snapshot table. When Oracle performs a complete refresh, the server replaces all the snapshot's current data with newer results from the defining query of the snapshot. Complete refreshes are possible on both simple and complex snapshots.

◆ **Fast.** Updates changed rows only. When Oracle performs a fast refresh, the server replaces only the information in the snapshot that has changed in the master since the most recent refresh of the snapshot. Fast refreshes are possible only for simple snapshots and only when a simple snapshot's base table has a snapshot log that tracks the snapshot refresh information. Fast refreshes are recommended when fewer than 25 percent of the rows are affected.

Snapshots can be refreshed from the primary site master either automatically at specified time intervals, or manually using the DBMS_SNAPSHOT or DBMS_REFRESH refresh procedures.

Advanced Symmetric Replication

Advanced update-anywhere symmetric-replication systems include updateable table snapshots or multimaster replication. These systems support several replication models, including dynamic-ownership and shared-ownership replication. A primary reason for using an advanced symmetric-replication system is to provide multiple (or varied) points of update access to table replicas. Features of advanced symmetric replication include the following:

◆ Propagation of deferred remote procedure calls (RPCs), which includes queued calls that are waiting to be processed from remote locations

◆ Initiated by standard PL/SQL stored procedure calls

◆ Efficient propagation at frequent intervals

◆ Replication on demand

◆ Replication at time-based intervals using built-in job queue

Symmetric replication supports both full table replication and replication of subsets of tables using two mechanisms:

◆ Updateable snapshots
◆ Multimaster replication

You can combine these two mechanisms in hybrid configurations to meet different needs.

Updateable Snapshots

Updateable snapshots use the features of "writeable" snapshots and *multimasters*, which are multiple master datasources, to provide a combination of their operating characteristics. You can create writeable and updateable snapshots by adding the FOR UPDATE keywords when the snapshot is created. A separate log is created and used as the synchronizing mechanism by tracking rows in the snapshot that have changed. In addition to the snapshot log at the slave location, a trigger captures events that occur against the snapshot. You can use writeable snapshots to implement "scratchable" snapshots, which are read-only databases that can be temporarily written to. Scratchable snapshots enable you to perform what-if analysis or to enforce the rule that any permanent changes must go through the master location. Figure 14.1 shows an updateable snapshot.

Updateable snapshots have several features that set them apart from other snapshots, including the following:

◆ They can be simple snapshots.

◆ They use AS SELECT * FROM syntax.

◆ They have no GROUP BY or CONNECT BY clauses.

◆ They do not use subqueries in the snapshot definition.

◆ They use joins or set operators.

◆ They do not reference LONG columns.

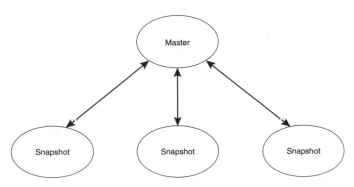

FIGURE 14.1 *This is an updateable snapshot showing the master and three snapshots.*

Multimasters/N-Way Replication

Multimasters, also called n-way replication, provide full-table, peer-to-peer broad cast replication between participating database locations. Multimaster replication propagates changes applied to any master table and applies them directly to all other master tables. Changes are broadcast to all other participating database locations. The replication facility queues changes at the originating location and periodically pushes them to other locations on a location-by-location basis. Failures during a push to one location do not affect pushes to any other location, and transactions remain in the queue for later propagation after error correction. The multimaster method resolves conflicts at every database location, with every location using the same routine in order to guarantee convergence.

Figure 14.2 shows the relationships between multimasters and the "n" possible ways that they can be represented.

Hybrid Configurations

Some sites can combine multimaster replication and updateable snapshots in hybrid configurations to meet different needs. Specifically, you can multimaster replicate a snapshot master (see Figure 14.3). This allows you to combine full-table and table subset replication in one system. Snapshots can be remastered for greater fault tolerance.

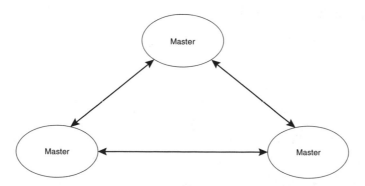

FIGURE 14.2 *The relationships between multimasters and the "n" possible ways that they can be represented.*

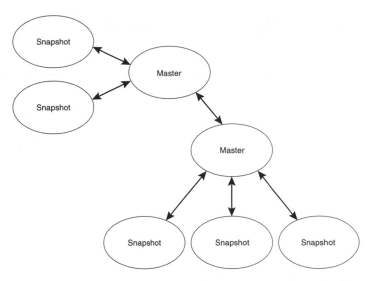

FIGURE 14.3 *Hybrid configurations showing two masters, each with several snapshots.*

Performance

In any replication system, there are two components to performance:

◆ **Storing**—The act of recognizing and recording the information necessary to replicate a transaction. Not related to how many locations will receive the eventual transaction; related only to events that need to be replicated. Should not have to deal with any other database activities. Failure to record a transaction should have minimal impact on the operation of the source database.

◆ **Forwarding**—The act of delivering and applying transactions at remote locations. Its performance depends on the relative speeds of the delivering and receiving systems, as well as the network throughput. It needs to enforce transactional ordering and guarantee the delivery of replicated transactions. Forwarding should compress as much information as possible into a stream of deliverable information. Should be able to handle intermittent network failures and provide robust restart and throttling options.

In a synchronous system, these procedures are combined into a single operation. Both the store and forward must occur within the transaction to make sure real-time synchronous replication takes place. In asynchronous replication, the store and forward activities are de-coupled and can be measured independently.

Propagating Changes between Replicas

Oracle uses two primary mechanisms for asynchronously propagating data-level changes between replication sites: deferred transactions and snapshot refresh. Additionally, you can use row-level replication or procedural replication to propagate data changes among replicas. Both the row-level replication and procedural replication methods make use of deferred transaction queues.

Deferred Procedure Call Queue

Multimasters and updateable snapshots use Oracle's deferred-execution mechanism (deferred-transaction queue) for making data changes to replicated tables. The generic deferred-execution mechanism, which is asynchronous by definition, allows users to place information about procedures for execution at a later time at any server. The server also implements the deferred-transaction queue as a set of tables that is fully protected by all backup and recovery mechanisms.

Snapshot Refreshes

Snapshot sites use the deferred transaction mechanism to propagate data-level changes from updateable snapshots to their associated master table. Any changes made to the master table since the snapshot was created or previously refreshed are applied to the snapshot. Changes from multiple transactions are propagated in a batch-oriented operation. These are referred to as asynchronous snapshot refreshes.

Row-Change Replication

Row-change (or data) replication, which is synchronous, forwards row changes to all other interested locations. Data changes are recorded at the database row level. If both old and new values for the row are recorded, the forwarded information contains everything needed to identify potential conflicts in a shared-ownership model. Because row-change replication does not use a deferred transaction queue, you need a trigger at your current master or snapshot site and a package at each receiving master site. LONG and LONG RAW data types are not supported.

Procedure-Call Replication

Procedure-call (sometimes called *process*) replications replicate the call only to a stored procedure that updates a table. Procedure replication, which can be synchronous or asynchronous, does not replicate itself, but forwards procedure calls and argument lists to all other interested locations. The procedures run individually at each location. This is the best way to replicate an application's non-conflicting batch-oriented activities. For procedural replication, a wrapper procedure (SYS.DBMSOBJGWRAPPER) calls the actual replicated procedure. This procedure must be replicated at all master sites. The procedure call can be made either synchronously or asynchronously (using the deferred transaction queue).

Conflict Resolution

Applications employing asynchronous replication should use conflict-avoidance or -detection methodologies to ensure data convergence. Such applications should include the logic necessary to recognize that a conflict-avoidance methodology is being employed, and what data is owned (and hence can be updated) at a given site. Similarly, if business requirements demand that ownership be shared across multiple sites, the application needs to take into account the potential for update conflicts and their detection and resolution.

There are three conflict-avoidance techniques:

- ◆ **Data partitioning.** Data partitioning is a conflict-avoidance technique in which data subsets can be modified from only one location. This model is often called a primary site static ownership model.

- ◆ **Workflow.** This conflict-avoidance technique ensures that any individual data item can be modified from only one location at any given time. It is different from data partitioning in that the owning location can move from location to location. It is sometimes called a primary site dynamic ownership model.

- ◆ **Token passing.** With token passing, each data item contains an ownership token. Locations can broadcast their requests to "own" a data item and must get agreement from all other locations before acquiring the data item token.

Symmetric replication is designed to support replication models employing conflict avoidance, detection, and resolution. Applications employing conflict-avoidance models restrict updates to certain sites to prevent conflicts. Optionally, you can define database facilities such as views and triggers as "guards" to enforce exclusive ownership for primary site and dynamic models. For more advanced usage models, symmetric replication provides built-in, automatic conflict detection and resolution.

During the replication design phase, conflict-avoidance techniques can help prevent conflicts before they happen. However, once they happen, a good conflict-resolution method is needed to resolve them. A conflict-resolution method allows you to tell each database location what to do in case of an emergency. Part of the data collision problem has to do with what happens after a collision occurs. Should all replication to that node be suspended until the problem is resolved? Where will the problem be reported? Who will resolve the problem?

All asynchronous replication solutions for fail-over have the potential for transaction loss in some failure scenarios. As a result of its store-and-forward nature, it is possible for replicated changes to have been stored but not yet forwarded to the fail-over site when the failure occurs. The stored transactions might not be recoverable.

These three types of conflicts are detected by the symmetric replication facility:

◆ **Update.** Detects a conflict when there are differences between the old value of the replicated row and the current values of the same row at the receiving site.

◆ **Uniqueness.** Detects a conflict when a unique constraint is violated during an INSERT or UPDATE of the replicated row.

◆ **Delete.** Detects a conflict when you change a row at a remote site after you delete that row from the local site. The delete conflict occurs because the old values of the deleted row at the local site do not match the current values of the same row at the remote site.

These conflict-resolution methods are available through the symmetric replication facility:

◆ Minimum

◆ Maximum

◆ Earliest timestamp

◆ Latest timestamp

◆ Priority group

◆ Site priority

◆ Overwrite

◆ Discard

◆ Additive

◆ Average

The system-defined routines do not support the following situations:

◆ Delete conflicts

◆ Changes to primary key columns

◆ Nulls in the columns that you designate to resolve the conflict

◆ Referential integrity constraint violations

Although symmetric replication offers conflict detection and resolution, the best practice is to avoid conflicts completely. If they do occur and the system routines are not enough, you can build user-defined routines to extend the resolution capabilities.

Replication Analysis and Planning

Before choosing a replication architecture, it is important to understand the driving needs for replication within your organization. Developers who put together database applications without a detailed understanding of the system's overall requirements typically spend a great deal of time after deployment reengineering the system to meet the needs of their customers. The analysis and design phases of application development are especially important when you want to determine whether an application can benefit from a distributed-database system that replicates data.

Prior to implementing a replicated environment, you must do the following:

◆ Identify access requirements

◆ Identify quantity of information

◆ Identify frequency of updates

◆ Identify placement of data

◆ Identify schemas that qualify for replication

◆ Identify schema objects to be replicated

◆ Identify master sites and snapshot sites

◆ Identify the type of data access (read-only versus the capability to update)

◆ Identify data characteristics

◆ Identify data responsibilities with each business unit

◆ Identify the current system capabilities

◆ Identify the current network capabilities

◆ Identify the current technical expertise

◆ Identify the conflict resolution method (supplied or user defined)

◆ Identify the data entities of each business

◆ Decide which entities are best suited for replication

◆ Eliminate data redundancy

◆ Guard against the loss of data integrity

◆ Determine whether multiple masters are required

◆ Determine whether real-time replication is required

◆ Evaluate the budget

Keep these "rules of thumb" in mind while planning for replication:

◆ High volume writes are not good for replication.

◆ Replication increases archive logging.

◆ Network performance influences replication.

◆ Small transactions are best.

◆ Replicate only needed objects.

◆ Never rely on indexes to be created for you.

◆ Evaluate using minimum 4KB block size (high block sizes benefit both batch and online access).

◆ Use large rollbacks and temporary areas.

◆ Anticipate growth in tables, rows, and indexes.

◆ Release 7.2 of Oracle is the RDBMS minimum version to use for replication.

◆ You must have at least one background process running to execute your queued jobs. DBMS_JOB submits, changes, and removes jobs in a queue.

◆ Unique indexes are not allowed on updateable snapshots.

◆ Do not replicate tables, which are the targets of triggers.

NOTE

There are currently no automatic facilities that handle replication of and updates to data types that are up to 2GB. This means that LONG and LONG RAW data cannot be replicated with any replication option.

Network Considerations

When considering replication, it is important to determine the amount of data that will move across the network. In synchronous replication, changes to one database are immediately propagated to other servers as part of the same transaction. With asynchronous replication, changes to a database are recorded but are propagated to other databases only when an event occurs. Although asynchronous replication is the easiest to implement and is more common, managing its queues and scheduling of data bursts can be demanding.

Here are a few network issues to investigate:

◆ How does the information move: bi-directional or one-way?

◆ How much of the data does each application move across the network?

◆ How time-sensitive is the data?

◆ Can the current network architecture handle the amount of data to be transferred?

◆ How fast can the network route data?

◆ How is downtime handled?

◆ How will failed replication attempts be managed?

◆ What events trigger data transfer?

◆ Are time zones a consideration?

◆ How long will it take to transfer data under various conditions?

◆ Can scheduling help flatten the load?

◆ What changes can affect the operation and current performance of the current replication strategy?

◆ What business changes can affect the network?

Replication Initiation

In a single-server system, initially loading your system is relatively simple. In a replicated environment, loading a number of remote systems in a coordinated fashion is much more complex. *Instantiation* is the process of creating and loading a copy (or replica) of your system at a "remote" location. There are several ways to place your data copies at all locations participating in the replicated environment:

◆ **Pre-instantiation.** Copying all data to all locations before beginning the configuration of your replication environment is an easy way to guarantee identical data copies before allowing transaction activity. No activity can take place against the data until all locations are configured into the replication catalog.

◆ **Online instantiation.** Given an initial populated location with empty remote locations, replication can perform online instantiation. In this method, the replication facility creates objects over the network and copies their data to each location. This has the advantage of guaranteeing that all locations have the same data and gives the administrator a single point of control. However, there can be significant delay while data is copied over the network.

◆ **Offline instantiation.** An option is to configure a replication environment from one location and inform it that other locations will be joining at a later date. The initial location should "store" changes destined for future locations and push them to the other locations as they come online. Other locations can be loaded with data and synchronized with the initial location as they are registered into the replication catalog.

Using Oracle's replication options, all replicated schemas in the replicated environment must be queued before any administrative activity can take place. Pending changes must be completed against the "old" version of the database structure and any new changes must wait until all locations have the "new" version of the database structure. This means that there can be no changes to any data in any replicated schema (within the replicated environment) during the administrative period. Oracle's replication options allow an administrator to alter all locations using a single command that's broadcast to the remote locations.

Replication for Recovery

Businesses need mission-critical systems to remain available on a nonstop basis. The notion of nonstop systems is not restricted to 24×7 operations; it must also include uninterrupted operation during critical periods where failure of the database engine or hardware can lead to significant loss of revenue for the enterprise. Oracle's symmetric replication facility supports system survivability, thus enabling applications to run in spite of system or site failures. Applications are run on a fail-over system, accessing the same (or nearly the same) data as they were on on the primary system when it failed.

Asynchronous Replication Recovery Mechanisms

To protect against site failures, you can place a fail-over system in a geographically remote location, and use some form of asynchronous replication to maintain copies of a primary system's data on a secondary system for fail-over. One form of asynchronous replication is the transfer of the log files generated on the primary system to the secondary system site and the use of an Oracle recovery mechanism to apply the log changes to the fail-over system. This is an excellent method for offloading OLTP systems for decision support system reporting.

Symmetric Replication Recovery Mechanisms

The Oracle symmetric replication facility supports system survivability. For example, two sites maintaining n-way replicated master tables can serve as fail-over sites for one another. If one site fails, processing can continue on the surviving site against the data replicated from the failed system. When the failed system is restored, Oracle reestablishes consistency between the two databases. Transactions that had not been propagated to the fail-over site when the failure occurred can then be selectively reapplied.

When designing a fail-over system in a replicated environment, the symmetric replication facility must be able to keep up with the transaction volume of the primary system. Recently committed transactions at the primary site might not have been asynchronously propagated to the fail-over site when the failure at the primary site occurs. These transactions will appear to be lost. You must then deal with the lost transactions when the primary site is recovered. This can become further complicated by the fact that users might have reapplied these lost transactions.

Managing Replicated Environments

Just take a look at the hundreds of pages of Oracle Server documentation that address symmetric replication configuration to get an idea of the steps, commands, and procedures you have to use when you want to configure a symmetric replication system.

Simple, read-only replication environments are easy to configure and manage relative to symmetric replication environments. You do not want to use symmetric replication unless your business requires it. As easy as some people try to make symmetric replication sound, it is not something you implement overnight.

Advanced replication features are set up and administered using more than 90 procedures activated by REPCAT.SQL. More than 30 dictionary views are also provided for managing and monitoring all aspects of the replication facility. Given the complexity of these features, it is a good idea to have someone appointed as your replication administrator.

Replication Administrator

The replication administrator is the "control user" of all master replication environments on a particular database location. The replication administrator is a powerful database user, with the capability to create, drop, alter, and perform commands against any database object (in the case of a global administrator). Proper configuration of this user is essential for symmetric replication. Because many of the replication administrative activities are performed by a job in the Oracle Server job queue, and because jobs cannot inherit privileges through a database role, all privileges must be directly granted.

Snapshots

Snapshot rebuilds are faster than checking and comparing with SQL. For the best performance, set snapshots to run at low load times if possible. Unlike snapshots, views require no physical storage; however, multiple table join views can lead to poor performance.

Job Queue

You can schedule the deferred transaction queue to be pushed at periodic intervals by scheduling a job in the job queue. A background process wakes up at configurable intervals and executes any outstanding jobs. Job queues are also used by the symmetric replication facility to automatically refresh snapshot groups.

Stored Procedures

Much of the current replication features have been written using the Oracle Server PL/SQL stored procedure language. A keen understanding of PL/SQL is useful in tracking the tasks performed by Oracle replication.

Rollbacks

Oracle8 refreshes all group members as part of the same transaction. When a refresh group includes a large number of snapshots, the group's refresh transactions can generate a large amount of rollback data. When a refresh group generates excessively large refresh transactions, you might also consider changing the list of member snapshots to reduce the size of refresh transactions and improve the performance of group refreshes.

Primary Key Indexes

In order to replicate a table in a consistent manner, make sure that the name of the primary key index for your table and the name of the constraint are the same.

 NOTE

The disconnect between the name of the index and the name of the constraint typically occurs in environments that create unique indexes to enforce the primary key prior to creating the primary key constraint.

Dependencies

A common problem when replicating a group of objects is making sure that all referenced objects exist at the target database location. For example, in order to replicate a view, you must make sure you replicate the tables on which the view is based before copying the view definition to the target database location. The replication facility is intelligent enough to make sure objects appear in the correct order at the target database location, but you must make sure that any referenced objects outside the replicated set are installed prior to initiating the copy.

Network

SQL*Net is required for replication locations. Every location should be able to connect to every other location using an alias from the local Tnsnames.Ora file. It will ease administrative burdens if the Tnsnames.Ora file is global to the replicated environment, and each database location has only one alias.

Naming Collisions

When objects are registered with a replication facility and copied to other database locations, their complete structure (including their constraints) is sent over the network. Many customers created these tables. The Oracle Server also used system-generated names (such as SYS_C061591) for any constraints (in particular, NOT NULL is a constraint that also receives its own name). Because constraint names must be unique within a schema (not within a table), this might cause problems when these table structures are replicated to another database location, particularly when the schema at the target location has already "generated" constraints with the same name. The solution to this problem is to explicitly name all constraints (even NOT NULL) to avoid potential conflicts in system-generated names.

Referential Integrity Constraints

The Oracle server can enforce referential integrity constraints between tables to maintain business rules on data. Primary key constraints uniquely identify rows within tables and are used by some replication options to help identify conflicts. They also provide information for conflict resolution.

Scheduling

Issues that can affect scheduling include duration of data transfer, whether data is being transferred over time zones, time and event triggers, and the quality of the transferred data. If the data transfers can be scheduled during slow times, the duration of the transfer can be shortened because there will be less traffic competing for the network bandwidth. Customer usage patterns are important. With transcontinental time zones, the window of opportunity for transferring data might be extremely small.

Deferred Remote Procedure Calls (RPCs)

The deferred remote procedure call queues are in the system tablespace by default. It's a good idea to move them from the system into their own tablespace along with their indexes, disk, and channel. They will also become fragmented at their current sizes.

Items to Monitor

There are several items to monitor when managing replication. Here is a list of some to consider:

- Database alert log
- Background job process trace files
- Snapshot logs
- Snapshot DDL
- Many catalog packages, procedures, and views

Also consider these issues when scheduling items to monitor:

- Plan space to hold queues for planned outages
- Move deferred queue out of the system tablespace
- Automate log handling

Governing Init.Ora Parameters

The init.ora file has many parameters that can affect replication. Some of the more common ones include:

◆ JOB_QUEUE_INTERVAL (this is the frequency to propagate changes)

◆ SHARED_POOL_SIZE (set to a minimum 35MB)

◆ JOB_QUEUE_KEEP_CONNECTIONS

◆ DISTRIBUTED_LOCK_TIMEOUT

◆ DISTRIBUTED_TRANSACTIONS

◆ GLOBAL_NAMES

◆ OPEN_LINKS

◆ COMPATIBLE

◆ GLOBAL_NAMES

◆ DB_DOMAIN

◆ SNAPSHOT_REFRESH_PROCESSES

◆ SNAPSHOT_REFRESH_INTERVAL

◆ SNAPSHOT_REFRESH_KEEP_CONNECTIONS

Required Resources for Replication

This is a list of the resources needed in order for replication to function correctly:

◆ Minimum 30MB of system tablespace to store the packages and procedures

◆ Minimum 5MB of rollback space

◆ Minimum 25MB of SHARED_POOL_SIZE

◆ Additional server resources

◆ Accounts at every replicated site

◆ DB links to every other site

◆ Possibly another DBA

Security

It is relatively easy to define a security model that allows users to access and change data, while tracking and auditing their work. However, in a distributed replicated environment, there can be questions about how transactions are executed at remote locations. Should they be executed as the original user or as a generic replication user? Given the demands of user-by-user security and auditing against the convenience of having a single replication user, many security models can be implemented. Each of these models refers to how transactions execute when they are replicated to remote locations.

Global Access

In this model, the global replication administrator executes all replicated transactions. Keep in mind that the global replication administrator is a powerful user, and that any manually queued transactions will execute under this security domain at all remote locations. In this scenario, it is best to deny manual access to the queuing mechanism. Object users do not have to be mirrored on every location.

Single Schema Access

In this model, an object owner executes all replicated transactions. Database links are required from all object users to the object owner at the remote locations. Through these links, users have full access to the object owner schema. They are also limited to queuing transactions for one object owner schema only. However, no additional privileges are required. Object users do not have to be mirrored on every location.

Designated User Access

In this model, a designated user executes all replicated transactions. It is similar to the global access model, but allows the database administrator to specifically tailor the privileges of the designated user. The designated user can have privileges on multiple object owner schemas. Database links are required from all object users to the designated user at the remote locations. The designated user requires direct execution privileges on the replication support packages for all object owner schemas that are affected by any replicated transaction. Object users do not have to be mirrored on every location.

Mirrored User Access

In this model, the same user who initially submitted them executes all replicated transactions. Object users must exist on all remote locations. Those mirrored users require direct execution privileges on the replication support packages for all object owner schemas that are affected by any replicated transaction. Database links are required between mirrored users.

Summary

As databases continue to grow, you face the question of how to deliver, replenish, and extract data to and from data sources while not interfering with current business operations. This problem escalates when users require delivery of information in a timely, consistent, and meaningful manner. Oracle's replication technology makes it possible for distributed enterprises to place shared data at locations throughout an organization.

Although replication can help achieve a higher degree of availability for mission-critical systems, replication tends to multiply single-system challenges and risks by the number of systems participating in the replicated environment. Complicating the replication process is the diverse architecture within which the task must operate, including the amount of data being transferred, the transfer rates of networks, and the number of servers to be updated.

If your systems are already loaded with normal processing, replication will cause major problems. To minimize this transaction load while also meeting other types of organizational needs, you should provide various means of initiating and managing transactions. One of these options is a *two-phase commit*, which is a system that requires sources and targets to agree to provide the resources needed for the transaction. Although it is appropriate for some users, when multiple locations must agree to commit, it can quickly become impractical. As an alternative to two-phase commit, some products also offer choices of *push* or *pull*, with either a target or source database determining when updates are to be initiated.

If the application is primarily a decision support or a light OLTP situation, data that is hours or even days out of date might not be a serious impediment. More often, an organization will run a mix of applications—some requiring solid data integrity and others being more tolerant of inconsistencies. Like all other systems, replicated data increases in volume and complexity over time.

The many benefits of replication include the following:

- ◆ Replication can offload processing.
- ◆ Replication can be an important part of a data-warehousing strategy.
- ◆ Replication can consolidate data from multiple operational databases to a single data store for analysis.
- ◆ Replication can set the stage for quick disaster recovery and cost-effective load balancing on busy networks.

When replication is not properly planned, however, the results can be catastrophic. Data becomes unsynchronized; users can be locked out of applications while data is moved; performance erodes; and networks can quickly become clogged.

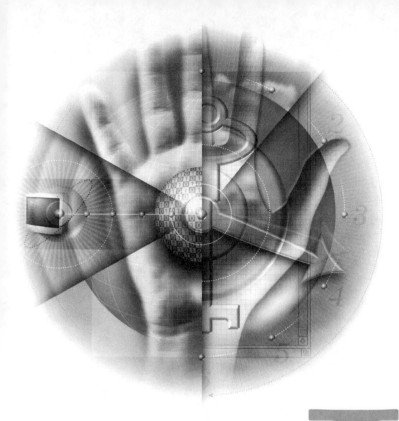

PART III

Supporting and Documenting Your Oracle Database

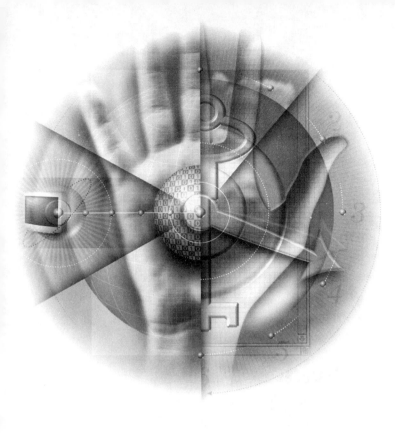

Chapter 15

ORACLE

Although phone support is usually the first resource DBAs try when in need of assistance, it's not a silver bullet by any means. For one reason, you must purchase support prior to the call. Even if you do have support, long hold times are usually par for the course. Half the time, DBAs determine the solution to the problem before the call is answered. This chapter looks at the available Oracle support alternatives beyond placing a call and logging a TAR (Technical Assistance Request).

Oracle Support Options

Oracle offers expanded support options from Large Systems Support (LSS), the Center of Expertise (COE), OracleExpert, and OracleMetals. The LSS staff works with the customer and the vendor to characterize and understand areas of risk and define a plan to assure reliability. The COE provides special expertise at the customer's site and at Oracle's to solve most difficult problems.

OracleExpert

`http://support.oracle.com` (then search for OracleExpert)

Most recently, Oracle has updated its offerings in the form of OracleExpert, which combines a variety of services. The ExpertONSITE support program provides on-site Oracle field service analysts and replaces the OracleONSITE program. The ExpertPACKAGES program focuses resources on short-term tasks such as installation, upgrades, reviews, or training. ExpertSATELLITE is comprised of a dedicated team that provides help-desk support on-site, at Oracle facilities, or both. ExpertONLINE is similar to ExpertONSITE with the exception that the resources are remote and remote standby.

OracleMetals

`http://support.oracle.com/metalink`

OracleMetals is one of Oracle's primary support mechanisms; it offers several levels of service packages, each discussed further in the following sections:

◆ OracleGOLD

◆ OracleSILVER

◆ OracleBRONZE

◆ OracleMERCURY

OracleGOLD

OracleGOLD support, which you access by calling (800) 440-4653, consists of the following:

◆ 24×7 phone support

◆ Priority response

◆ Information access and downloads

◆ Product maintenance and upgrades

◆ Management account reporting

◆ Operations readiness assessment

◆ Support account management

◆ Web support

◆ Support notes

OracleSILVER

For the majority of companies, OracleGOLD support is too expensive. OracleSILVER, which you access by phoning (800) 223-1711, is the next level of support. It consists of the following:

◆ 24×7 phone support

◆ Information access and downloads

◆ Product maintenance and upgrades

◆ Management account reporting

◆ Web support

◆ Support notes

OracleBRONZE

For sites that do not need 24×7 availability, Oracle offers OracleBRONZE, which you access by dialing one of the following numbers:

- ◆ East: (407) 240-8900
- ◆ Midwest: (719) 635-8900
- ◆ West: (650) 506-1500

OracleBRONZE support consists of the following:

- ◆ Phone support (standard hours)
- ◆ Information access and downloads
- ◆ Product maintenance and upgrades
- ◆ Web support
- ◆ Support notes

OracleMERCURY

For companies with workgroup products that want to research information and solutions to common problems, Oracle offers OracleMERCURY, which is licensed per user. You access OracleMERCURY by visiting **http://support.oracle.com/ OracleMERCURY**. OracleMERCURY support consists of the following:

- ◆ Install information
- ◆ A tech support database
- ◆ A technical forum

Subscribers receive Web-based support for products within a specified area:

- ◆ OracleMERCURY for tools products
- ◆ Limited WWW support for trial products
- ◆ Workgroup tool support
- ◆ Workgroup database support

OracleINCIDENT

`http://support.oracle.com` (then search for OracleExpert)

OracleINCIDENT provides telephone access during normal business hours for sites that want to pay for support on a per-incident basis. Product upgrades are not included. Oracle incident-based support is available 7 a.m. to 5 p.m. Pacific time, except on New Year's Day, Memorial Day, Independence Day, Labor Day, Thanksgiving (two days), and Christmas. Support is $200 per incident. See Oracle's support home page for the latest phone number.

OracleFOUNDATION

OracleFOUNDATION is a grouping of products for sites that do not require a high level of support. OracleFOUNDATION support is through Oracle's grouping of electronic online services, 24 hours per day, 365 days per year. Oracle-FOUNDATION also offers telephone access using OracleINCIDENT, which provides BRONZE-level telephone support on a pay-as-you-go basis. OracleFOUNDATION does not include product upgrades. See Oracle's support home page for the latest phone number.

Oracle Electronic Information Resources

Oracle maintains several electronic information resources, as discussed in the next sections.

OracleMetaLink

```
http://support.us.oracle.com/metalink
```

OracleMetaLink gives OracleMetals customers access to customer support through the Web, including product alerts, de-support notices, step-by-step installation instructions, installation manuals, release notes, patches, a technical forum, TAR submittal and tracking, and the technical support knowledge base. The knowledge base is a search engine that provides access to technical support bulletins, problem/fix data, technical alerts, white papers, release notes and installation instructions, product documentation, and lists of supported product versions.

Virtual Support Analyst (VSA)

http://support.oracle.com (then search for Virtual Support Analyst or VSA)

The Virtual Support Analyst (VSA) service provides an Internet e-mail–based system by which customers can access the Oracle customer support systems. This service is available to U.S. customers with an OracleMetals support agreement.

VSA features include the following:

- Ability to access CSIs (Oracle's assigned Customer Support Identifier)
- Order updates
- Access and manage TARS/TAR reports
- Product change requests
- 24-hour availability

 NOTE

SUPREQ subscriptions are not automatically converted to VSA accounts; SUPREQ users must submit a new registration.

Global Solutions Exchange (GSX)

MetaLink customers can obtain information on known solutions using the Fax-on-Demand service, which includes an electronically accessible repository. Oracle customers can access Global Solutions Exchange (GSX) using OracleMER-CURY and Oracle MetaLink to retrieve technical information for researching known problems. Through GSX, users can access information about changes and enhancements to Oracle products, and access technical bulletins containing articles, technical tips, and new release information.

Incident Tracking System (ITS)

http://support.oracle.com/ (then search for ITS)

The Incident Tracking System (ITS) allows MetaLink customers to log and manage TARs and view Oracle bulletins. ITS can be accessed using the telephone at (415) 598-9350 or the Web.

Oracle SupportInSite

http://support.oracle.com/insite/

SupportInSite is one of the most up-to-date information sources on Oracle support, and it's available free of charge. With SupportInSite, you can:

◆ Explore the available support resources and alternatives

◆ Locate information such as support bulletins, bug queries, solutions, and white papers in ways that best suit their needs

 NOTE

The information on SupportInSite's Web site is also available on a CD-ROM Support-InSite produces.

SupportNotes

http://support.oracle.com/ (then search for SupportNotes)

The SupportNotes CD-ROM, available to OracleMetals customers, contains a variety of information, including the following:

◆ Problem/Solution database

◆ Technical bulletins

◆ Product availability

◆ SupportNews newsletters

◆ Messages and codes

◆ Electronic Support Services User Guide

◆ U.S. Customer Support Center Users Guide

◆ Support information

Oracle EASI InfoFax

You can obtain information about Oracle education services using the Fax-on-Demand service, which includes an electronically accessible repository. Dial (800) 405-6336. Free of charge and available 24 hours a day, this service handles

◆ Course information and schedules

◆ Computer-based training (CBT) ordering

◆ Education catalog requests

◆ Oracle channel and classroom locations

For installation assistance with trial products, try the Workgroup 2000 Fax-Back Services at (415) 506-8438.

Oracle Published Resources

These resources include magazines, quick reference guides, Oracle Press books, as well as other documentation.

Oracle Documentation

To purchase additional or hardcopy documentation for a licensed product or to receive an automated fax-back price list, call Oracle documentation at (800) 252-0303. You can purchase the following items from Oracle documentation.

◆ Oracle manuals

◆ Oracle manuals on CD-ROM

◆ Searchable documents

◆ Printable online documents

Oracle Press Books

http://www.osborne.com/oracle/

Formed in conjunction with Oracle Corporation, Oracle Press provides cutting-edge information on Oracle's rapidly expanding family of products. The following is a list of some of the more popular books:

◆ *Advanced Oracle Tuning and Administration*

◆ *Oracle8 Architecture*

◆ *Oracle8: A Beginner's Guide*

◆ *Oracle8: Backup & Recovery Handbook*

◆ *Oracle8 DBA Handbook*

◆ *Oracle8 PL/SQL Programming*

◆ *Oracle8: The Complete Reference*

◆ *Oracle8 Tuning*

◆ *Oracle Backup and Recovery Handbook*

◆ *Oracle: A Beginner's Guide*

◆ *Oracle: The Complete Reference, Electronic Edition*

◆ *Oracle: The Complete Reference, Third Edition*

◆ *Oracle Data Warehousing*

◆ *Oracle DBA Handbook, 7.3 Edition*

◆ *Oracle Designer/2000 Handbook*

◆ *Oracle Developer/2000 Handbook*

◆ *Oracle Networking*

◆ *Oracle PL/SQL Programming*

◆ *Oracle Power Objects Developer's Guide*

◆ *Oracle Power Objects Handbook*

◆ *Oracle Troubleshooting*

◆ *Oracle Web Application Server Handbook*

◆ *Oracle Workgroup Server Handbook*

◆ *Tuning Oracle*

Periodicals, Magazines, and Newsletters

Magazines and newsletters can be efficient resources for Oracle professionals. A magazine article can provide tips, solutions, or quick references to recent bugs and problems. For many Oracle professionals, magazines can be obtained through a free subscription. Many publishers provide extra content on the Web.

There are several Oracle magazines, but the two that stand out above the rest are:

◆ Oracle *PROFIT* Magazine. http://www.oracle.com/oramag/ (then click on PROFIT Magazine)

◆ Oracle Magazine. http://www.oracle.com/oramag/ (then click on Oracle Magazine)

Other magazines worth noting are *Select, Database Programming & Design,* and *DBMS Online* (see the next sections).

Select

`http://www.ioug.org/` (then click on Select)

This IOUG quarterly newsmagazine, produced by the International Oracle User's Group, provides a full range of technical information, user tips, and technical and management-related articles. Also covered are updates on member benefits, volunteer opportunities, enhancement voting, and alliance partner and global Oracle meetings. Articles and features from the current and past issues of *Select* are available online. Membership ID number and last name are needed as a login and password.

Database Programming & Design

`http://www.dbpd.com`

Database Programming & Design is the magazine for managers, developers, and administrators. It features in-depth articles offering techniques, design methods, insights, product analyses, and commentary by leading practitioners and technology experts in the field. *Database Programming & Design* also sponsors four conferences:

- ◆ Business Rules Summit
- ◆ VLDB Summit
- ◆ Data Mining Summit
- ◆ Object/Relational Database Summit

DBMS Online

`http://dmreview.com`

DBMS Online is a monthly magazine devoted to database, client/server, and Internet/intranet application development solutions. The publication focuses on front-end development tools, RDBMS servers, client/server middleware, and the strategies for making these things work together. *DBMS Online* includes an "Internet Systems" supplement every other month; the supplement focuses on developing Internet and intranet database applications. The magazine also reviews development tools, DBMSs, and new productivity and data analysis tools.

Cobb Group Newsletters

http://www.cobb.com/eod

The *Exploring Oracle RDBMS*, *Developer/2000*, and *Designer/2000* newsletters give you a tour of all the features of Oracle. The Cobb newsletters present short-cuts and advice from computer experts who cover every aspect of Oracle. They include time-saving strategies and practical solutions to Oracle questions through in-depth articles.

Additional Oracle Numbers

The following are additional Oracle phone numbers that you might use in the course of administrating your Oracle database.

◆ OracleGOLD RDB support: (800) 909-9985

◆ OracleSILVER RDB support: (800) 909-9985

◆ OracleBRONZE RDB support: (719) 577-6000

◆ DMD Federal (for information on sales to federal government offices): (800) 633-0584

◆ Oracle Consulting Services: (800) 578-4672

◆ Oracle User Groups: (415) 506-4064

Summary

This chapter, although brief, was designed to familiarize you with some of the resources available for support while you are implementing and maintaining your Oracle databases. This chapter did not include many of the resources available on the Internet; the next two chapters focus on those types of resources.

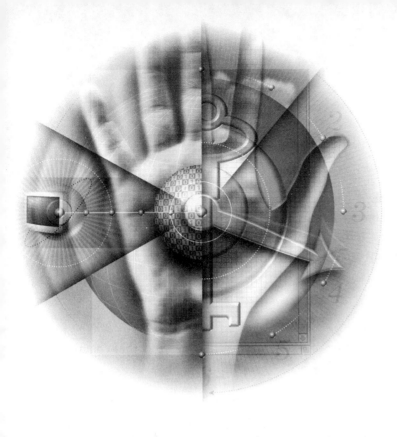

Chapter 16

WWW Dot Oracle Dot Com

ORACLE

When you are in need of Oracle support, the Internet is a very good resource. This chapter contains a collection of Web and FTP links, as well as newsgroups and frequently asked questions sites that you might find useful in your day-to-day Oracle experiences.

Web Sites

This section lists and describes some of the more popular Web sites that contain information about Oracle.

 NOTE

Chapter 17, "More WWW Dot Oracle Dot Com," is also dedicated to listing hundreds of Web sites that deal with Oracle.

Oracle's Web Sites

Oracle's own Web sites are probably the single most important resource sites on the Internet for Oracle. The following are some of the more important ones.

Oracle's Corporate Web Site

`http://www.oracle.com`

Oracle's corporate Web page contains an abundance of up-to-date information, including:

- Free trial software
- The latest news on Oracle products, services, education, and events
- Brochures and data sheets
- A place to register for Oracle's educational classes
- Links to related Web sites

Worldwide Customer Support Web Page

http://support.oracle.com

Oracle's support home page enables you to:

◆ Obtain the latest product information and installation instructions
◆ Perform text searches against Oracle's internal support databases
◆ Post questions and share ideas in technical forums
◆ Connect to OracleMERCURY and OracleMetaLink

In addition, you can visit the Oracle Worldwide Customer Support Guide at **http://support.oracle.com/**.

Certification Tracks

http://technet.oracle.com/training/certification/

The Oracle Certified Professional Program helps you understand more and more about Oracle and Oracle products. By demonstrating a high level of competence using Oracle products, you will be able to do your job better and with more confidence. Being an Oracle Certified Professional also gives you more visibility and greater access to more Oracle related challenges.

Oracle Education

http://education.oracle.com

Hundreds of courses are available for Oracle products and Oracle-based technologies through Oracle's educational services ([800] 633-0575). Also available is a line of self-paced training programs that teaches users how to use Oracle products and related technologies through Media Based Training (MBT) Technical Support, ([800] 887-0180). The Oracle educational Web site offers:

◆ Internet-based training
◆ Oracle channel information (live satellite broadcasts)
◆ Available coursework, including course schedules and class locations
◆ Course registration
◆ Education e-news service
◆ Computer Based Training (CBT)

Oracle Technology Network (OTN)

http://technet.oracle.com/

The Oracle Technology Network is a substantial online collection of diverse technical resources for Oracle users. It includes these items:

◆ A product information library that contains data sheets, white papers, and code samples

◆ A technology library that provides code, product usage information, and Oracle strategies

◆ A documentation library that contains a huge amount of online documentation for core Oracle products, including—but not limited to—Oracle 7.*x* and Oracle 8.0

◆ Forms, reports, graphics, and various platform-specific installation and user guides

◆ A support library containing problem reports, technical bulletins, and code written by Oracle Support Services in response to frequently asked questions from users

◆ Technical articles providing insight into Oracle and its products

OTN is a good resource for any professional who needs information about Oracle technologies. OTN has valuable information for DBAs, developers, analysts, managers, support staff, engineers, and executives at all experience and skill levels.

The OTN site is updated regularly. In addition, OTN members can receive *DevBlast*, an e-mail newsletter that highlights new information and additions to the OTN site.

Oracle-Sponsored Sites

These sites are found as links from the Oracle corporate site. They contain a vast array of information contained in online type magazines, journals, and books.

Oracle Publications Site

http://www.oracle.com/publications

Oracle Publications offers some of the best white papers from some of Oracle's own professionals. Oracle Publications' papers offer principles of Oracle server technology, thus helping you optimize performance while maintaining an almost perfectly available database system. Oracle Publications also offers:

◆ Application implementation

◆ Web searches for Oracle information

OracleProfessional *Online Site*

http://www.oracleprofessionalnewsletter.com/

OracleProfessional Online is a digital resource for subscribers of *OracleProfessional* Online and for professional developers working with Oracle. *OracleProfessional* Online contains an article index, free tips and techniques, and downloads available to subscribers only. A user name and password unlock each issue for downloads.

OraWorld Site

http://www.oraworld.com

OraWorld provides a fee-based site. With a membership, access includes:

◆ Seven training modules or a free test drive

◆ Articles and tips

◆ Utilities

◆ Listings of events

Oracle Frequently Asked Questions (FAQ)

The following Web sites list answers to the most frequently asked questions regarding Oracle.

David T. Bath FAQ Site

http://www.bf.rmit.edu.au/Oracle

http://www.bf.rmit.edu.au/OracleFAQ

Although this Australian site, one of the first Web sites and FAQs to appear on the Web, is becoming outdated, it still offers a good repository of useful information.

The Official Oracle Underground FAQ Site

`http://www.onwe.co.za/frank/faq.htm`

`http://www.onwe.co.za/frank/download/orafaq.zip`

This site offers a wealth of information on Oracle, including questions/answers, source code, reference materials, links to other sites, and more.

The New DBA FAQs by Kevin Loney

`http://www.osborne.com/oracle/dbafaq/dbafaq1.htm`

This site by Osborne offers one of the most current Oracle DBA FAQs from author Kevin Loney. The New DBA FAQs are in HTML format or can be downloaded in text form.

Publishers of Materials about Oracle

To find a new book or supplementary information for a book you already purchased, try these next few Web sites:

- Addison-Wesley: http://www.aw.com/aw/
- O'Reilly & Associates: http://www.ora.com/publishing/oracle
- Coriolis: http://www.coriolis.com/
- Sybex: http://www.sybex.com/
- PrimaTech Publishing: http://www.prima-tech.com
- Sams: http://www.mcp.com/sams/

NOTE

Through the IOUG-A store, presented by The Primary Key, IOUG members receive discounts of up to 25 percent off the latest Oracle and information technology–related materials. Members can take advantage of this program at IOUW and year-round through the IOUG-A store catalog listing in *Select*, the IOUG-A Web site, and the CompuServe forum.

Search Engine Sites Dedicated to Oracle

This section contains search engine sites that can help you find more information about Oracle.

Yahoo!

http://www.yahoo.com/Computers_and_Internet/Software/Databases/Oracle

This search engine is one of the first places to start looking for Oracle sites and information.

Alta Vista

http://www.altavista.com/

This search engine can sift through more than 4,000,000 articles from 14,000 Usenet groups.

DejaNews

http://www.deja.com/usenet

This engine allows you to search by any keyword to find relevant information. You can access facts about a company or a competitor, as well as other information.

Liszt Select

http://www.liszt.com

This directory of e-mail discussion groups allows users to enter any word or phrase to search a large directory of mailing lists—includes 66,692 listservs, list-procs, majordomos, and independently managed lists from 2,348 sites.

JCC Consulting Oracle Site

http://www.jcc.com

The search engine at this site contains indexed newsgroups. It enables you to more easily search for information that those resources contain.

Other Oracle Sites

The following are some miscellaneous sites that you'll most likely want to save in your Favorites folder.

OAUG DataWarehouse SIG

`http://www.oaug.org`

Currently, the OAUG Data Warehouse SIG (special interest group) is in the formative stage. The SIG addresses topics relevant to the installation, configuration, implementation, maintenance, and continued support of multidimensional and relational Oracle data warehouse products.

Virginia Tech Research and Graduate PL/SQL Site

`http://gserver.grads.vt.edu`

This site focuses on PL/SQL (via the Oracle Web server), as well as the use of Perl and Java. From this site, you can also subscribe to the RGS sample mailing list, which discusses PL/SQL in general as well as WebCyS development with Oracle's Web application server. The archive is accessible on the Web at **http:// gserver.grads.vt.edu/mail-archive/sample**.

Troy Cheramie Unofficial Oracle Web Server Site

`http://www.geocities.com/SiliconValley/Peaks/9111`

This site provides tips, suggestions, and tutorials on the development of applications and administration of the Oracle Web server.

Sites for User Groups and Events

The following listings contain Oracle user groups and upcoming events that deal with Oracle.

IOUG-A

`http://www.ioug.org`

> International Oracle Users Group-Americas
> 401 N. Michigan Avenue
> Chicago, IL 60611-4267
> Phone: (312) 245-1579
> Fax: (312) 527-6785
> E-mail: iouga@ioug.org

The International Oracle Users Group-Americas (IOUG-A), part of the International Oracle User Group (IOUG), is comprised of more than 10,000 members in North, Central, and South America. IOUG's purpose is to provide communications, networking, and educational forums for Oracle customers on Oracle-related products and services (but is not part of Oracle Corporation). IOUG's primary mission is to create and deliver education through new technologies and face-to-face meetings and to provide a voice to Oracle Corporation on both strategic and technical concerns.

Some of IOUG's services include:

◆ The IOUG conference

◆ *Select* magazine

◆ Voting on Oracle enhancements

◆ Vendor discounts

◆ Access to past IOUG conference papers

◆ Access to regional user groups

ODTUG

http://www.odtug.com/

> Oracle Development Tools User Group
> CompuServe: 102351,1311
> 2840 South College Road, Suite 151
> Wilmington, NC 28412
> Phone: (910) 452-7444
> Fax: (910) 452-7834
> E-mail: odtug@wilmington.net

The Oracle CASE Special Interest Group (OCSIG) changed its name to the Oracle Development Tools User Group (ODTUG). This is the international user group for information systems professionals who use Oracle's Designer/2000,

Developer/2000, and Discoverer. Members' interests cover all aspects of the system development lifecycle, including business process re-engineering, analysis, modeling, design, and development.

Current benefits of membership include the following:

◆ Timely access to the latest technology and information

◆ Access to early, pre-production, and trial releases of new products

◆ A direct feedback mechanism to Oracle development, enhancements, and comments through the Web

◆ Quarterly journal, the *ODTUG Technical Journal* (formerly *briefCASE*)

◆ Discounts to semiannual conferences

EOUG

```
http://www.eoug.com
```

Brigittenauer Laende 50-54, A-1203 Vienna,

Phone: +43 1 33777 870

Fax: +43 1 33777 873

E-mail: eoug_at@oracle.com

The primary task of the Europe, Middle East, and Africa Oracle Users Group (EOUG) is to provide existing Oracle customers with the information they need to make the best return on their investment in Oracle products. The EOUG arranges a conference and exhibition for the benefit of Oracle customers in Europe, the Middle East, and Africa.

ECO

```
http://www.oracle-users.com
```

ECO, or East Coast Oracle, was formed to provide a platform for the exchange of technical Oracle information. Experienced users and managers annually organize the ECO conference. It is often one of the best technical Oracle developers' conferences around. Attendance is limited to fewer than 1,000 people to allow plenty of opportunity to have questions answered.

OAUG

http://www.oaug.org

> Oracle Applications Users Group
> 415 East Paces Ferry Rd., NE
> Suite 200
> Atlanta, GA 30305
> Phone: (404) 240-0897
> Fax: (404) 240-0998
> E-mail: OAUG@mindspring.com

The Oracle Applications Users Group (OAUG) was formed in the San Francisco Bay Area in May 1990. Since then, meetings have been held in the spring and fall of each year. OAUG produces two periodicals: *OAUG Forum*, a semiannual magazine, and *OAUG Insight*, a quarterly newsletter. These publications are available online for OAUG members. OAUG also publishes an annual *Product and Service Supplier Directory*, which is mailed to the organization's key contacts each year. Conference proceedings are available to both members and non-members.

The OAUG, which is independent of Oracle Corporation, does the following:

◆ Provides a forum for sharing information about the use of Oracle applications

◆ Provides a collective means of prioritizing service and product directions

◆ Serves as a worldwide communications channel to Oracle Corporation

◆ Supports education and training related to Oracle Application products

Conference Events

It's not enough to read books and articles; interacting with other professionals leads to a better understanding of Oracle. With the rapidly changing technologies, Oracle professionals need to keep up to date, share ideas, network with their peers, and exchange their understanding and hands-on knowledge. Many events offer this experience each year. The following Web sites provide information about various Oracle events.

IOUG-A Live

http://www.ioug.org

IOUG-A Live is the most widely recognized IT-focused conference devoted to the most pressing issues facing the Oracle community. IOUG-A Live offers a knowledge source for Oracle users and database professionals, providing practical, in-depth knowledge for Oracle users, consultants, product managers, and developers. Abstracts, technical sessions, mini lessons, and IOUG-A University seminars are available online. Session papers are available to registered attendees online prior to the conference.

Features and focus areas in the conference include the following:

◆ IOUG-A Live campgrounds (talk directly to key Oracle product managers, developers, and others)

◆ Database Administration Track

◆ Developer/2000 and Application Development Products Track

◆ Data Warehousing Track

◆ Designer/2000 and Modeling Tools

◆ Web-Enabled Computing Track

◆ New Technology and Trends

◆ Technical Manager Focus Areas (planning and implementing shifts in Oracle technology)

Oracle OpenWorld

http://www.oracle.com/corporate/seminars_and_events

Oracle OpenWorld is one of the largest sources of education and training on almost every Oracle product and technology. Network with Oracle product managers and employees, form business alliances, and learn about the latest Oracle product technology from this site.

Key components of Oracle OpenWorld include:

◆ Keynote sessions from industry gurus and Oracle executives

◆ Technical sessions about Oracle products

◆ Technology campgrounds (get direct access to Oracle product managers and developers for questions)

◆ Hands-on training about Oracle products

◆ Free evaluation software

◆ A one-year membership to the Oracle Developer Program

◆ Hands-on sessions for test-driving pre-release software

Oracle FTP Sites

The File Transfer Protocol (FTP) is not new; it allows users to log in to a remote computer and browse directories, select files, and then transfer them to a local machine. Following are some FTP sites that relate to Oracle.

Oracle Corporation

```
ftp://oracle-ftp.us.oracle.com/
```

```
ftp://ftp.oracle.com
```

The World Wide Support portion of the Oracle FTP site is divided into three major competencies:

◆ **Apps.** Applications (manufacturing, financials, auto-install, AOL)

◆ **Dev_tools.** Development tools (OLAP)

◆ **Server.** Server technologies (RDBMS, Unix, networking)

Each competency contains an anonymous upload/download area, and a separate area for patches:

◆ **Incoming.** For non-Oracle individuals to upload files

◆ **Outgoing.** For Oracle employees to upload files for public consumption

◆ **Patches.** For patches

University Oldenburg Germany Site

```
ftp://ftp.Informatik.Uni-Oldenburg.DE/pub/oracle
```

This German university's FTP site was one of the first Internet Oracle FTP sites with FAQs. Although it's getting outdated and the site is in German, the site still offers a good repository of useful information.

Computing Centre of Russian Academy of Sciences Site

`http://www.cas.ru/`

The Russian Computing Centre is a research institute of the Russian Academy of Sciences. This site offers a variety of Oracle information in English and Russian.

Oracle Newsgroups

Usenet is a group of specialized newsgroups on the Internet that is organized by specific interest areas. Usenet consists of more than 14,000 newsgroups, many of which are superb places to expand knowledge, solicit feedback to questions, or communicate with other Oracle professionals. Participating in electronic forums can help you reduce the amount of effort you might otherwise expend when attempting to solve problems that others have already solved. Try these newsgroups for information pertaining to Oracle:

- ◆ **comp.databases.oracle.server**: Oracle database administration/server topics
- ◆ **comp.databases.oracle.tools**: Oracle database tools/applications
- ◆ **comp.databases.oracle.marketplace**: Oracle-related jobs, resumes, and so on
- ◆ **comp.databases.oracle.misc**: Oracle miscellaneous topics
- ◆ **comp.databases.rdb**: Oracle RDB
- ◆ **comp.databases**: General database discussions
- ◆ **comp.databases.theory**: Database theory
- ◆ **comp.databases.olap**: Analytical processing and data warehousing

 NOTE

If you have any doubt as to a particular group's focus, check the group's FAQ section. It should provide a prescription for successful interaction in that newsgroup.

Summary

Just two years ago, few resources were available online other than those offered by Oracle. With the explosion of the Web, however, there has been an exponential increase of Oracle information available. Use this power to open new avenues that will help you find information about your Oracle problems.

The next chapter contains a large list of Oracle Web sites that might prove to have just the information you are looking for!

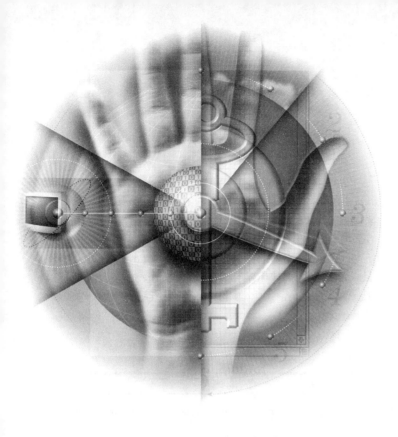

Chapter 17

More WWW Dot Oracle Dot Com

ORACLE

This chapter contains a list of more than 200 Web sites that deal with implementing and managing your Oracle database or application. This chapter is, in a way, a continuation of the last, and makes a great reference to keep next to your computer. The previous chapter mentioned some of the more popular sites and gave you an idea about what you'd find there; this chapter simply lists the Oracle-related sites that the authors and others have visited over the years. Sites are categorized into pertinent topics.

Oracle WWW Sites

Site Name	URL
Download Oracle Product Patches	ftp://suppftp:suppftp@www.uk.oracle.com/patch/std
Oracle Asia Pacific	http://www.oracle.com.sg
Oracle Australia	http://www.oracle.com.au
Oracle Brazil	http://www.oracle.com.br
Oracle Business Alliance Program	http://alliance.oracle.com
Oracle Canada	http://www.oraclecanada.com
Oracle Corporation	http://www.oracle.com
Oracle Corporation, by FTP	ftp://ftp.oracle.com/pub
Oracle Documentation	http://technet.oracle.com/docs/
Oracle Education	http://education.us.oracle.com
Oracle Europe, Middle East, and Africa	http://www.uk.oracle.com
Oracle InterMedia	http://www.oracle.com/intermedia
Oracle Japan	http://www.oracle.co.jp
Oracle Magazine Interactive	http://www.oramag.com
Oracle Press Releases	http://www.oracle.com/corporate/press
Oracle Publications	http://www.oracle.com/publications
Oracle Search Form	http://www.oracle.com/cgi-bin/searchForm

Oracle South Africa Support Server	http://www.oracle.co.za
Oracle Store	http://oraclestore.oracle.com/
Oracle Support	http://www.oracle.com/support
Oracle Trial Software	http://technet.oracle.com/software
Oracle United States	http://www.us.oracle.com
Oracle US Support	http://www.oracle.com/support
Oracle Consulting Services	http://www.oracle.com/consulting

Oracle User Groups

Site Name	URL
Americas International Oracle Users Group	http://www.ioug.org
Austrian Oracle Users Group	http://www.eoug.com/aoug
Chicago Oracle Users Group	http://www.roman.com/coug
Dallas Oracle Users Group	http://www.doug.org
Delaware Valley Oracle Users Group	http://www.oug.com/devoug/
Detroit Oracle Users Group	http://www.doug-mi.org/
Europe, Middle East, and Africa Oracle Users Group	http://www.eoug.com
German Oracle Users Group	http://www.doag.org
Japan's Oracle User Group	http://www.oracle.co.jp
Oracle Users Group Finland	http://www.ougf.fi
South Australian Oracle Users Group	http://www.odg.on.net/saoug
Swiss Oracle Users Group	http://www.soug.ch
United Kingdom Oracle Users Group	http://www.oracleuser.co.uk

Oracle Special Interest Groups (SIGs)

Site Name	URL
Data Warehousing SIG	http://www.oaug-dwsig.org/
Designer 2000 Special Interest Group	http://www.elmwood.com/oracle/d2ksig
The IOUG-A Linux Special Interest Group	http://www.oug.com/linuxsig/index.html

MAOP - DBA SIG	http://www.maop.org/sig-dba/
Oracle Applications Users Group	http://www.oaug.org
Oracle Development Tools User Group	http://www.odtug.com
Oracle MVS Special Interest Group	http://www.mvsoraclesig.org/
Oracle Technology SIG	http://www.gcpcug.org/sigs/oracle.htm
Oracle Windows NT User Group	http://www.geocities.com/SiliconValley/Heights/6616
Oracle Worldwide Internet Special Interest Group	http://www.communicata.co.uk/Oracle

Oracle Frequently Asked Questions (FAQ)

Site Name	URL
David T Bath's General Oracle FAQ Pages	http://www.bf.rmit.edu.au/OracleFAQ
Kevin Loney's Oracle DBA FAQ	http://www.osborne.com/oracle/dbafaq/dbafaq1.htm
Oracle General FAQ	http://www.bf.rmit.edu.au/~orafaq
Oracle's FAQ's	http://www.orafaq.org/faq.htm
The Underground Oracle FAQ List	http://www.onwe.co.za/frank/faq.htm

Oracle Usenet Newsgroups

Site Name	URL
Analytical Processing and Data Warehousing	news:comp.databases.olap
Client/Server Issues	news:comp.client-server
Database Theory	news:comp.databases.theory
General Database Discussions	news:comp.databases
General Object Databases	news:comp.databases.object
Job Postings	news:comp.databases.oracle.marketplace
Oracle Database Administration Server Topics	news:comp.databases.oracle.server
Oracle Database Tools Applications	news:comp.databases.oracle.tools
Oracle Miscellaneous Topics	news:comp.databases.oracle.misc
Oracle RDB	news:comp.databases.rdb
Oracle-Related Jobs, Resumes, and so on	news:comp.databases.oracle.marketplace

Oracle FTP Archives

Site Name	URL
Euro-Asian Oracle Users Group's (EAOUG) FTP Area	http://www.ccas.ru/pub/DataBase/Oracle
Oldenburg University's Computer Science Department	ftp://ftp.Informatik.Uni-Oldenburg.DE/pub/oracle
Oracle Corporation via FTP	ftp://ftp.oracle.com/pub
Oracle Utilities	ftp://ftp.Informatik.Uni-Oldenburg.DE/pub/oracle

Oracle Books

Site Name	URL
Books for Oracle Developers	http://www.rbsbooks.com
Oracle Press (Osborne/McGraw-Hill)	http://www.osborne.com/oracle/
O'Reilly Books & Software	http://www.ora.com/catalog/oracle2
The Illuminations Book Store	http://www.illumine.com/
Prima Tech Publishing	http://www.prima-tech.com

Oracle Magazines

Site Name	URL
Exploring Oracle DBMS	http://www.cobb.com/dbm
Exploring Oracle Developer/2000 and Designer/2000	http://www.cobb.com/eod/
DBMS Magazine	http://www.dbmsmag.com
DM Review	http://www.dmreview.com/
Data Management Review	http://www.dmreview.com
DB2 Magazine	http://www.db2mag.com/
Disaster Recovery Journal	http://www.drj.com
Quarterly Journal Published by IOUG	http://www.ioug.org/public/select/
Oracle Magazine Interactive	http://www.oramag.com
Oracle Professional	http://www.oracleprofessionalnewsletter.com/

Oracle Magazine	http://www.oracle.com/oramag/ (click on Oracle Magazine)
Profit Magazine	http://www.oracle.com/oramag/ (click on Profit Magazine)
TeraData Review	http://www.teradatareview.com/
Enterprise Systems Journal	http://www.esj.com

Oracle Training

Site Name	URL
Oracle Certified Professional	http://education.oracle.com/certification/index.html
Animated Learning—Multimedia Courseware	http://www.animatedlearning.com
Prepare for the DBA Certification Exam	http://www.docsoftware.com/dbademo.htm
Computer Based Training	http://cbt.oracle.com/
Oracle User Resource	http://www.oracle-users.com

Oracle Jobs/Career Opportunities

Site Name	URL
Just Oracle Job	http://www.justoraclejobs.com/
Oracle Placement Specialists	http://ipa.com/queen
Oracle Job Network	http://www.oracjobs.com/
Oracle Jobs Online	http://jobs.oracle.com/
Oracle Job Opportunities on the Internet	http://www.internet-solutions.com/itjobs/oracle
The Oracle Job Network	http://www.oracjobs.com
OraSEARCH.COM	http://www.orasearch.com
The Software Job Home Page	http://www.softwarejobs.com

Oracle Web Development

Site Name	URL
General WWW Developer Info	http://www.steview.com
Oracle Internet Server Products	http://www.olab.com

Oracle User Forum and Fan Club	http://www.orafans.com/
ORALink	http://oradb1.jinr.dubna.su/software/ORALink
Overview Oracle-WWW	http://www.w3.org/hypertext/WWW/RDBGate/Overview.html
The Unofficial Oracle Web Server Site	http://www.geocities.com/SiliconValley/Peaks/9111
Web to Oracle Interface	http://www.mowi2.com

Oracle-Related Vendors

Company Name	Description	URL
Platinum Technology	Oracle monitoring and database reorganization	http://www.platinum.com
Eventus Software	Oracle database tools	http://www.eventus.com
Embarcadero Technologies	Oracle database tools	http://www.embarcadero.com/
BMC Software	Database and application management tools and agents	http://www.bmc.com
Cronos Web Pages	Belgian Oracle solutions company	http://www.cronos.be
Database Acceleration Systems	Performance solutions for database applications	http://www.desdbx.com/
JCC Consulting, Inc.	SQL standards, press releases, search through archives, and so on	http://www.jcc.com
CDS	Custom database solutions	http://www.customdb.com
RECON Technologies	Oracle and client-server applications	http://www.recon.com
Imperial Technology	Oracle performance acceleration	http://www.imperialtech.com
Kumaran Systems	Oracle forms VAR	http://www.kumaran.com
TUSCS	Database consulting, training, and VAR	http://www.tusc.com

RevealNet	Information tools for mastering Oracle and DB2	http://www.revealnet.com
Smart Corporation	Graphical tools (SMART DB Workbench)	http://www.smartdb.com
TechnoSolutions	Server management and programming tools	http://www.technosolutions.com
Precise Software Solutions	Precise SQL tools	http://www.precisesoft.com
Diversified Consultants	Oracle partner	http://www.divcomp.com
Savant Corporation	Q diagnostics	http://www.savantcorp.com
Noblestar Systems	Oracle consulting firm	http://www.noblestar.com
Solutron	Dynamic publishing solutions for Oracle Designer/2000	http://www.solutron.com

Database Vendors (Non-Oracle)

Site Name	URL
Advanced Oracle Access Solutions	http://www.crlab.com/home.html
Informix	http://www.informix.com
Microsoft (MS Access, FoxPro, SQL Server)	http://www.microsoft.com
Powerbuilder Home Page	http://www.sybase.com/products/powerbuilder

SQL-Related Information

Site Name	URL
Oracle SQL Info	http://www.spnc.demon.co.uk/index/oracle.htm
Query Optimization	http://sunsite.ust.hk/dblp/db/dbimpl/qo.html
SQL Interpreter & Tutorial	http://www.sqlcourse.com/
SQL-Programmer	http://www.sfi-software.com/
SQL Standards	http://www.jcc.com/sql_stnd.html
SQL Tutorial	http://w3.one.net/~jhoffman/sqltut.htm

Oracle Tips & Scripts

Site Name	URL
Biji's Oracle DBA Page	http://www.bijoos.com/oracle/index.htm
DBA Support.Com	http://ora.dbasupport.com/
Dieter's Oracle Toolbox	http://www.geocities.com/doberkofler
G & J Piper	http://www.ozemail.com.au/~gpiper/
Ken Atkins' Oracle Database Tip of the Week	http://www.arrowsent.com/oratip/frames.htm
Large River Oracle	http://www.ieighty.net/~davepamn/display.html
Oracle Bookmark	http://www.vb-bookmark.com/vbOracle.html
Oracle Notes	http://www.oraclenotes.com
Oracle Geeks	http://www.interealm.com/orageeks/
Ora World	http://www.oraworld.com/
Solv-IT, Inc.	http://www.solvit.net/dbscripts/
Steve Rae's Tips	http://www.uaex.edu/srea/

Oracle Scripting Languages

Site Name	URL
Oracle via Perl	http://www.aphis.usda.gov/~mmoxcey/scripts/ora_tut
OraTCL Interface to Oracle	http://www.rhic.bnl.gov/html/local/oracle/oratcl.html
REXX SQL Interface to Oracle	http://www.gu.edu.au/gwis/the/rexxsql.html

Oracle Database Standards and Research

Site Name	URL
ANSI—American National Standards Institute	http://www.ansi.org
Database Systems Laboratory	http://www-ccs.cs.umass.edu/db.html
DBTG—University of Zurich	http://www.ifi.unizh.ch/groups/dbtg/
ISO—International Organization for Standardization	http://www.iso.ch/
ODMG—Object Database Management Group	http://www.odmg.org
SQL Standards	http://www.jcc.com/sql_stnd.html
The Computer Security Institute	http://www.gocsi.com

Oracle User Group Conferences

Site Name	URL
IOUG-A Oracle International User Group—America	http://www.ioug.org
OAUG Oracle Applications User Group	http://www.oaug.org
ODTUG Oracle Development Tools User Group	http://www.odtug.com

Oracle Miscellaneous Sites

Site Name	URL
Advanced Oracle Access Solutions	http://www.crlab.com/home.html
Carnac Systems	http://www.carnac.com
CASE Tools Overview	http://osiris.sunderland.ac.uk/sst/casehome.html
Computer Economics, Inc.	http://computereconomics.com
Database Administration Web App	http://www.geocities.com/BourbonStreet/2481
Database Systems Lab, Univ of Massachusetts	http://www-ccs.cs.umass.edu/db.html
Database Tips Home	http://www.platinum.com/dbtips
DBTG—University of Zurich	http://www.ifi.unizh.ch/groups/dbtg/
Envive Corporation	http://www.envive.com
Facts About Object-Relational Databases	http://www.odbmsfacts.com
G. C. Daley & Associates	http://web2.airmail.net/gcdaley/oralinks.htm
Great Oracle Sites to Visit	http://www.onwe.co.za/frank/faqlink.htm
Hot-Oracle.com	http://www.hot-oracle.com/index.html
Informant Communications Group, Inc.	http://www.informant.com
Informatica Corporation	http://www.informatica.com
META Group Collaborative IT Decision Making	http://www.metagroup.com
NetSmith's Oracle Links Page	http://www.netsmith-tx.com/odbc.asp
NYOUG—Download	http://www.nyoug.org/nyoug/download.htm
ODMG Object Databases Management Group	http://www.odmg.org
Oracle Humor	http://www.oraclehumor.com/
Oracle8i Data Dictionary	http://www.divcomp.com/dcc_odd/

Oracle Resource Stop	http://www.orsweb.com/
Oracle Resources Center at TechnoSolutions	http://www.technosolutions.com/oracle.html
Oracle Technology Network	http://technet.oracle.com
Oracle User Forum and Fan Club	http://www.orafans.com
Oracle User Resource, Inc.	http://www.oracle-users.com
OraWorld—Everything Oracle	http://www.oraworld.com
OraWorld: Utilities	http://www.oraworld.com/utilitie.htm
Ralph Kimball Associates Home Page	http://www.rkimball.com
Saraswati Systems Corporation	http://www.saraswati.com/
SMART Sites	http://www.smartdb.com/links.html
SQL Forum Home Page	http://www.sqlforum.com
The SSC Developer Resource	http://www.saraswati.com/dev/devtxt.htm
The Telox Guide	http://www.telox.no
Third-Party Add-On Tools: Oracle	http://www.hallogram.com/menus/Oracle.html
TOAD—Tool for Oracle Application Development	http://www.toadsoft.com/
Tom's World of Oracle	http://home.wtal.de/dromas/orcllink.htm
Yahoo Database Links	http://www.yahoo.com/Computers_and_Internet/Software/Databases

Summary

"Wow!" You are probably saying about now, "What a list of good Oracle resources!" True, this chapter has definitely put together a list of online resources that should prove to be valuable in your career as an Oracle professional.

You've almost reached the end of the book! The next chapter is all about *application service providers* (ASPs) who provide software and other services to subscribers over private networks or the Internet. Chapter 18 will help you understand all about this new and quickly expanding area.

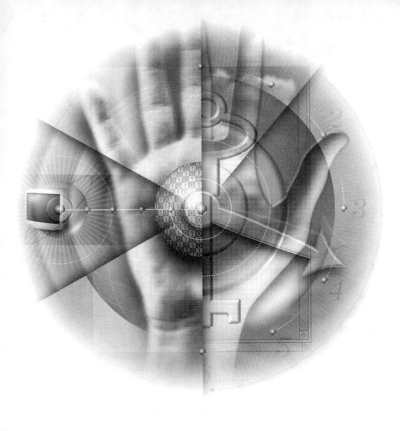

Chapter 18

What Does It Take to Be an Application Service Provider?

ORACLE

For a monthly or yearly fee, most *application service providers* (ASPs) provide software and other services to subscribers over private networks or the Internet. There are, however, variations on the types of services and software ASPs provide, because each company struggles to gain market share and visibility. Some ASPs provide global application solutions to customers, whereas others provide core services, such as Internet access and network management. Other ASPs might provide vertical solutions specific to an industry such as health care or online banking. Many companies consider ASP to be a cost-effective solution for meeting the demands of e-business, and for offsetting capital expenditures, platform ownership and upgrades, software investments, implementation challenges, and competitiveness.

Benefits of Using an ASP

As companies become increasingly dependent on complex and rapidly changing e-business information systems, many are strongly considering the ASP approach. Many companies enlist an ASP to quickly deploy applications at an affordable cost but without sacrificing security and risk of the corporate brand. ASPs can help companies deploy applications that might otherwise involve significant investments in software, hardware, deployment time, and IT resources. The goal of the ASP is to make the technology as transparent and reliable as the ordinary telephone.

Companies considering ASPs are primarily cost motivated, but secondarily consider these benefits when making the decision:

◆ **Accelerated implementation deployment**. The ASP has the hardware, applications, and resources to provide the service, in addition to the capability to quickly respond to business change or growth.

◆ **Application-skilled resources.** By outsourcing application management, companies can focus critical resources on their business instead of on mundane operational issues, and reduce the need to compete for hard-to-find and expensive-to-retain IT personnel.

◆ **Competitive edge.** Companies can partner with an ASP to get an edge on the competition.

◆ **Financial benefits.** By using an ASP, companies can reduce costs and lower expenditures for hardware, applications, and resources.

◆ **Leading technology access.** ASPs can be thought of as libraries of available technologies that can be tried without significant investment.

◆ **Maintenance, updates, and configuration management.** The ASP is managing the applications, customization, and maintenance, not the client's in-house application development staff. This reduces the need for application development, Q/A, and change-management resources.

◆ **No IT infrastructure required.** IT infrastructure costs, including personnel, hardware, and equipment, usually exceed software costs when applications are deployed in-house. Transition to an ASP requires minimal to no in-house IT infrastructure, so these costs are reduced or eliminated.

◆ **Performance improvements.** An ASP maintains a skilled staff whose expertise on hosted applications is more extensive than normally at a customer's site. Also, an ASP's infrastructure is designed to provide reliable, high-performance application access and response.

◆ **Risk reduction and transfer.** With no capital expenditure on software, hardware, and the like, companies can "test" new technology with no impact on their existing production environment.

ASP Categories

Most ASPs can host, manage, and support a wide array of applications, including major enterprise resource planning (ERP) and customer relationship management (CRM) packages, as well as payroll, accounting, and other software. Some ASPs can act as an independent software vendor that hosts their own products, whereas others host third-party products. In most cases, ASPs separate into these four categories:

◆ **Application infrastructure providers (AIPs).** These ASPs provide the e-business platform, bringing together the disparate business processes, applications, and enterprise management of applications.

◆ **Full-service application service providers (FSASPs).** These ASPs provide it all—software, hardware, networks, databases, storage, security, resources—everything.

◆ **In-house application solution providers (IASPs).** These service providers host custom-built software solutions. They also can host preexisting in-house company-built applications.

◆ **Third-party software solution providers (TSSPs).** These ASPs host third-party software such as enterprise resource planning (ERP) packages, front-office packages, customer relationship management (CRM) packages, and so on.

Types of ASP Services

Because all application service providers are not equal, you need to evaluate each one based on its capability to meet your company's business requirements. Doing so requires an understanding of the different services offered by each. Note that this list is not definitive because new ASPs go online each day with new offerings.

◆ **Customer relationship management provider (CRM).** These provide customer relationship management applications over the Internet and/or host a company's system using virtual private networks (VPNs).

◆ **Data center provider (DCP).** These outsourcers host a company's servers and disk farm at their facility. This usually includes all environmental, clean power, HVAC, fire suppression, equipment racks, redundancy, and physical access control. The applications might not be included as part of the agreement.

◆ **Desktop application provider (DAP).** These ASPs host and/or maintain desktop applications packages such as Microsoft Office, contact-management packages, and personal organization-management packages over the Internet.

◆ **E-mail application provider (EAP).** These ASPs provide e-mail service over the Internet and/or host and maintain clients' e-mail servers and storage.

◆ **Enterprise resource planner (ERP).** Because of their complexity, interdependencies, and implementation challenges, the majority of ASPs target this offering. Most enterprise application offerings are for dot-coms and other companies that do not have existing infrastructures or ERP applications requiring integrating. Older established companies, on the other hand, require the proper e-business platform to source and integrate all their systems and data, which the ASP might not provide. These types of providers typically offer managed ERP, CRM, data warehousing, business-intelligence portals, total Web management and personalization, desktop applications, finance, accounting, sales, distribution, manufacturing, logistics, and human-resource applications.

◆ **Financial application provider (FAP).** These ASPs provide Internet access to tax-preparation and bill payment-type packages for a monthly fee.

◆ **Internet service provider (ISP).** This, the other common service provider, typically offers Internet access, Web conversion, hosting, e-mail, and management services.

◆ **Management system provider (MSP).** Similar to outsourcers, these service providers concentrate on the enterprise management and monitoring of companies' servers, networks, applications, databases, Web servers, and security through the use of a systems-management framework. They typically provide administration support for specific operating systems, upgrades, fail-over sites, OS hardening, equipment replacement/installation, and disaster recovery.

◆ **Multitainment provider (MTP).** These ASPs provide Internet access, storage, and rental of content such as movies, music, multimedia, and gaming.

◆ **Network service provider (NSP).** These ASPs manage wide area network (WAN) and local area network (LAN) connectivity, including routers, switches, network load balancers, directory services, virtual private networks (VPNs), and firewalls.

◆ **Online storage/backup provider (OSP).** These ASPs provide secure remote storage that you can attach as a Web drive on which to back up or store data and programs so that you can access them from any computer on the Internet.

◆ **Traditional IT outsourcer.** These ASPs provide services to monitor, maintain, and manage your entire IT infrastructure.

◆ **Web infrastructure provider (WIP).** These ASPs provide Internet consulting services, Internet application architecture assistance, Internet application development, and middleware integration.

◆ **Web hosting provider (WHP).** These ASPs provide Web-server monitoring and management, including upgrades, e-mail services, commerce servers, merchant-services support (credit-card authorization), catalog services, managed caches, controlled content-distribution services, load balancing, and streaming-media services.

As you can see, comparing and selecting an ASP is not as simple as you might have thought. Due diligence on your company's part is an important step prior to selecting an ASP.

Identifying Your Company's Requirements

Determining which ASP to use requires a well-thought-out requirements analysis. Without knowing your company's business goals, IT requirements, budget allocations, resource skill set, and allocation, it is literally impossible to properly select an ASP partner.

Before evaluating ASPs, you need to assess your company's requirements, and evaluate potential tradeoffs between in-house operations and outsourced deployments. For example, determine whether you will receive a better financial return by outsourcing existing in-house solutions, or by deploying new ones through an ASP. In addition, your company should fully investigate and understand all cost aspects of the application-rental model. Companies must consider the total price of outsourcing the software over a specific period of time, because an ASP's contract might require a minimum usage or contract period.

When compiling the company's list of requirements, ask yourself these questions:

- Does the savings of internal infrastructure and resources reduction outweigh the ASP costs?
- Will the ASP enable improved access to mission-critical applications?
- Does the ASP reuse current company best practices?
- Does using the ASP expose the company to new security risks because the new solution involves moving highly confidential information off of the company premises?
- Will the financial department experience an increased workload in order to deal with the contracts and tracking of service level agreements?
- Does the ASP service the applications itself, or is there another vendor that will have to be dealt with for each application, platform, or network area?
- What are the business's activities and priorities?

◆ Which applications are being considered for outsourcing (be sure to identify any linkages to suppliers, affiliates, partners)?

◆ What application-integration/customization needs need to be addressed to meet the company's business needs?

◆ What is the estimated number of application users, as well as the number of users expected over the next 1–3 years?

◆ What is the forecasted cost of hardware/upgrades to meet new business demands?

◆ What is the forecasted cost of software/upgrades to meet new business demands?

◆ What is the forecasted cost of network/upgrades to meet new business demands?

◆ What is the forecasted cost of storage to meet new business demands?

◆ What is the forecasted cost of additional resources/training to maintain all the new hardware, software, and networks, as well as business analysts to analyze all the new business data?

◆ What level of reliability and service is required to grow as well as sustain business and maintain customer satisfaction?

◆ Are there any concerns about company brand and the risks garnered by using an ASP?

◆ Has enough information been compiled to compare the costs and benefits of the applications being considered?

After performing the internal-requirements analysis, it is important to then gather the operational and business data about the ASPs you want to compare to see which ones meet your company's business requirements.

Selecting an ASP to Meet Your Business Requirements

When deciding whether to outsource or rent applications, a company should look for partners who understand its business and can provide technology and services that help it quickly expand its existing business or quickly move into a new market model. During an ASP evaluation, it's important to ask questions about the

ASP's business background, business partners, and longevity. Questions should cover the following:

◆ Operational readiness

◆ Business readiness

Operational Readiness

You should ask any prospective ASP the following questions related to operational readiness:

◆ **Architecture.** Is the ASP architecture model capable of handling current business demands as well as projected growth? Is it modular, open, and scalable? Or is it proprietary?

◆ **Migration.** Does the ASP use and offer open tools and technologies that enable easy migration to the ASP model without requiring rewriting of current applications, or ones that easily and quickly source the data from existing systems of record to populate new applications?

◆ **E-business management.** Does the ASP use integrated but modular open tools that handle management of servers, networks, databases, applications, the Web, storage facilities, and security, or does it use proprietary in-house scripted systems?

◆ **E-business applications.** Does the ASP use integrated but modular open tools that handle application lifecycle tracking, change and configuration management, business intelligence/reporting, enterprise resource planning, customer relationship management, and project management, or does it use proprietary in-house coded applications?

◆ **Performance monitoring and management.** Does the ASP use integrated but modular open tools that handle centralized console, event management and correlation, alerts, alarms and notification, root cause analysis, preventive and predictive analysis, load balancing, high availability, redundancy, and disaster planning, or does it use proprietary in-house scripted systems?

Understanding ASP Architectures

Most in-house systems rely on a fixed architecture inherent to the company's past business processes. Companies considering ASPs must carefully consider all business requirements; not all business processes are suitable for outsourcing. For applications that aren't easily outsourced, an ASP should have an architecture design that is scalable, reliable, and maintainable in addition to providing robust network connections to deliver the required services.

Because the delivery mechanism is a network or leased line, it is the primary limiting factor. Consequently, ASPs typically use one of these four architectures:

◆ Web server/browser-based applications

◆ Thin client/server architectures

◆ Thick client/server architectures

◆ Java-based applications

Browser-Based Architectures

Browser-based architectures enable ASPs to deliver services through a browser or portal interface. Clients access Web applications through a browser from a variety of platforms. Most legacy platforms can now have their data sourced and enabled in a browser, thus replacing hardwired leased line terminal connections. This architecture can take advantage of inexpensive network computing hardware for the desktop.

Although a good a way to deploy applications to almost to any user on any desktop, the browser application still requires management as well as an infrastructure. Pinpointing the root cause of a problem can be difficult without an integrated enterprise management solution that covers the server, network, application, database, Web server, and desktop.

Client/Server-Based Computing

Client/server-based computing (thick or thin) better addresses network bandwidth and client-management issues. Many ASPs control their operations from a central data center to the subscribers' desktops using clients connected over leased lines or the Internet. This architecture provides a simpler integration where an ASP will use an enterprise management-based delivery mechanism to centrally monitor, administer, troubleshoot, and maintain the applications. Because applications are run locally at the client's site with the network transporting inputs and updates, a larger desktop-hardware investment is required as compared to browser-based architectures.

Java-Based Applications

Java applications can reduce the issues of individual desktop management as well as control application versioning. In Java architecture, a client downloads an application that runs locally on a desktop. Known for its portability, Java works across multiple operating systems and computer platforms. However, Java is a changing standard with performance issues compared to client/server computing. Bandwidth required for Java applications can also result in higher network-services costs.

Table 18.1 outlines the pros and cons of the various ASP architectures.

Table 18.1 ASP Architecture Comparison

Architecture Type	Pro	Con
Application server/Web applications	Applications sent to the browser	Training required for legacy users
	Browser can be on almost any platform	Lack of Security
	Browser is easy to use	Bandwidth usage can vary
	Portal customizable to business	License tracking
	Lowered support requirements	Root cause problem identification
Thin client	Delivers to most clients	Client management and upgrades
	Custom business-specific applications	Network reliant
	Windows application	Client customization
	Lowered support requirements	Lack of security
Thick client	Low network usage	Client management
	Custom business-specific applications	Increased support requirements
	Good security	Increased development
Java	Can be almost any platform	Performance challenges
	Minimizes version control	Bandwidth usage can vary
	Portability	SDK version control
	Reusable libraries	Standards still in development

Because ASPs must choose from one of these architectures, companies must fully understand each one to determine how well the ASP is prepared to deliver mission-critical enterprise applications.

Migration

Companies that have decided to move to the ASP model should understand and have an outlined plan on how application and data migration will be performed prior to signing a contract. The ASP you choose must be able to support your company's migration requirements. Important questions to ask include the following:

◆ Does the ASP support the company's data-modeling tools, or do other methods have to be used?

◆ Does the ASP have tools or resources to help identify and track dependent application data?

◆ Does the ASP have tools or resources to load and unload data?

◆ Does the ASP have a data repository infrastructure?

◆ Does the ASP have tools or resources to clean and transform data?

E-Business Management

Although most think ASPs have their own data centers, some contract with third-party capacity service providers for infrastructure services. For either scenario, you must analyze the ASP's infrastructure on which your company's applications will run. Ask about the types of hardware, operating systems, networking products, databases, applications, Web servers, and tools used. Also be sure to determine the number of skilled resources on permanent staff or contract; whether your applications will be run on dedicated or shared servers; how they are delivered to the Internet and/or leased lines; and so on. If the ASP does contract out services, determine whether the vendors have a process or plan to address and resolve issues.

When requesting information about the ASP hosting site, ask the following questions:

◆ Does the ASP own the data center and facilities management? If not, who else has access to company data? Is there a fail-over site in case of a disaster, and in what order are customers restored?

◆ Is the data center completed, or is it under construction? Is capacity being added that can possibly disrupt production operations? Is there on-site capacity for the company's future growth?

◆ How secure is the data center? What physical security measures are in place?

Staffing

Because ASPs typically host clients' applications off-site at their own data centers, they should have a staff of skilled experts. Potential ASPs should be requested to provide a list of their staff and their credentials. Skills should include the following:

◆ Enterprise systems management

◆ Enterprise network management

◆ Enterprise database management

◆ Enterprise security management

◆ Enterprise Web management

◆ Enterprise workload/load-balancing management

◆ Enterprise storage and recovery management

◆ Project management

◆ Enterprise applications management (specific to the applications your company is interested in having hosted or renting)

◆ Data access

◆ Change management and control

When requesting information about ASP support levels, staffing, and skill sets, ask the following questions:

◆ Does the ASP provide support and staffing for existing company systems at its site and host the existing applications back over the Internet or from other communication links? Or does it require the company to export all its data into the ASP's systems and applications?

◆ Does the ASP offer all the services, staffing, and skill sets necessary to fully deliver the applications?

◆ Does the ASP supply all levels of support, or is it reliant upon other outsourcers or partners?

◆ Does the ASP have staff experts for applications it provides, or does it obtain that expertise from an external source?

◆ Does the ASP have dedicated or shared staff for supporting the application services?

◆ What is the staff turnover rate and training initiatives for new technologies?

Security and Management

An ASP should have a solid and safe security infrastructure, especially if the ASP delivers sensitive company data over the Internet. Security management encompasses enterprise information risk analysis and the mitigation of such risk through a variety of means and measures. When requesting information, ask the following questions:

◆ What is the ASP's data security policy or function?

◆ Does the ASP offer different levels of security?

◆ Does the ASP offer separated hosting by company, or is it a shared environment?

◆ What measures are in place by the ASP to prevent unauthorized access, updating, malicious acts, and auditing of sensitive data?

◆ What measures are in place for intrusion detection, logging, reporting, and change control for security policies?

◆ Does the ASP have VPN, firewalls, encryption, virus protection, or security authentication and access systems?

E-Business Applications

When requesting information about the applications available through the ASP, ask the following questions:

◆ Does the ASP have experience installing, managing, and supporting the application being considered? Is it certified to do so?

◆ Does the ASP support any applications the company might choose in the future?

◆ Once the company's data is at the ASP's data center, what ownership rights exist to change, move, or copy data?

◆ Does the ASP offer usage-based, leasing, or subscription-based applications?

◆ Does the client hold title to the application that passes through to the ASP?

◆ Does the ASP purchase the application but remit royalties for client use?

◆ Will the ASP permit the application it manages to integrate or source data from other systems or software it doesn't manage?

◆ Will the ASP provide the upgrades?

◆ If an existing company application needs to be customized for hosting, does the ASP offer that service?

◆ Is there a contract clause that limits how much the ASP can raise the cost of the services?

Data is the most important asset to e-business companies today. As such, it is important that the ASP has the methods and tools in place to ensure its availability, optimization, management, security, and protection. Important questions to ask are as follows:

◆ Does the ASP offer commercial relational database management engines?

◆ Does the ASP enterprise database management infrastructure provide active or predictive database problem identification and drill down to the actively transacting SQL?

◆ Does the ASP offer automated offline and online reorganization of database data?

◆ Which mechanisms are in place to prevent data loss? In the event of data loss, how is it recovered and how quickly?

◆ Does the ASP have high-performance I/O or caching architectures for optimal database performance?

Performance Monitoring and Management

Enterprise performance monitoring and management is the only way to ensure optimal service levels and customer satisfaction. Before you consider an ASP, be sure to investigate its strategy to ensure its infrastructure matches your company's requirements. When requesting information, ask the following questions:

◆ Does the ASP have management down to the individual device level?

◆ Does the ASP have active and predictive threshold monitoring?

◆ Does the ASP have object performance trending and capacity planning?

◆ Does the ASP have real-time performance analysis for troubleshooting and diagnostics?

◆ Does the ASP have historical data collections for determining operational, environmental, or managed object status or change?

◆ What infrastructure is in place to track and measure service levels and correlate them across all the domains?

- ◆ Does the ASP offer performance reports? If so, how are they delivered to the customer?

- ◆ Does the ASP have an integrated collection and correlation of the information to the operations, trouble ticket system, and help desk?

Business Readiness

You should ask any prospective ASP the following questions relating to business readiness:

- ◆ **Service levels.** What service levels, available support staff, help desks, and problem-resolution mechanisms does the ASP have available? Are they reactive or do they offer predictive capabilities of resolving the issue before it affects the service agreement?

- ◆ **Future growth or reduction.** Does the ASP have a solid strategy and five-year plan to ensure that clients' applications keep up with future technological innovation? Or if a company downsizes, can it adjust as well with minimal impact or cost?

- ◆ **Payment types.** Companies need to fully understand the different ASP types, offerings, and payment methods. Because many companies are unable to incur huge up-front technology costs, they choose ASPs as an alternative. However, those costs might end up being passed on to the clients in the form of overpriced ASP fees or long-term contracts, as well as penalties for early termination.

In addition, you'll want to get a handle on the ASP's capabilities in the areas of project implementation as well as process analysis, change management, and problem resolution.

Project Implementation Management

When selecting an ASP, it is important to identify tools, resources, or practices that assist in an accelerated implementation. Implementation management is the planning and coordination required for deploying the application and infrastructure to meet clients' requirements. Important questions to ask in preparation for implementation are as follows:

- ◆ Who establishes the project acceptance criteria?

◆ Does the ASP perform a requirements impact analysis based on a company's application requirements?

◆ When is the application successfully installed and turned over?

◆ Does the ASP have a project function or organization implemented?

◆ Who performs the implementation design?

◆ Does the ASP have a design or document review?

◆ Does the ASP assume application vendor relationships once the implementation is complete?

Process Analysis, Change Management, and Problem Resolution

Any successful IT operation requires processes and procedures that enable the staff to meet the business and operational objectives while minimizing production risks. Important questions to ask in this area are as follows:

◆ Does the ASP have "best practices" management methods?

◆ How does the ASP introduce change and how often does the ASP permit change in the environment?

◆ In the complex Web delivery architecture, what problem-resolution and escalation practices exist?

◆ Does the ASP perform everything manually, or is there repetitive automation?

◆ Does the ASP require standardization of tasks across all customers?

◆ Does the ASP have standards and practices for application response time, network availability, mean time between failures, mean time to respond to failures, and mean time to restore service?

◆ When and how are upgrades done? How are they triggered?

◆ Does the ASP provide a problem-resolution system, and have documented procedures to log, track, report, and close support incidents?

Pricing ASP Services

Because of the varied services offered by ASPs, it can be difficult for larger companies to perform comparisons; therefore, larger companies are best served by the formal RFP (requests for proposal) and bid processes. For smaller companies, however, assessing ASP cost can be as simple as comparing monthly fees across ASPs. A typical client can pay a fixed monthly amount, normally based on the number of users or, as new technologies permit, on terms such as the number of transactions, click stream, or the amount of usage time. There might also be a one-time setup fee.

In either case, a company needs to be clear on all activities above and beyond those that can incur a fee, such as adds, deletes, or moves. Proper billing management is also required if charge-backs are negotiated based upon service-level expectations. ASPs can offer a variety of payment options, such as these:

◆ Based on transaction volume

◆ Based on concurrent users

◆ Based on a number of users

◆ Based on application time usage

◆ Quality of service guarantees

◆ Rent-to-own

◆ Strategic partnerships

Like any other software contract, companies should always review the fine print. Even if your company implements a standard, it should still consider the likelihood of business process changes over the long run. Change usually equates to additional charges or triggers a new contract and pricing. ASPs typically impose heavy charges for configuration changes after implementation.

Cost should not be the only determining factor in deciding whether to use an ASP. After performing a company's requirements analysis and gathering information about the ASP's reputation, size, liquidity, experience, and existing customer base, review the ASP's key partners and investors. Ask for a customer reference list to determine whether the ASP is meeting other customers' needs. Visit the ASP's data center for a thorough inspection. The goal is to identify an ASP that is viable and meets your company's needs, both current and future.

Companies should also make sure that the ASP has written service levels, performance guarantees, and problem-escalation procedures in place. And if a problem does occur, such as poor response time or downtime, make sure there is remediation or reimbursement for loss of service.

It is important that a company retain the proper skilled resources to identify and select potential Application Service Providers and outsourcers to ensure successful engagement and service-level agreements. Resources can be leveraged from existing staff or temporarily retained consultants until the activity is complete, after which point, mechanisms, measurements, and processes must be in place to monitor and maintain service-level compliance.

Summary

Data is the asset that runs e-business. Without meaningful, available, and responsive data, companies risk the loss of customers or possibly their entire business. It is this dependency on data that has raised the role of the Database Administrator (DBA) from operator to that of a data steward. Different from the days of the "Glass House," the DBA is now an integral part of the business process. Gone are the days of a database operator picking up a phone to call a systems analyst when a flag or an alarm appears on the screen. Today's DBA job role now encompasses much of what used to be performed by the systems analyst, along with some systems and network administration.

Not only has e-business n-Tier architecture changed IT job roles, it has also changed the rules. A typical DBA now works a minimum of 55 hours per week with no rest from an ever-buzzing pager or ringing cell phone. Without the proper support of a backup DBA, tools, staffing, or time off, DBAs quickly tire, becoming a new risk that must be mitigated by an organization. A burned-out DBA sees no clear career path and typically decides to either move to a less stressful role or to look for an employer who is more willing to pay even a greater amount for their time.

As the demand increases for DBAs, so do the openings, as fewer and fewer IT graduates are willing to work the long hours while sacrificing weekends and vacations to being "on call." As such, recruiters quickly dip back into companies they just placed at, further increasing the bounty upon a head. All the while, human resource departments still think that DBAs are merely operators and attempt to attract and hire on compensation packages that clearly indicate to a candidate that this company has yet to enter the 21st century. Those companies that have figured out the importance of the DBA as part of the new business process are the ones who are able to attract, retain, and succeed in business.

Oracle database administration goes far beyond installation and tuning of the database, as the majority of books well cover. But with the DBA getting involved as part of the business process, architecture, and planning, there may be more to do upfront, but in the end there is less chaos and more time away from work. To better prepare those who are up to the new e-business challenges, the chapters in book were organized with information to not only provide IT professionals with information that can be applied for a more challenging and successful career, but also for those companies that are trying to attract and retain them.

This book was intended to guide both beginners and professionals through the course of becoming more familiar with the different areas of the Oracle database and application development. You can use this book as a reference in addition to employing the templates, checklists, and scripts found in the appendixes to help you in your day-to-day activities. So start out tomorrow and make a difference in your Oracle environment with the skills and knowledge you have learned in this book!

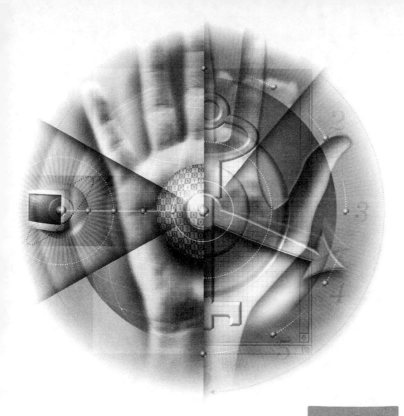

PART IV

Appendices

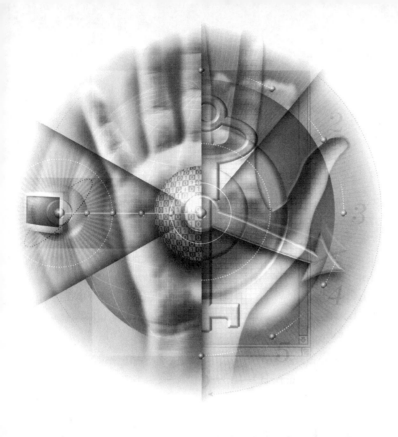

Appendix A

DBA Templates and Checklists

ORACLE

This appendix contains two templates, two checklists, and two quick scripts to aid you in areas during your day-to-day work. The two templates are 1) a sample tool evaluation template that helps in comparing two or more software tools, and 2) a disaster recovery plan template, which can serve as a guideline in writing a plan for recovering from a disaster. The two checklists complement the various options presented when installing Oracle RDBMS and Oracle's Enterprise Manager. The two quick scripts are derived from the checklists used to create the example databases in this book.

Copy these pages or download the templates and checklists off of the Prima Web page at http://www.prima-tech.com/book.asp?ID=4809.

Sample Tool-Evaluation Template

This template can be used over and over again for any tool that you need to evaluate. Simply fill out the appropriate information under each section for a comparison of your software tool(s).

Purpose

The purpose of this template is to effectively and consistently evaluate recognized/recommended database tools—either in-house or commercial—in order to determine whether the tool in question:

- Is available for database maintenance and monitoring
- Can be reused
- Has a vendor-support infrastructure to support 24×7 manufacturing operations
- Is cost effective
- Can be used with current system architectures
- Leverages existing skill expertise with little or no training

Database Tool Overview

This section of your tool-evaluation plan should discuss high-level requirements and include an overview of the desired database tool. This section should also list:

- Database tool name and version
- Database tool description
- Database tool features
- Licensing cost and yearly support fees
- System requirements
- Who developed the database tool (in-house or commercialized database tool)
- Available platforms
- System requirements
- Vendor support quality
- Performance
- Scalability
- Documentation quality
- Target customer
- How long the tool has been in the market (production)
- Number of customers
- Training availability
- Security
- Networking and communication functionality—SQL*Net, and so on
- How easily the tool can be integrated and reused

Reason for Evaluation

This section should explain why this database tool is being evaluated. Ask yourself the following questions:

- Who recommends the evaluation?
- Why is this database tool being considered?
- Is this database tool currently in use?

◆ Is this a shrink-wrapped solution, or does it require creation of a custom database tool?

◆ Can this database tool most likely be reused?

User's Perspective

From the user's point of view (if applicable), evaluate the database tool based on the following categories:

◆ Ease of use

◆ Number of allowed users

◆ Responsiveness

◆ Reliability

◆ Recoverability

◆ Performance

◆ Online help

◆ User skills required for use

◆ Benefits and drawbacks

Administrator's Perspective

From the administrator's point of view, evaluate the database tool based on the following categories:

◆ Reliability in a 24×7 manufacturing environment

◆ Maintainability in a 24×7 manufacturing environment

◆ Configurability

◆ Scalability

◆ Configuration management

◆ Security

◆ Administrative tasks (full/part time)

◆ Maintenance required once established (high/medium/low)

◆ Administrator skills required for use

◆ Benefits and drawbacks

Developer's Perspective

From the developer's point of view, evaluate the database tool based on the following categories:

◆ Openness of technology used

◆ Appropriateness of technology used for given system

◆ Extensibility of the system

◆ Design quality

◆ Developer skills required for integration

◆ Benefits and drawbacks

Features/Functions

In this section, discuss the features and functions being offered in this database tool:

◆ Automation

◆ Ease of use

◆ Portability

◆ User interface

◆ Ease of integrating the tool into existing systems

◆ Networking communication capabilities

Defects and Problems

In this section, reveal any weaknesses of the database tool:

◆ Bugs found while evaluating

◆ Poor documentation or support

◆ Difficulty of use

Recommendations and Conclusion

Provide your conclusions about the database tool:

◆ The strengths

◆ The weaknesses

◆ Alternatives

◆ The functions and features to consider for the new project

◆ The possibility of reuse

◆ Other comments, such as cost

Checklists

Fill in the following two checklists for each of the tools you evaluate. These can be used as a side-by-side comparison.

Comparison Checklist

Tool Champion/Date

Tool Name and Version

Tool Description

Initial Licensing Cost and Yearly Support Fees   _____

Who Developed the Tool (In-House or COTS)   _____

Available Platforms/Platform Evaluated

Minimum System Requirements

Product Type (User, Developer)

How Long It Has Been on the Market (Production) _____

Number of Installed Sites/Company Sites   _____

Training Availability

Comments

Ratings Checklist

	High	Med	Low	N/A
Vendor support quality	[ ]	[ ]	[ ]	[ ]
Comments:				
Vendor support availability	[ ]	[ ]	[ ]	[ ]
Comments:				
Performance of the product under load	[ ]	[ ]	[ ]	[ ]
Comments:				

Quality and abundance of tool features	[ ]	[ ]	[ ]	[ ]
Comments:				
Quality of the documentation	[ ]	[ ]	[ ]	[ ]
Comments:				
Scalability of the production version	[ ]	[ ]	[ ]	[ ]
Comments:				
Security of the product	[ ]	[ ]	[ ]	[ ]
Comments:				
Networking/communication functionality	[ ]	[ ]	[ ]	[ ]
Comments:				
Ease of integration and reuse	[ ]	[ ]	[ ]	[ ]
Comments:				
Availability of the source code	[ ]	[ ]	[ ]	[ ]
Comments:				
Size of required skill set	[ ]	[ ]	[ ]	[ ]
Comments:				
Ease of use and learning curve	[ ]	[ ]	[ ]	[ ]
Comments:				

Disaster Recovery Plan Template

Use this template to create a disaster recovery plan that you store on location. Place a copy of the plan next to the system for which the plan was developed, and another copy in an easily accessed off-site location. This template is only a guide; there are no hard and fast rules about what to put into your plan. Use your common sense and put some time and thought into the plan so that if disaster strikes, you have the upper hand.

NOTE

Note that the *<your_company_name_here>* inserts are inserts that you could globally replace with your company's name. Also note that the entire template is sample text and can be used like it is, or with any number of modifications.

Preface

This is the *<your_company_name_here>* Disaster Recovery Plan.

This plan addresses the main issues necessary for a complete Computer System Disaster Recovery. The *<your_company_name_here>* Business Resumption plan references this plan.

The System Administration Guides and LAN Configuration Guide have more detailed information with regard to rebuilding the *<your_company_name_here>* systems. The Administration guides have detailed instructions so that individuals with fewer technical skills can assist in rebuilding the systems.

The Project/Department Impact Assessment will be further developed by the *<your_company_name_here>* staff to help prioritize business resumption efforts. This step is very important to a thorough plan. Management must be involved in determining issues, such as identifying the most critical parts of the business and how quickly the computing functions must be operational before the business functions are adversely affected.

This plan assumes off-site facilities will be available and that management will determine priorities at the time of disaster recovery. To increase the effectiveness of the Business Resumption Plan, be sure to consider these issues prior to any disaster.

You must consider and document the most critical business functions ahead of time so that the highest priority items can be addressed appropriately.

Disaster Recovery Plan Overview

Scope

These guidelines are set forth to all *<your_company_name_here>* mission-critical applications residing on *<your_company_name_here>* networks, but specifically those in the *<your_company_name_here>* facility.

This Disaster Recovery Plan (DRP) provides the procedures to follow in the event of a disaster situation such as a fire, tornado, or any unanticipated event that makes <*your_company_name_here*>'s computers or networks unusable or compromises the integrity of the hardware, data, or software on the systems for any extended period of time. The purpose of these procedures is to ensure the continuity of <*your_company_name_here*>'s business and engineering operations. This is done by providing access to pertinent data; minimum system configurations with respect to hardware, software, and data; and personnel to restore the critical computing needs in a timely and orderly fashion.

Responsibilities

It is the responsibility of each employee to strive toward prevention of disastrous effects to <*your_company_name_here*>, its employees, and its customers. <*your_company_name_here*> recognizes that family emergencies related to any disaster that affects <*your_company_name_here*> are possible, and will be dealt with properly.

The DRP team is responsible for managing disaster recovery for the plant. Additionally, each department is responsible for completing or contributing to its own DRP.

Risk Prevention

The Disaster Recovery Plan performs two functions. It aids in the recovery of data during a real disaster. It also prevents disasters from happening. Even in the event of a disaster, proper prevention efforts can help minimize the effect of the disaster on <*your_company_name_here*> 's financial assets, customer satisfaction, legal obligations, and corporate image.

Minimizing Adverse Effects Using Risk Assessment

1. Power supply and conditioning
   A. Equipment on the generator and UPS equipment
   B. UPS/Line Monitoring

2. Off-site storage
   A. Meet or exceed <*your_company_name_here*>'s policy on off-site storage of data
   B. Keys to data-storage boxes located in fireproof safe

3. Proper on-site storage

   A. Store interim data in fireproof safe at *<your_company_name_here>* until it can be sent to off-site storage facility

   B. Protect on-site tapes from smoke and water damage: Fireproof safe or plastic waterproof containers

4. On-site storage in fireproof safe

5. Copy of backup procedures and administration guides

6. Documented software/scripts/programs

7. Redundancy of equipment

8. Research fire-fighting methods of data centers

Testing the DRP

1. Have a stand-alone system and perform the following functions:

   A. Install system

   B. Install OS

   C. Install application(s)

   D. Restore data from off-site backups

   E. Create new users/groups

   F. Run applications

   G. Print output if necessary

   H. Back up new configuration on to new backup tapes

2. Possibly use a test system to test the plan.

Cross-Training Personnel

1. Have many personnel cross-trained in their tasks so that, in their absence, the tasks aren't missed.

2. Rotate common or routine duties between administrators, manager, and/or engineers.

3. Have some members of Disaster Recovery Team on your evacuation team and/or trained in fire safety.

Outside Assistance

1. List contractors or *<your_company_name_here>* approved consultant companies to assist in DRP.

2. List software available for all platforms that can assist in Disaster Recovery Planning.

Project/Department Impact Assessment

The Project/Department Impact Assessment details the priorities in the event of different kinds of disasters. These items are specific to *your_dept_name_here's* role in *<your_company_name_here>*'s success with regards to possible or probable impacts to the company's financial status, customer satisfaction, legal or contractual obligations, and image. The *your_dept_name_here* staff is responsible for the Project/Department Impact Assessment documentation.

Disaster Recovery Procedure

Incident Notification

This section details in concise, one-line action statements the various steps that you need to notify of an incident. This process is generally initiated by on-site personnel, managed by the group, and includes problem determination, escalation sequence, communication to management, activation of recovery personnel, and recovery site and communication/coordination with applications and user areas.

This document also lists the names and work, home, and pager phone numbers of all those who might need to participate in the recovery.

In the event of a disaster, the management team is responsible for coordinating and overseeing the high-level management of the disaster and its subsequent recovery. This includes damaged data collection, incident assessment, recovery team activation, disaster declaration, application coordination, and communication within the corporation.

The primary site restoration team, functioning under the direction of the management team, is responsible for performing the initial damage assessment and then restoring the primary site to an operational condition.

The contingency site recovery/operation teams are responsible for recovering and operating the systems and networks at the recovery site(s).

Disaster and Recovery Teams Members

Be sure to list the following team members and their phone or pager numbers:

- ◆ Management team members
- ◆ Site Restoration team members
- ◆ Contingency site recovery/operation team members

Minor Loss

Minor loss is a loss of part or all the computer room, but not your entire company or facility. In the event of a minor loss *<your_company_name_here>*, you need to take the following steps:

1. Locate all available disaster and recovery personnel. Request additional assistance. Ensure safety and well-being of all participants.
2. Determine extent of damage. Determine whether further threat is likely. Determine the correct plan of attack.
3. Secure disaster site.
4. Begin salvage.
5. Contact all interrelated operations about the situation (on a need-to-know basis only) and request necessary assistance. Reference the company *<your_company_name_here>* phone list.
6. Locate the new area.
7. Transport loaned, leased, salvaged, or otherwise available equipment to the new location.
8. Double-check current priorities with available management/leaders.
9. Contact hardware and software vendors and inform them of your needs.
10. Get supplies necessary for initial startup.
11. Get clean power to the new area.
12. Get cable and network hardware to the new area.
13. Retrieve off-site data.
14. Duplicate off-site data and send it off-site.
15. Secure new location(s).
16. Begin hardware installations based on priority.
17. Begin software installations based on priority.

18. Begin application installations based on priority.
19. Begin data restoration based on priority.
20. Update management and project leaders.
21. Establish hotline for users.
22. Ensure network connectivity and security.
23. Reestablish data backups.
24. Reestablish mail.
25. Reestablish printers.
26. Start actions for permanent solutions to all.

Major Loss

Major loss is the loss of most or all of your company or facility. In the event of a major loss, you should take the following steps:

1. Locate all available personnel. Request additional assistance. Ensure safety and well-being of all participants. Identify and notify disaster recovery personnel.
2. Determine extent of damage. Determine whether further threat is likely. Determine the correct plan of attack for correcting the situation.
3. Secure disaster site.
4. Begin salvage.
5. Contact all interrelated operations about the situation (on a need-to-know basis only) and request necessary assistance. Reference the *<your_company_name_here>* company phone list.
6. Locate new facilities.
7. Transport loaned, leased, salvaged, or otherwise available equipment to the new location.
8. Double-check current priorities with available management/leaders.
9. Contact hardware and software vendors and inform them of your needs.
10. Get supplies necessary to initial startup.
11. Get power to new facility.
12. Get cable and network hardware to new facility. Make sure to prioritize according to business impact assessment.

13. Retrieve off-site data.

14. Duplicate off-site data and send it off-site.

15. Secure new location(s).

16. Begin hardware installations based on priority.

17. Begin software installations based on priority.

18. Begin application installations based on priority.

19. Begin data restoration based on priority.

20. Update management and project leaders.

21. Establish hotline for users.

22. Ensure network connectivity and security.

23. Activate off-site work environments.

24. Reestablish data backups.

25. Reestablish mail.

26. Reestablish printers.

27. Start actions for permanent solutions to all.

Recovery Facilities

This section documents the locations, phone numbers, hardware, software, and activation procedures of a prearranged recovery location. The type of recovery approach is usually determined by the importance of the business. This in turn drives the speed of recovery. A relatively lower priority system, with a small network and a recovery requirement of 72 hours or longer, can effectively be recovered by acquiring replacement hardware and relocating to an employee cafeteria or conference room, or even by renting facilities in a hotel or conference center.

For more critical and larger systems, however, you need to set up special arrangements with a hot site services company or establish a reciprocal agreement with another site, in another location. This other site should, of course, have similar equipment and be willing to give it up or share it for a few days in the event of a disaster. The recovery sites should have peer-to-peer network linkage capability. Critical business areas should test their disaster recovery plans yearly.

In some cases, you can establish recovery facilities before a disaster occurs. However, *<your_company_name_here>* planning for a large space can prove to be expensive and inefficient. Therefore, the acquisition process for recovery facilities in large organizations is done after a disaster occurs. The following list represents the issues that you need to resolve after you select a location:

◆ Directions to the recovery site

◆ Important facts/statistics about recovery site, such as maximum number of employees allowed, door size, power, cooling, and so on

◆ Hardware inventory present at recovery site

◆ Software inventory present at recovery site

System Recovery Plans

This section contains all the step-by-step action points and procedures that you need to perform at the recovery site in order to restore the *<your_company_name_here>* systems and their applications. This includes hardware, software, operating system, cabling, and network requirements. The detailed steps used to recover the system and applications as well as operating procedures and documentation are also listed in this section. The most critical applications are recovered first. Document application interdependency. If capacity is constrained, the most critical users can access the system first.

In the event of a disaster, you should ensure the following events occur:

1. Inventory and salvage all systems.
2. Notify support vendors of disaster and obtain needed systems.
3. Begin hardware installations based on priority.
4. Software recovery based on priority.
5. Begin application recovery based on priority.
6. Begin data restoration based on machine and application priority.

LAN Environment Recovery Plans

This section contains all the step-by-step action points and procedures that you need to perform at the recovery site in order to restore the LAN and its applications. This includes hardware, software, operating system, cabling, and network requirements. The detailed steps used to recover the system and applications as well as the operating procedures and documentation are also contained in this section. The most critical applications are usually recovered first. Document application interdependency. If capacity is constrained, the most critical users can access the system first.

LAN recovery specifics need to be documented in the your <*your_company_ name_ here*> LAN Configuration Guide. The following tasks will occur in the event of a disaster:

1. Inventory and salvage all networking equipment.
2. Notify support vendors of disaster.
3. Build LAN topology based on priority.

Cabling

Restore net cabling copper/fiber.

Routers

Restore configuration; establish link to wide area if possible.

Network Hubs

Restore subnets in this order:

1. Subnet 1
2. Subnet 2
3. Subnet 3
4. And so on…

Terminal Servers

Restore terminal servers based on determined priority.

Servers

Restore servers in this order:

1. Backup servers

2. E-mail servers

3. Application server

Workstations

Restore individual workstations based on determined priority .

System Backup/Restore Procedures

The daily, weekly, and monthly backup procedures need to be documented in the *<your_company_name_here>* Administration Guide, in the *<your_company_name_here>* Backup Guide, and the *<your_company_ name_here>* LAN Configuration Guide. Be sure to store your backed-up data at an off-site facility. This section also explains how to restore the backed-up data as well as how to recall the off-site tapes. Remember, any data that is not backed up and stored off-site can be lost forever in the event of a disaster.

All system configuration needs to be referenced in the *<your_company_ name_here>* Administration Guide.

Software Recovery and Installation

This section should be referenced in these guides:

- ◆ *<your_company_name_here>* Administration Guide
- ◆ *<your_company_name_here>* Backup Guide
- ◆ LAN Configuration Guide
- ◆ Workstation Guide
- ◆ System Specifics Guide

This section should contain information such as, but not limited to:

- ◆ OS
- ◆ Backup/restore software
- ◆ Backup scripts
- ◆ Licensing information
- ◆ Scripts

◆ Batch jobs

◆ Mail servers

◆ Security issues

◆ Third-party application software

Software Recovery

In the event of a disaster, data recovery is paramount. However, not only do personnel need to follow restoration procedures; they must also initiate the backup procedures. Specific backup information should be listed in the <*your_company_name_here*>'s Administration Guide, <*your_company_name_here*> Backup Guide, <*your_company_name_here*>'s LAN Configuration Guide, and the <*your_company_name_here*>'s System Specifics Guide.

List the areas the company stores its data. For example, <*your_company_name_here*> stores data in three major locations:

◆ Immediate proximity (tape drives, tape cabinet)

◆ On-site (fireproof safe)

◆ Off-site

Immediate Proximity

In the event of a minor disaster, such as a power failure, which does not physically harm the media containing backup data, the data can be restored from the most immediate source. The tapes used on a daily basis are stored in the tape cabinet. If the tapes in the immediate proximity are available, restoration is more straightforward. For example, if the system goes down or data gets destroyed and these tapes are available, you can restore the system to the previous day's data.

On-Site Storage

You should store data away from the immediate proximity of your Oracle database, perhaps updating it on a weekly basis, to minimize the effect of a localized disaster. Data can be stored in a file cabinet down the hall or in a locked safe on the other side of your building, and still be considered on-site. Data restoration can take place based on the previous week's cycle.

Off-Site Storage

On a bi-weekly basis, the data backed up onto tapes must be sent to an off-site facility for safekeeping. In the event of a major disaster, such as losing the entire site (in which case the immediate proximity and on-site storage are destroyed), it will be necessary to restore data from the off-site location. This unfortunately means that the recovered data might be up to a week old.

Special Forms and Supplies Lists

The lists contained in this section are used to gather any special forms, manuals, and supplies that are kept at off-site locations for transport to the recovery site.

Vendor Lists

This section lists all vendors—hardware, software, network, support services, and so on—that might need to be contacted in the event of a disaster. Document corporate names, addresses, day and night phones, and FAX numbers. Also list names and home phone numbers of sales support and service personnel.

Inventory and Other Required Information

This section contains miscellaneous documentation: detailed hardware, network infrastructure and backbone configurations, inventory lists, and warrantee information. Disaster Recovery Manual update procedures include a list of who has each Disaster Recovery Manual for control and update purposes and a contents/checklist of what is stored off-site and thus has to be relocated in the event of a disaster. A current list of the changes made to the system can be very helpful during the recovery process.

Master Phone Lists

This section lists the business, home, and pager numbers of all personnel who might need to be contacted in the event of a disaster. List police and fire departments, hospitals, airlines, hotels, catering services, and so on. Also included are the phone and fax numbers at the recovery site or alternative operation facilities.

Miscellaneous Supplies Lists

The lists contained in this section are used to gather any special items that might be kept at off-site locations for transport to the recovery site. It should include

- ◆ Disaster Recovery Notebook
- ◆ Tapes: magnetic or optical
- ◆ CD-ROMs
- ◆ Fire safe combination
- ◆ Master phone list
- ◆ Duty pager phone list
- ◆ Copy of licenses

Documentation

Enclosed with this DRP is a floppy disk containing information that will be critical at startup time. Items of interest on the floppy disk include:

1. How to load and read the disk using the `fbackup` command or Acrobat.
2. Locations of other sources for this information and additional copies.
3. Online location of recovery information to aid in the event of a disaster.

Recovery Team/Immediate Contact Listing

The following lists members of the *<your_company_name_here>* Recovery Team, and interrelated operations that need to be contacted immediately about the situation.

The *<your_company_name_here>* department's recovery team includes the following personnel:

- ◆ Management team members
- ◆ Site restoration team members
- ◆ Contingency Site Recovery/Operation team members

A copy of their phone and pager numbers are included in the phone list. A copy is also stored in the fireproof safe.

Vendor Listing and Recovery Commitments

Be sure to list vendors' names, phone numbers, and expected recovery times. The following is an example.

XXX is responsible for disaster recovery of the computers. Current response time is four hours.

> 1-800-*XXX-XXXX*   Access #

Special Forms and Supplies Listing

This listing contains the special forms, manuals, and supplies that are kept off-site for transport to the recovery site in the event of a disaster.

Forms

These forms might include the following: nondisclosure forms, <*your_company_name_here*> account forms, purchase requests, petty cash forms, visitors authorization forms, and property pass forms.

Manuals

Because of the nature of change within a typical company, it is unwise to use a paper-based system to maintain software manuals. Much of the needed information is available online, either through FTP, the Web, or other means.

Restoration Devices/Media

This includes:

◆ Tape drives
◆ Blank tapes to allow for immediate backup procedure resumption
◆ CD-ROM drives to allow for reinstallation of O/S or reading of online documentation

Hardware Tools for Rebuilding Network

This includes modems and SCSI adapters/cables, and other networking hardware tools. Also included in the section might be tools such as wire strippers, network cables, crimpers, and extra connectors or jacks. If the network goes down, it may be time to strip out the old cables and replace them.

Portable Devices

These include:

◆ Laptops

◆ Radios

◆ Cellular phones

Financial Signature Authority

Determine who has the authority to get people in/out or sign for petty cash expenditures.

Off-Site Storage Areas Listing

All backup tapes older than one month are stored off-site. Number of off-site location should be listed. Be prepared to give:

◆ Your name

◆ Account number

◆ Your ID number

Unix backup tapes less than two weeks old are stored on-site in a fireproof safe with a hard copy of the monthly logs. A soft copy of the logs resides on the volume of the *<your_company_name_here>* server entitled UNIX BACKUP LOGS.

Disaster declaration can be made by:

◆ Code 1—Authorization key contacts for *<your_company_name_here>*'s account

◆ Code 2—Authorization includes data retrieval

◆ Code 3—Authorization only includes signing for scheduled service times

Deliveries

Be sure your company has a regularly scheduled pickup and delivery date. However, special deliveries can be requested using the following criteria:

◆ Critical: Within 1 1/2 hours

◆ Emergency: Within 3 hours

◆ Unscheduled: When customer requires a pickup on a day other than their regularly scheduled day

◆ Holiday: 7 days notice required—holiday rates apply

Records

Records of tapes sent off-site are kept and recorded using an Excel spreadsheet, and are located on the *<your_company_name_here>* server.

Emergency and Miscellaneous Phone Listing

This listing is provided in the event of a disaster to allow *<your_company_name_here>* personnel to contact the police, fire departments, hospitals, airlines, hotels, catering services, and so on. The following are areas that need to have readily available and accurate phone numbers:

◆ Emergency contacts

◆ Hospitals

◆ Disaster recovery resources

◆ Vendor contacts

◆ Non-emergency contacts

Oracle8i Enterprise Edition 8.1.6.0.0

The following checklist includes all the possible items or choices that are available when installing an Oracle8i Enterprise 8.1.6.0.0 database.

RDBMS Product Options Installation Checklist

DBA's Name: _____

Date/Time of Installation: _____ _____

Oracle Home: _____

Global Database Name & SID: _____ _____

Oracle SID: _____

[ ] Oracle8i Server

    [ ] Oracle Database Configuration Assistant

    [ ] Oracle Data Migration Assistant

    [ ] Oracle Database Demos

    [ ] Advanced Replication

    [ ] Migration Utility

    [ ] Oracle Intelligent Agent

        [ ] Paging Service Agent Extensions

    [ ] Oracle Partitioning

    [ ] Generic Connectivity Using ODBC

    [ ] Generic Connectivity Using OLEDB

[ ] Oracle Products Options

    [ ] Oracle Time Series

        [ ] Oracle Database Configuration Assistant

        [ ] Oracle Data Migration Assistant

        [ ] Oracle Database Demos

        [ ] Advanced Replication

        [ ] Migration Utility

        [ ] Oracle Intelligent Agent

            [ ] Paging Service Agent Extensions

        [ ] Oracle Partitioning

[ ] Generic Connectivity Using ODBC

[ ] Generic Connectivity Using OLEDB

[ ] Oracle Visual Information Retrieval

    [ ] Oracle Database Configuration Assistant

    [ ] Oracle Data Migration Assistant

    [ ] Oracle Database Demos

    [ ] Advanced Replication

    [ ] Migration Utility

    [ ] Oracle Intelligent Agent

        [ ] Paging Service Agent Extensions

    [ ] Oracle Partitioning

    [ ] Generic Connectivity Using ODBC

    [ ] Generic Connectivity Using OLEDB

[ ] Oracle Spatial

    [ ] Oracle Database Configuration Assistant

    [ ] Oracle Data Migration Assistant

    [ ] Oracle Database Demos

    [ ] Advanced Replication

    [ ] Migration Utility

    [ ] Oracle Intelligent Agent

        [ ] Paging Service Agent Extensions

    [ ] Oracle Partitioning

    [ ] Generic Connectivity Using ODBC

    [ ] Generic Connectivity Using OLEDB

[ ] Oracle COM Automation Feature

    [ ] Oracle Database Configuration Assistant

    [ ] Oracle Data Migration Assistant

[   ] Oracle Database Demos

[   ] Advanced Replication

[   ] Migration Utility

[   ] Oracle Intelligent Agent

    [   ] Paging Service Agent Extensions

[   ] Oracle Partitioning

[   ] Generic Connectivity Using ODBC

[   ] Generic Connectivity Using OLEDB

[   ] Oracle Advanced Security

[   ] Oracle interMedia

    [   ] Oracle Database Configuration Assistant

    [   ] Oracle Data Migration Assistant

    [   ] Oracle Database Demos

    [   ] Advanced Replication

    [   ] Migration Utility

    [   ] Oracle Intelligent Agent

        [   ] Paging Service Agent Extensions

    [   ] Oracle Partitioning

    [   ] Generic Connectivity Using ODBC

    [   ] Generic Connectivity Using OLEDB

[   ] Net8 Products

    [   ] Net8 Client

    [   ] Net8 Server

    [   ] Oracle Names

    [   ] Oracle Connection Manager

    [   ] Oracle SNMP Agent

    [   ] Oracle Protocol Support

[ ] Oracle Utilities

    [ ] Oracle Performance

    [ ] Oracle Database Utilities

    [ ] SQL*Plus

[ ] Oracle Java Products

    [ ] Oracle JDBC Drivers

        [ ] Oracle JDBC/OCI Driver fro JDK 1.1

        [ ] Oracle JDBC/OCI Driver fro JDK 1.2

        [ ] Oracle JDBC Thin Driver fro JDK 1.1

        [ ] Oracle JDBC Thin Driver fro JDK 1.2

    [ ] Oracle SQLJ

    [ ] Oracle Java Tools

[ ] Oracle Enterprise Manager Products

    [ ] Oracle Intelligent Agent

        [ ] Paging Service Agent Extensions

    [ ] Oracle Management Server

        [ ] Oracle Applications Manager Server Extensions

        [ ] Oracle Enterprise Manager Migration Assistant

    [ ] Oracle Enterprise Manager Client

        [ ] Oracle Enterprise Manager Integrated Applications

            [ ] Oracle interMedia Text Manager

            [ ] Oracle Enterprise Security Manager

            [ ] Oracle Developer Server Forms Manager

            [ ] Net8 Integration

            [ ] Oracle Application Server Manager

            [ ] Oracle Parallel Server Manager

            [ ] Oracle Replication Manager

[ ] Oracle Spatial Index Advisor

[ ] Oracle Directory Manager

[ ] Oracle Applications Manager

[ ] Oracle Enterprise Manager Migration Assistant

[ ] Oracle DBA Management Pack

    [ ] Oracle Schema Manager

    [ ] Oracle Storage Manager

    [ ] Oracle Security Manager

    [ ] Oracle Instance Manager

    [ ] SQL*Plus Worksheet

    [ ] Oracle DBA Studio

[ ] Oracle Enterprise Manager Web Site

    [ ] Oracle Application Server Listener

[ ] Oracle Enterprise Manager Quick Tours

[ ] Oracle Configuration Assistants

    [ ] Oracle Data Migration Assistant

    [ ] Oracle Database Configuration Assistant

    [ ] Oracle Web Publishing Assistant

[ ] Development Tools

    [ ] Oracle Call Interface

    [ ] Object Type Translator

    [ ] Oracle Objects for OLE

    [ ] Oracle ODBC Driver

    [ ] Oracle Provider for OLE DB

[ ] Oracle Installation Products

    [ ] Oracle Universal Installer

[ ] Oracle Migration Workbench

>   [ ] Oracle JDBC/OCI Driver fro JDK 1.1

>   [ ] Oracle JDBC/OCI Driver fro JDK 1.2

>   [ ] Oracle JDBC Thin Driver fro JDK 1.1

>   [ ] Oracle JDBC Thin Driver fro JDK 1.2

>   [ ] MS Access Plug-in

>   [ ] MS SQL Server 6.5 Plug-in

>   [ ] MS SQL Server 7.0 Plug-in

>   [ ] Sybase Adaptive Server 11 Plug-in

>   [ ] Oracle ODBC Driver

[ ] Oracle Services for Microsoft Transaction Server

[ ] Oracle Administration Assistant for Windows NT

Oracle8i Enterprise Manager 2.1.0.0.0

The following checklist includes all the possible items or choices that are available when installing the Oracle8i Enterprise Manager 2.1.0.0.0 database toolkit.

Product Options Installation Checklist

DBA's Name: _____

Date/Time of Installation: _____   _____

Oracle Home: _____

Global Database Name & SID: _____   _____

Oracle SID: _____

[ ] Oracle Enterprise Manager Packs and Management Infrastructure 2.1.0.0.0

Required

>   [ ] Oracle Management Server

>   >   [ ] Oracle Applications Manager Server Extensions

>   >   [ ] Oracle Enterprise Manager Migration Assistant

[ ] Oracle Enterprise Manager Web Site

    [ ] Oracle Application Server Listener

[ ] Oracle Enterprise Manager Quick Tours

[ ] Oracle Diagnostics Pack

    [ ] SQL Server Monitoring Option

[ ] Oracle Tuning Pack

[ ] Oracle Change Management Pack

[ ] Oracle Universal Installer

Optional

[ ] Oracle Enterprise Manager Integrated Applications

    [ ] Oracle interMedia Text Manager

    [ ] Oracle Enterprise Security Manager

    [ ] Oracle Developer Server Forms Manager

    [ ] Net8 Integration

    [ ] Oracle Application Server Manager

    [ ] Oracle Parallel Server Manager

    [ ] Oracle Replication Manager

    [ ] Oracle Spatial Index Manager

    [ ] Oracle Directory Manager

    [ ] Oracle Applications Manager

[ ] Oracle Enterprise Manager Migration Assistant

[ ] Oracle DBA Management Pack

    [ ] Oracle Schema Manager

    [ ] Oracle Storage Manager

    [ ] Oracle Security Manager

    [ ] Oracle Instance Manager

    [ ] SQL*Plus Worksheet

    [ ] Oracle DBA Studio

Quick Scripts

The following two quick scripts are good starting points that you can print and modify for documentation purposes. The quick scripts include detailed installation steps that were used to make the example databases for this book. These scripts include details and options about the databases for this book. You might not choose the same options.

The quick scripts include:

◆ Installing Oracle8i on Windows NT/2000

◆ Installing Oracle8i on Sun Solaris (Unix platform)

Installing Oracle8i on Windows NT/2000

The following quick script was used by the authors to create an Oracle8i database on the Windows NT/2000 platform.

Installation Items

1. Run the installer on the CD.

2. Choose D:\ORA8_HOME for Oracle Home.

3. Choose Oracle8i Enterprise Edition.

4. Choose Custom.

5. Choose the following for the installation:

   A. Oracle8i Server—keep all checked

   B. Oracle Product Options—check Spatial & Time Series

   C. Net8 Options—keep all checked (default)

   D. Oracle Utilities—keep all checked (default)

   E. Oracle Configuration Options—check DB Assistant but not Migration Assistant

   F. Development Tools—uncheck all

   G. Java Products—uncheck all

   H. Oracle Enterprise Manager Client—check all

   I. Oracle Enterprise Manger Web Client—uncheck all

   J. Oracle Quick Tours—check all

K. Oracle Installation Products—check all

L. Solaris Documentation—check all

6. Component Locations—take the defaults.

7. Management Server Repository—set to Require a New Repository.

8. Create Database—Set to Yes—use the tool (make this the default).

9. Database Identification:

A. Global Database Name: COLBYDB.world

B. SID: COLBYDB

10. Oracle Protocol Support—select Next.

11. Summary—press Install, sit back, relax, and wait.

Net8 Configuration

1. Configure manually.

2. Select No for Directory Service.

3. Take the defaults for Listener.

4. Select No for Named Configurations.

Database Configuration Assistance

1. Set concurrent users to 20.

2. Set to Shared Server Mode (can set later to undo MTS).

3. Options: Select SQL*Plus Help only.

4. Database Info—take the defaults.

5. Control files:

A. C:\oradata\COLBYDB\control01.ctl

B. D:\oradata\COLBYDB\control02.ctl

C. D:\oradata\COLBYDB\control03.ctl

6. Tablespaces:

A. SYSTEM, 100MB, C:\oradata\COLBYDB\system01.dbf—take defaults

B. TOOLS, 15 MB, D:\oradata\COLBYDB\tools01.dbf—take defaults

C. USERS, 20MB, C:\oradata\COLBYDB\users01.dbf—take defaults

    D. RBS, 100MB, D:\oradata\COLBYDB\rbs01.dbf—take defaults and check unlimited

    E. COLBY_INDEX, 60MB, C:\oradata\COLBYDB\indx01.dbf—take defaults

    F. TEMP, 100MB, D:\oradata\COLBYDB\temp01.dbf—take defaults

7. Redo Logs:

    A. C:\oradata\COLBYDB\redo01.ctl

    B. D:\oradata\COLBYDB\redo02.ctl

    C. D:\oradata\COLBYDB\redo03.ctl

8. Logging Information—take defaults.

9. SGA Parameters—take defaults except set Processes to 200.

10. Trace File Directory—left default on C:\.

11. Create the database!

    A. When it's done, the message should say:

       i. Global DB Name: COLBYDB.world

       ii. SID: COLBYDB

       iii. SYS/change_on_install

       iv. SYSTEM/manager

Repository Manager

1. Log in as system/manager COLBYDB.world.

2. Repository Information. Create user: COLBYDBRepUsr password: xxxxxxxxxx.

3. Create New OEM_Repository tablespace.

4. Summary: finish.

Finished

Installation finished. Save this printout for future documentation.

Installing Oracle8i on Sun Solaris (Unix Platform)

The following quick script was used by the authors to create an Oracle8i database on the Sun Solaris (Unix) platform.

Preinstallation Items

1. Create the oinstall group.
2. Create the Oracle account and the COLBYDBA account.
3. Make the two accounts: Primary GUI = oinstall group and the Secondary GUI = dba.
4. Give permission to both accounts read/write.

    A. To check this, type `umask`

    B. If 022 is returned, great, if not, set umask to 022 for Oracle and COLBYDBA

5. Set environment variables:

    A. DISPLAY (set to DISPLAY=:0.0)

    B. PATH (/bin:/usr/bin:/usr/ucb:/etc:/disk1/ora8_home/bin)

    C. ORACLE_HOME (/disk1/ora8_home)

    D. ORACLE_SID (COLBYDB)

    E. And others (look in manual—but these are optional and worked without them)

6. Put the following variables in the /etc/system file:

    A. Set shmsys:shminfo_shmmax=4294967295

    B. Set shmsys:shminfo_shmiseg=10

    C. Set shmsys:shminfo_shmmni=100

    D. Set shmsys:shminfo_shmmin=1

    E. Set shmsys:shminfo_semmns=200

    F. Set shmsys:shminfo_semmni=100

    G. Set shmsys:shminfo_semmsl=100

    H. Set shmsys:shminfo_semopm=100

    I. Set shmsys:shminfo_semvmx=32767

    These variables are in the documentation and can be cut/pasted from there.

7. Reboot the system for these SGA variables to take effect (#init 0, and then >ok boot).

Installation Items

1. Run the installer on the CD.
2. Choose /disk1/ora8_home for Oracle home.
3. Choose Oracle8i Enterprise Edition.
4. Choose Custom.
5. Choose the following for the installation:

   A. Oracle8i Server—keep all checked

   B. Oracle Product Options—uncheck all

   C. Net8 Options—keep all checked (default)

   D. Oracle Utilities—keep all checked (default)

   E. Oracle Configuration Options—check DB Assistant—not Migration Assistant

   F. Development Tools—uncheck all

   G. Java Products—uncheck all

   H. Oracle Enterprise Manager Client—check all

   I. Oracle Enterprise Manger Web Client—uncheck all

   J. Oracle Quick Tours—check all

   K. Oracle Installation Products—check all

   L. Solaris Documentation—check all

6. Component Locations—take the defaults.
7. Privileged Operation Systems Groups: Set both to oinstall (make this the default).
8. Management Server Repository—set to Require a New Repository.
9. Create Database—set to Yes—use the tool (make this the default).
10. Database identification:

    A. Global Database Name: COLBYDB.world

    B. SID: COLBYDB

11. Database File Location—set directory to /disk2.
12. Oracle Protocol Support—go to Next.
13. Summary—press Install, sit back, relax, and wait.

Net8 Configuration

1. Configure manually.
2. Select No for Directory Service.
3. Take the defaults for Listener.
4. Select No for Named Configurations.

Database Configuration Assistance

1. Set concurrent users to 20.
2. Set to Dedicated Server Mode (can set to MTS later).
3. Options: Select SQL*Plus Help only.
4. Database Info—take the defaults.
5. Control files:

    A. disk1/oradata/COLBYDB/COLBYcontrol01.ctl

    B. disk2/oradata/COLBYDB/COLBYcontrol02.ctl

    C. disk3/oradata/COLBYDB/COLBYcontrol03.ctl

6. Tablespaces:

    A. SYSTEM, 100MB, disk2/oradata/COLBYDB/system01.dbf—
    take defaults

    B. TOOLS, 15 MB, disk3/oradata/COLBYDB/tools01.dbf—
    take defaults

    C. USERS, 40MB, disk2/oradata/COLBYDB/users01.dbf—
    take defaults

    D. RBS, 100MB, disk3/oradata/COLBYDB/rbs01.dbf—
    take defaults and check unlimited

    E. COLBY_INDEX, 60MB, disk2/oradata/COLBYDB/COLBY_
    index01.dbf—take defaults

    F. TEMP, 100MB, disk3/oradata/COLBYDB/temp01.dbf—
    take defaults

7. Redo logs:

    A. disk1/oradata/COLBYDB/COLBYredo01.ctl

    B. disk2/oradata/COLBYDB/COLBYredo02.ctl

    C. disk3/oradata/COLBYDB/COLBYredo03.ctl

8. Logging Information—take defaults.

9. SGA Parameters—take defaults (left Processes at 50; 200 caused memory problems).

10. Trace File Directory—left it to default on disk1.

11. Create the database.

    A. When it's done, the message should say:

       i.   Global DB Name: COLBYDB.world

       ii. SID: COLBYDB

       iii. SYS/change_on_install

       iv. SYSTEM/manager

Repository Manger

1. Log in as system/manager COLBYDB.world.

2. Repository Information. Create user: COLBYDBRepUsr password: xxxxxxxxxxx.

3. Create New OEM_Repository tablespace.

4. Summary: finish.

Finished

Installation finished. Save this printout for future documentation.

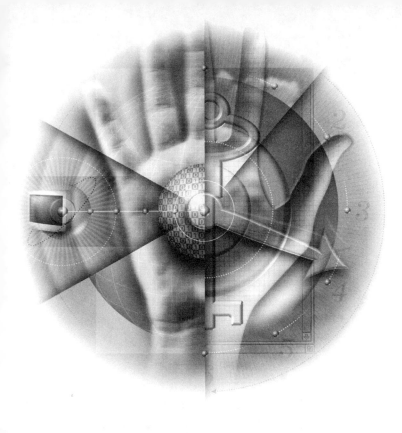

Appendix B

**Usage,
Performance,
and Other
Oracle Scripts**

This appendix is divided into different scripts that can be used to measure or report on various areas within your database. These scripts are categorized into various areas, thus making it easier to find scripts for the task you need to accomplish.

This appendix lists the title of the script with a definition and then shows the script itself. Look through the topic headings and familiarize yourself with them. Try some of the scripts and see whether they make some of your day-to-day tasks a bit easier.

 NOTE

Some of these scripts are duplicated from other chapters in the book. They are reproduced here for convenience's sake. You can also find these at http://www.prima-tech.com/book.asp?ID=4809.

Database System/Object Scripts

The following categories of scripts deal primarily with the system itself and the objects within the system.

Control Files, Datafiles, and Redo Logs

The following script dumps the control files, datafiles, and redo logs of your Oracle database.

Script

```
set pagesize 80
set heading off
set feedback off
set verify off
column file_name format a40
```

```
column bytes format 999,999,999,999
set echo off
select 'Physical information for database : ', name from v$database
/
set heading on
break on report on tablespace_name
compute sum of bytes on report
select 'online redo log group number :' tablespace_name, b.group#
    file_id, b.member file_name, a.bytes
from v$log a, v$logfile b where a.group# = b.group#
union
select 'controlfile number : ' tablespace_name, rownum file_id, name
    file_name, 1048576
from v$controlfile
union
select tablespace_name, file_id, file_name, bytes from dba_data_files
order by tablespace_name
/
```

All Object Types in Database

This script provides you with a listing of all the object types in the database, ordered by user name.

Script

```
SELECT username,
        COUNT(DECODE(o.type#, 2, o.obj#, '')) Table_count,
        COUNT(DECODE(o.type#, 4, o.obj#, '')) View_count,
        COUNT(DECODE(o.type#, 8, o.obj#, '')) Funct_count,
        COUNT(DECODE(o.type#,12, o.obj#, '')) Trigr,
        COUNT(DECODE(o.type#, 5, o.obj#, '')) Synmn,
        COUNT(DECODE(o.type#, 1, o.obj#, '')) Index_count,
        COUNT(DECODE(o.type#, 6, o.obj#, '')) Seque,
        COUNT(DECODE(o.type#, 7, o.obj#, '')) Procd,
        COUNT(DECODE(o.type#, 9, o.obj#, '')) Packg
FROM sys.obj$ o, sys.dba_users U
```

```
WHERE u.user_id = o.owner# (+)
GROUP BY username
/
```

DB Links

This simple script shows the DB links in the database.

Script

```
select * from sys.dba_db_links
/
```

Profiles

This simple script lists the profiles in the database.

Script

```
Select * from sys.dba_profiles
/
```

Roles

This simple script lists the roles in the database.

Script

```
Select * from sys.dba_roles
/
```

Functions

This script shows the current functions in the database.

Script

```
select * from dba_objects where object_type = 'FUNCTION'
/
```

Triggers

This script shows the current triggers in the database.

Script

```
select * from dba_objects where object_type = 'TRIGGER'
/
```

Stored Procedures

This script shows the stored procedures in the database. Be sure to replace XXX with the owner of the database in question.

Script

```
select owner, object_name, created, last_ddl_time, timestamp from
    dba_objects
where object_type = 'PROCEDURE'
and owner like XXX
/
```

Sequences

This script determines the number and types of sequences on the system.

Script

```
select * from dba_objects where object_type = 'SEQUENCE'
/
```

Database Storage Scripts

The next set of scripts is grouped together because they all pertain to the database storage for Oracle.

Tablespace Usage and Percentage of Free Space

This script shows the percentage of free space in the tablespaces. They are listed in order of the amount of free space left in the tablespaces.

Script

```
set pagesize 60
set line 130
clear breaks
clear computes
column "Total Bytes" format 9,999,999,999
column "Bytes Free" format 9,999,999,999
column "% Free" format 999.99
ttitle left "*******   Database:  "dbname", Current Tablespace
    Usage ( As of: "xdate" )    *******" skip 1
select  substr(fs.FILE_ID,1,3) "ID#", fs.tablespace_name,
          df.bytes "Total Bytes", sum(fs.bytes) "Bytes Free",
          (100*((sum(fs.bytes))/df.bytes)) "% Free"
from sys.dba_data_files df, sys.dba_free_space fs
where df.file_id(+) = fs.file_id
group by fs.FILE_ID, fs.tablespace_name, df.bytes
order by "% Free"
/
title off
```

Next Possible Extent Failures

This script detects possible extent failures. These possible extent failures include cases in which the next chunk of memory is smaller than the next allocated extent. If these extents try to grab the next chunk of memory, Oracle will automatically resize the tablespace (whether or not you have disk space available), assuming that the automatic tablespace grow feature is on. If this is the case, Oracle produces an error complaining about trying to extend a tablespace with no available memory.

Script

```
select
substr(sg.tablespace_name,1,30) Tablespace,
substr(sg.segment_name,1,30) Object,
sg.extents extents,
sg.next_extent next,
max(sp.bytes) available
from dba_free_space sp, dba_segments sg
```

```
where sp.tablespace_name = sg.tablespace_name
having max(sp.bytes) < sg.next_extent
group by sg.tablespace_name,
sg.segment_name,sg.extents,sg.next_extent
order by 1,2
/
```

Table Fragmentation Script

The following script lists the all tables in the database that are in need of frag-mentation correction (with the exception of the tables owned by SYS).

Script

```
select substr(de.owner,1,8) "Owner", substr(de.segment_type,1,8)
"Seg Type",
          substr(de.segment_name,1,35) "Table Name (Segment)",
          substr(de.tablespace_name,1,20) "Tablespace Name",
          count(*) "Frag NEED", substr(df.name,1,40) "DataFile
Name"
from sys.dba_extents de, v$datafile df
where de.owner <> 'SYS' and de.file_id = df.file# and
de.segment_type = 'TABLE'
group by de.owner, de.segment_name, de.segment_type, de.table-
space_name, df.name
having count(*) > 1
order by count(*) desc
/
```

Database Performance Scripts

The following section of scripts is meant to help you with performance issues. These scripts are often classified as tuning scripts.

Most Active Stored Procedures

This script lists the most active stored procedures or functions running when the script is run. This script lists, by decreasing number of times they were reloaded, the stored procedures and packages that are most frequently moved in and out of memory, because these actions can lead to shared pool fragmentation. The goal is to keep the big objects in memory.

Script

```
REM Most Active Stored Procedures run during the day
column name format A50
column K format 9990
set numwidth 8
select c.owner || '.' || c.name name, round(c.sharable_mem / 1024) K,
          c.loads, c.executions, c.kept
from v$db_object_cache c, sys.obj$ o, sys.user$ u
where u.name = c.owner and u.user# = o.owner#
          and o.name = c.name and o.type# in (7, 8, 9) and c.loads > 1
order by 3 desc
/
```

Faster Needed Indexes

The following script searches for the tables and columns that need indexes to improve performance.

Script

```
COL table_name format A20 head 'TABLE_NAME'
COL constraint_name format A20 head 'CONSTRAINT_NAME'
COL table2 format A20 head 'TABLE_TO_BE_INDEXED'
COL column_name format A20 head 'COLUMN_TO_BE_INDEXED'
SET linesize 100
SELECT t.table_name,c.constraint_name,c.table_name table2
          ,acc.column_name
FROM all_constraints t, all_constraints c
          , all_cons_columns acc
WHERE c.r_constraint_name = t.constraint_name
  AND c.table_name =acc.table_name
  AND c.constraint_name = acc.constraint_name
  AND NOT EXISTS ( SELECT '1' FROM all_ind_columns aid
```

```
WHERE aid.table_name = acc.table_name
  AND aid.column_name = acc.column_name)
ORDER BY t.table_name, c.constraint_name
/
```

DB Buffer Ratio

The DB buffer ratio is one of the more important ratios for determining performance. The Init.Ora parameter DB_BLOCK_BUFFERS controls the amount of memory allocated for the data cache. When an application requests data, Oracle first attempts to find it in the data cache. When Oracle finds the requested data in memory, a physical I/O does not have to take place. This improves overall performance. Under normal circumstances, this ratio should be greater than or equal to 95 percent. Set the DB_BLOCK_BUFFERS size initially to be 20–50 percent of the size of the SGA.

Script

```
select round((1-(pr.value/(bg.value+cg.value)))*100,2) "Buffer
Cache Hit"
from v$sysstat pr, v$sysstat bg, v$sysstat cg
where pr.name = 'physical reads' and bg.name = 'db block gets' and
cg.name = 'consistent gets'
/
```

Dictionary Cache Efficiency

The Init.Ora parameter SHARED_POOL_SIZE controls the amount of memory allocated for the shared buffer pool. The shared buffer pool contains SQL and PL/SQL statements that are located in the library and data dictionary caches. They provide information on database sessions. This percentage will never equal 100 percent because the cache must perform an initial load when Oracle boots up. The percentage, however, should continually get closer to 100 percent as the system remains on.

Initially set the SHARED_POOL_SIZE to be 50–100 percent the size of the Init.Ora parameter DB_BLOCK_BUFFERS and then fine-tune the parameter to get it closer to 100 percent.

Script

```
select round(sum(gets)/(sum(gets)+sum(getmisses)) * 100,2) from
v$rowcache
/
```

Library Cache Efficiency

This script results in the percentage of a SQL statement that does not need to be reloaded because it was already in the library cache. For maximum efficiency, no SQL statement should be reloaded and reparsed.

Script

```
select round(sum(pinhits)/sum(pins) * 100,2) from v$librarycache
/
```

Sort Area Efficiency

This script results in the percentage of sorts performed in memory as opposed to sorts performed in temporary segments on a system's disk. This is of course will lead to better performance by utilizing the system's fast memory as opposed to the slow disk access. This too, should be greater than 95 percent if possible.

Script

```
select round((sum(decode(name, 'sorts (memory)', value, 0))
         / (sum(decode(name, 'sorts (memory)', value, 0))
         + sum(decode(name, 'sorts (disk)', value, 0)))) * 100,2)
from v$sysstat
/
```

Useless Database Indexes

The following query lists the indexes within your database that are most likely useless. As a rule of thumb, an ordinary (as opposed to a bitmap) index is useless (meaning the index access is slower than the table scan) if a key value returns more than 12 to 15 percent of the rows. The bigger the table, the smaller the percentage should be.

Script

```
column "TABLE" format A35
column "USEFUL INDEX?" format A25
break on "TABLE" on "ROWS"
select u.name || '.' || ot.name "TABLE", t.rowcnt "ROWS",
        oi.name "USEFUL INDEX?", i.distkey "KEYS"
from sys.user$ u, sys.tab$ t, sys.obj$ ot, sys.ind$ i, sys.obj$ oi
where ot.owner# = u.user# and i.bo# = ot.obj#
        and nvl(t.rowcnt, 0) > 100 and i.bo# = t.obj#
        and i.distkey < 7 and oi.obj# = i.obj# and oi.owner# != 0
order by 1
/
```

Cached Tables

This script lists all tables that are currently cached.

Script

```
SELECT owner, table_name, cache
FROM all_tables
WHERE owner not in ('SYS', 'SYSTEM') AND cache not like '%N%'
```

Coalesced Tablespace(s)

The following query shows the number of extents in each tablespace that have been coalesced.

Script

```
SELECT tablespace_name, total_extents, extents_coalesced,
    percent_extents_coalesced
FROM dba_free_space_coalesced
/
```

Invalid Objects Script

This script displays all the objects in the database that are currently invalid or ones that, if called upon to perform or be used, would produce an error.

Script

```
column invalid_object format A30
column likely_reason format A35 word_wrapped
set recsep off
break on type on invalid_object
select owner || '.' || object_name invalid_object, '-- ' ||
    object_type || ' --' likely_reason
from dba_objects where status = 'INVALID'
union
select d.owner || '.' || d.name, 'Non-existent referenced db link
    ' || d.referenced_link_name
from dba_dependencies d
where not exists (select 'x' from dba_db_links where owner in
    ('PUBLIC', d.owner)
        and db_link = d.referenced_link_name)
        and d.referenced_link_name is not null
        and (d.owner, d.name, d.type) in (select owner, object_name,
    object_type
        from dba_objects where status = 'INVALID')
union
select d.owner || '.' || d.name, 'Depends on invalid ' || d.referenced_type || ' '
        || d.referenced_owner || '.' || d.referenced_name
from dba_objects ro, dba_dependencies d
where ro.status = 'INVALID' and ro.owner = d.referenced_owner
        and ro.object_name = d.referenced_name and
    ro.object_type = d.referenced_type
        and d.referenced_link_name is null
        and (d.owner, d.name, d.type) in (select owner,
    object_name, object_type
        from dba_objects where status = 'INVALID')
union
select d.owner || '.' || d.name, 'Depends on newer ' ||
    d.referenced_type || ' '
        || d.referenced_owner || '.' || d.referenced_name
from dba_objects ro, dba_dependencies d, dba_objects o
where nvl(ro.last_ddl_time, ro.created) > nvl(o.last_ddl_time, o.created)
```

```
                and ro.owner = d.referenced_owner and ro.object_name =
        d.referenced_name
                and ro.object_type = d.referenced_type and
        d.referenced_link_name is null
                and d.owner = o.owner and d.name = o.object_name
                and d.type = o.object_type and o.status = 'INVALID'
union
select d.owner || '.' || d.name, 'Depends on ' || d.referenced_type || ' '
                || d.referenced_owner || '.' || d.referenced_name
                || decode(d.referenced_link_name, NULL, '', '@' ||
        d.referenced_link_name)
from dba_dependencies d
where d.referenced_owner != 'PUBLIC'  — Public synonyms generate noise
                and d.referenced_type = 'NON-EXISTENT'
                and (d.owner, d.name, d.type) in (select owner, object_name,
        object_type
                from dba_objects where status = 'INVALID')
union
select d.owner || '.' || d.name invalid_object,
                'No privilege on referenced ' || d.referenced_type || ' '
                || d.referenced_owner || '.' || d.referenced_name
from dba_objects ro, dba_dependencies d
where not exists (select 'x' from dba_tab_privs p
                where p.owner = d.referenced_owner
                and p.table_name = d.referenced_name
                and p.grantee in ('PUBLIC', d.owner))
                and ro.status = 'VALID' and ro.owner = d.referenced_owner
                and ro.object_name = d.referenced_name
                and d.referenced_link_name is not null
                and (d.owner, d.name, d.type) in (select owner, object_name,
        object_type
                from dba_objects where status = 'INVALID')
union
select o.owner || '.' || o.object_name, e.text from dba_errors e, dba_objects o
where e.text like 'PLS-%' and e.owner = o.owner
                and e.name = o.object_name and e.type = o.object_type
                and o.status = 'INVALID'
/
```

Most Reloaded Stored Procedures in Shared Pool

This script lists, by decreasing number of times they were reloaded, the stored procedures and packages that are most moved in and out of memory. This can lead to shared pool fragmentation. The larger objects should be kept in memory.

Script

```
column name format A50
column name format A50
column K format 9990
set numwidth 8
select c.owner || '.' || c.name name, round(c.sharable_mem / 1024) K,
          c.loads, c.executions, c.kept
from v$db_object_cache c, sys.obj$ o, sys.user$ u
where u.name = c.owner and u.user# = o.owner#
          and o.name = c.name and o.type# in (7, 8, 9) and c.loads > 1
order by 3 desc
/
```

Database Usage Scripts

The following scripts inform you how your database is being used, how much space is available, and who is using the database.

Number of Users in Database

The following script determines the maximum number of unique users that have access to the production system.

Script

```
select count(*) from dba_users where default_tablespace = 'USERS'
order by username
/
```

Table Records

The following script lists the number of records in each table. Substitute your table name for XXX in the following script.

Script

```
Select Table_Name, Num_Rows
From All_Tables
Where Owner = XXX
order by Num_Rows
/
```

Dirty Queue Length

This script lists the dirty queue length, or how much data is queued up and ready to be committed. The longer the queue length, the more trouble the database writer DBWR has keeping up with its writing.

Script

```
set pagesize 66
column   "Write Request Length" format 999,999.99
select sum( decode (name, 'summed dirty queue length', value)) /
          sum( decode (name, 'write requests', value)) "Write Request Length"
from v$sysstat where name in ( 'Summed dirty queue length', 'write
requests') and value > 0
/
```

Foreign Key Usage

This script provides information on foreign key usage. The first script lists the foreign keys. The second script lists foreign keys that have missing indexes on the foreign key columns in the child table. If the index is not in place, share lock problems can occur on the parent table.

Scripts

```
ttitle 'All Foreign Keys'
SELECT a.owner , a.table_name , c.column_name , b.owner ,
   b.table_name , d.column_name
FROM dba_constraints a, dba_constraints b, dba_cons_columns c,
   dba_cons_columns d
WHERE a.r_constraint_name = b.constraint_name AND   a.constraint_type = 'R'
        AND b.constraint_type = 'P' AND a.r_owner=b.owner
```

```
                    AND a.constraint_name = c.constraint_name
                    AND b.constraint_name=d.constraint_name
                    AND a.owner = c.owner AND a.table_name=c.table_name
                    AND b.owner = d.owner AND b.table_name=d.table_name
/

ttitle 'Foreign Keys with Indexes Missing on Child Tables'
SELECT acc.owner||'-> '||acc.constraint_name||'('||acc.column_name ||'['||
    acc.position||'])'||' ***** Missing Index'
FROM   all_cons_columns acc, all_constraints ac
WHERE   ac.constraint_name = acc.constraint_name AND ac.constraint_type = 'R'
            AND   (acc.owner, acc.table_name, acc.column_name, acc.position)
            IN (SELECT acc.owner, acc.table_name, acc.column_name, acc.position
            FROM all_cons_columns acc, all_constraints ac
            WHERE ac.constraint_name = acc.constraint_name AND
    ac.constraint_type = 'R'
            MINUS SELECT table_owner, table_name, column_name, column_position
            FROM all_ind_columns)
            ORDER BY acc.owner, acc.constraint_name, acc.column_name,
acc.position
/
```

User with Most Physical Disk Reads

This script shows which user has performed the most physical disk reads. This may be good to know to keep an eye out for someone who is hogging all the system resources and degrading the system performance.

Script

```
SELECT ses.sid, ses.serial#, ses.osuser, ses.process
FROM v$session ses, v$sess_io sio
WHERE ses.sid  = sio.sid AND nvl(ses.username,'SYS') not in ('SYS',
'SYSTEM')
            AND sio.physical_reads = (SELECT MAX(physical_reads)
            FROM v$session ses2, v$sess_io sio2
            WHERE ses2.sid = sio2.sid AND ses2.username NOT IN
('SYSTEM', 'SYS'))
/
```

Rollback Usage

This script shows who is accessing the rollback segments. This may be important when certain rollback segments continually get filled; you can identify who is filling the rollback segments and thus resolve the problem with the individual.

Script

```
column "Rollback Segment" format a20;
column "User Name" format a30;
ttitle 'Current Rollback Segment Usage'
set heading off
select r.name "Rollback Segment Name", p.spid "Process ID",
          s.username||'('||l.sid||')' "Oracle User Session",
   sq.sql_text
from v$sqlarea sq, v$lock l, v$process p, v$session s, v$rollname r
where l.sid = p.pid(+) and s.sid = l.sid
          and trunc(l.id1(+) / 65536) = r.usn and l.type(+) = 'TX'
          and l.lmode(+) = 6 and s.sql_address = sq.address
          and s.sql_hash_value = sq.hash_value
order by r.name
/
```

SGA Memory

This script lists key SGA memory usage. Knowing the SGA and its statistics will help in predicting or identifying upcoming problems.

Script

```
SELECT * FROM v$sgastat
WHERE name IN ('free memory', 'db_block_buffers', 'log_buffer',
          'dictionary cache', 'sql area', 'library cache')
```

Table Storage Usage

This script lists the percentage of storage that a table is currently using. This is important so that you can identify how much data is filling each table. When running this script, you are required to enter the table name.

Script

```
Select Blocks Allocated_Blks, Count(Distinct Substr(T.Rowid,1,8)
          || Substr(T.Rowid,15,4)) Used, (Count(Distinct
Substr(T.Rowid,1,8)
          || Substr(T.Rowid,15,4)) / Blocks) * 100 Pct_Used
From Sys.Dba_Segments E, &Tab_Name T
Where E.Segment_Name = Upper ('&Tab_Name') And E.Segment_Type = 'Table'
Group By E.Blocks
/
```

Waiting Users

This script lists all waits currently occurring on the system. The script also lists who is waiting.

Script

```
Select ses.username || '('||sw.sid||')' users, event
From v$session ses, v$session_wait sw
Where ses.sid = sw.sid
/
```

Monitoring Script

This script is a repeat from Chapter 11, "Monitoring Your Oracle Database." Presented here is the bare script without all the remarks. This script dumps information about the datafiles, size allocations, free space, tablespace configuration, rollback segments, and status.

Script

```
column segment_name jus cen hea 'Segment Name '
column segment_id jus cen hea 'ID' for 999
column status jus cen hea 'Status'
column next_extent jus cen hea 'Next' for 9,999,999,999
column max_extents jus cen hea 'Max|Extents' for 9,999,999,999
column min_extents jus cen hea 'Min|Extents' for 999
column mb jus cen hea 'Largest|Extent' for 9,999,999,999
column pct_increase jus cen hea '%|Incr' for 999
```

```
column initial_extent jus cen hea 'Initial' for 9,999,999,999
column total jus cen hea 'Total Amount|Remaining' for 9,999,999,999
column tablespace_name jus cen hea 'TableSpace|Name ' for a11
column Pieces jus cen hea 'Pieces'
column d_file jus cen hea "Data File" form a50
select substr(file_name,1,50) d_file, tablespace_name,
round((bytes/1024)/1024) MEG
from sys.dba_data_files
order by tablespace_name
/
select tablespace_name,
round(sum((bytes/1024)/1024)) MEG
from sys.dba_data_files
group by tablespace_name
/
select tablespace_name,count(*) Pieces,sum(bytes) total,max(bytes)
mb
from sys.dba_free_space
group by tablespace_name
/
select tablespace_name,initial_extent,next_extent,
min_extents,max_extents,pct_increase,status
from sys.dba_tablespaces
order by tablespace_name
/
select substr(segment_name,1,15) segment_name, tablespace_name,
segment_id,
          next_extent,initial_extent,pct_increase,
          substr(status,1,7) status
from sys.dba_rollback_segs
order by tablespace_name, segment_name
/
```

Miscellaneous Oracle Scripts

This last section is always the most read. Many times you are looking for a script that simply does something that you can't put your finger on, and doesn't belong in any other category. The following scripts are just that—the miscellaneous scripts that don't fit into any other area.

Undocumented Init.Ora parameters

This script lists all undocumented Init.Ora parameters. These are the Init.Ora features that are carried over into the latest release of Oracle but are not documented because the latest version of Oracle wants you to use new, documented features.

Script

```
SELECT name, value
FROM v$parameter
UNION ALL
SELECT ksppinm, ksppdesc
FROM x$ksppi
WHERE SUBSTR(ksppinm,1,1) = '_'
/
```

Database Duplicate Records

The purpose of this script is to find duplicate records within the tables.

 NOTE

This sample script was run on a table with fields person_ID, last_name, first_name, birth_date, and others. You must, of course, substitute your own field names for those in the example. Field names that should be replaced are in italic.

Script

```
set pagesize 80
set verify off
set echo off
select person_ID, last_name, first_name, birth_date, rowid
from person a
```

```
where rowid > (select min(rowid) from person b where
b.last_name=a.last_name and
          b.first_name=a.first_name and b.birth_date=a.birth_date)
order by 1,2,3
/
```

Verify the Oracle 7.3.4 for 8.1.x Upgrade

This collection of scripts checks various aspects of your Oracle7 database to determine whether it is ready to be converted to Oracle8. This particular script checks Oracle version 7.3.4 (the last official version of Oracle before version 8).

Script

```
spool verify73to81.lst
Prompt ++++++++++++++++++++++++++++++++++++++++++++++++++
Prompt Check PL/SQL is Installed - Install if NOT
Prompt ++++++++++++++++++++++++++++++++++++++++++++++++++
select * from v$version
/
Prompt ++++++++++++++++++++++++++++++++++++++++++++++++++
Prompt Check for user or role named MIGRATE and OUTLN
Prompt Drop if any rows are returned on this script
Prompt ++++++++++++++++++++++++++++++++++++++++++++++++++
select username from dba_users
where username in ('MIGRATE', 'OUTLN')
/
select role from dba_roles
where role in ('MIGRATE', 'OUTLN')
/
Prompt ++++++++++++++++++++++++++++++++++++++++++++++++++
Prompt Check for Tablespaces that are not online. Turn them online or
Prompt make sure they are offline normal.
Prompt ++++++++++++++++++++++++++++++++++++++++++++++++++
select tablespace_name, status from dba_tablespaces
where status != 'ONLINE'
/
```

```
Prompt ++++++++++++++++++++++++++++++++++++++++++++++++++
Prompt Check for datafiles that are not online but have read write permis-
sions.
Prompt ++++++++++++++++++++++++++++++++++++++++++++++++++
col name format a40
select name, status, enabled from v$datafile
where status != 'ONLINE' or enabled != 'READ WRITE'
/
Prompt ++++++++++++++++++++++++++++++++++++++++++++++++++
Prompt Check SYSTEM rollback segment. OPTIMAL should not be set.
Prompt Check to see If MAXEXTENTS should be above 121
Prompt Check to see If NEXT extent is not too small; should be >= 128K
Prompt ++++++++++++++++++++++++++++++++++++++++++++++++++
alter rollback segment SYSTEM shrink
/
select next_extent, max_extents, pct_increase, optsize
from dba_rollback_segs, v$rollstat
where  segment_name = 'SYSTEM' and usn = segment_id
/
Prompt ++++++++++++++++++++++++++++++++++++++++++++++++++
Prompt Make sure the AUD$ table is in SYSTEM tablespace
Prompt ++++++++++++++++++++++++++++++++++++++++++++++++++
select table_name, tablespace_name from dba_tables where table_name =
'AUD$'
/
Prompt ++++++++++++++++++++++++++++++++++++++++++++++++++
Prompt Make sure default tablespace for SYS is SYSTEM
Prompt ++++++++++++++++++++++++++++++++++++++++++++++++++
select default_tablespace, temporary_tablespace
from dba_users where username = 'SYS'
/
Prompt ++++++++++++++++++++++++++++++++++++++++++++++++++
Prompt Make sure SYS owned dictionary objects are not In other table-
spaces.
Prompt If they are, try to run catproc.sql and catalog.sql with SYS
default tablespace as SYSTEM
Prompt ++++++++++++++++++++++++++++++++++++++++++++++++++
col segment_name format a30
```

```
col segmmet_type format a10
col tablespace_name format a30
select segment_name, segment_type, tablespace_name
from dba_segments where owner = 'SYS'
        and tablespace_name != 'SYSTEM' and segment_type != 'ROLLBACK'
/
Prompt +++++++++++++++++++++++++++++++++++++++++++++++++++
Prompt Make sure you have 100MB free.  If not, then double the amount
Prompt of space used in SYSTEM tablespace and make It available.
Prompt +++++++++++++++++++++++++++++++++++++++++++++++++++
COLUMN tsname FORMAT a17
COLUMN bytes FORMAT 999,999,999
COLUMN Tot_Size FORMAT 9,999,999 HEADING "TOTAL (M)"
COLUMN Tot_Free FORMAT 9,999,999 HEADING "FREE (M)"
COLUMN Pct_Free FORMAT 999 HEADING "FREE %"
SELECT a.tablespace_name TSNAME, SUM(a.tots)/1048576 Tot_Size,
        SUM(a.sumb)/1048576 Tot_Free,
        SUM(a.sumb)*100/sum(a.tots) Pct_Free
FROM (SELECT tablespace_name, 0 tots, SUM(bytes) sumb
        FROM dba_free_space WHERE tablespace_name = 'SYSTEM'
GROUP BY tablespace_name
UNION
SELECT tablespace_name, SUM(bytes) tots, 0
        FROM dba_data_files WHERE tablespace_name = 'SYSTEM'
GROUP BY tablespace_name) a WHERE a.tablespace_name = 'SYSTEM'
GROUP BY a.tablespace_name
/
PROMPT +++++++++++++++++++++++++++++++++++++++++++++++++++
Prompt Check the INITIAL and NEXT extents of SYSTEM tablespace to ensure
Prompt they are 128K or higher and that the maxextents is also high enough
(> 249K).
PROMPT +++++++++++++++++++++++++++++++++++++++++++++++++++
select initial_extent, next_extent, max_extents, pct_increase
from dba_tablespaces where   tablespace_name = 'SYSTEM'
/
PROMPT +++++++++++++++++++++++++++++++++++++++++++++++++++
Prompt These are the control files of this database, make sure you have enough
```

```
Prompt free space available in the file system. Oracle8 creates large control
    files
PROMPT ++++++++++++++++++++++++++++++++++++++++++++++++
select value from v$parameter where name = 'control_files'
/
PROMPT ++++++++++++++++++++++++++++++++++++++++++++++++
Prompt Connect as SYS to run this next query. Make sure there are no uncommitted
Prompt transactions and any uncommitted distributed transactions.
Prompt If there Is no problem, then there will be no returned rows.
PROMPT ++++++++++++++++++++++++++++++++++++++++++++++++
select kttvstnm "TABLESPACE_NAME" from sys.x$kttvs where kttvstnm IS NOT null
/
select * from sys.pending_trans$
/
select * from sys.pending_sessions$
/
select * from sys.pending_sub_sessions$
/
PROMPT ++++++++++++++++++++++++++++++++++++++++++++++++
Prompt Oracle suggests that all tablespaces except SYSTEM, TEMP, and RBS
Prompt should be set to READ ONLY.
PROMPT ++++++++++++++++++++++++++++++++++++++++++++++++
spool off
```

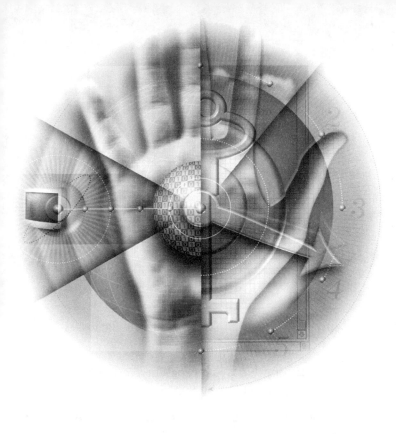

Glossary

5-Nines—5-Nines is the capability to provide a minimum of 99.999 percent availability to a database, typically to support e-commerce applications, which normally run 24×7.

A

Advanced replication—The capability of Oracle to replicate or update databases that are located on remote hosts or on a separate Oracle instance.

Asynchronous—In the context of replication, this is the capability to log SQL operations targeted for another site for later processing by that site.

Availability—In the context of this book, this is the time that a system is available to users. (See also 5-Nines.)

B

Bidirectional replication—In this form of replication, both the publishing and subscribing site can update a particular data object. Also referred to as *symmetric*.

Blocks—The basic unit of storage, both physical and logical, for all Oracle data.

C

Clustering—The physical act of grouping tables and data together to minimize the number of I/Os (inputs and outputs) that must be performed.

Control files—A database's overall physical structure or architecture is maintained by its control files. Control files hold all the information about the files within the database.

CSI#—A CPU Support Identification (CSI) number is issued to Oracle support customers and must be used each time you log a fault with Oracle support.

D

Data block buffer cache—A cache in the System Global Area (SGA) used to hold the data blocks that are read from data segments in the database. Segments include tables, clusters, and indexes.

Data dictionary—A printout of a database's tables and their corresponding fields.

Data mining—A multistage business process leading to the automated detection of cause-and-effect relationships in data. This process involves the mathematical analysis of numerical data, and the search for various types of statistical relationships among variables that might yield useful knowledge that can be applied to future decision-making situations.

Database link—An object stored in one database (local) that identifies a remote (non-local) database and the path needed to connect to the remote database.

Datafile—Each tablespace is comprised of one or more files called *datafiles*, which are located on a specific disk. Datafiles are unique and can belong to only one tablespace.

DBA—Database administrator. This is the person in charge of administering the Oracle database.

DBWR—The Oracle database writer is an Oracle background process created when you start a database instance. The DBWR writes data from the SGA to the Oracle database files.

DDL—Data Definition Language. A language used by database management systems, which allow users to define the database, specifying data types, structures, and constraints on the data.

Dedicated server—A server that has protocols and instructions assigned to only one user or transaction. Multithreaded is the opposite of dedicated.

Deferred transaction—One or more deferred RPCs submitted within one local transaction that are propagated and applied as one transaction at the destination database.

Downtime—The amount of time that a computer or server sits while not being powered up or connected to users. Downtime should be zero when it comes to a 24×7 operation. (See also uptime for the opposite definition.)

Dynamic performance tables—Oracle's internal tables (V$ tables) that constantly collect performance information about the Oracle instance.

E

Extents—An extent is a contiguous space allocated to a segment in a tablespace. The size of an extent is controlled by storage parameters used when you `CREATE` or `ALTER` the segment, including `INITIAL`, `NEXT`, and `PCT_INCREASE`. (See also blocks.)

H

Heterogeneous—This term refers to replicating data among different DBMSs.

I

iFS—Oracle's Internet File System allows one to store files in an Oracle database.

Init.Ora—A database system parameter file that contains specific information that is used when starting up the Oracle database.

Instance—A set of memory structures and background processes that access a specific set of database files. Within an Oracle database, there can be one or more Oracle instances.

J

Job queue—PL/SQL code scheduled for periodic execution by a background process.

L

LGWR—The LGWR (LoG WRiter) process writes redo log entries from the SGA to the online redo logs.

License—Oracle license that specifies usage conditions and named users. When an Oracle instance starts, Oracle license limits are read and these limits govern how many sessions and users are licensed for the particular instance.

N

Network—A connection between two or more computers that enables them to communicate with each other.

Normalization—Implementing your database to be fully relational is known as normalization. A normalized database eliminates functional dependencies in the data so that when it comes time to update the database, the task is efficient and trouble-free.

O

Object—A named item or element in an Oracle database such as a trigger, table, index, or procedure.

OFA—Optimal Flexible Architecture is an Oracle standard for file placement.

OLTP—On-Line Transaction Processing. OLTP systems capture, validate, and store large amounts of transactions. These systems are optimized for general data entry operations.

ORACLE_BASE—An environment variable used as base directory for an Oracle OFA installation.

ORACLE_HOME—An environment variable pointing to the directory underneath which all Oracle software is installed.

P

PL/SQL—PL/SQL is Oracle's procedural language extension to SQL.

Publisher—The originator of a replicated database change. Note that a publisher can also be a subscriber in bi-directional schemes.

Pull replication—Scenario in which the subscriber sites determine when they want to receive replication transactions.

Push replication—Scenario in which a publisher site controls when replication occurs and "pushes" the changes to the subscribers.

R

RDBMS—See Relational Database Management System.

Redo log—A sequential log of actions that is reapplied to the database if it is not written to the disk drive.

Refresh—This is a process whereby one or more tables at one of the subscriber sites are completely restored or updated.

Relational Database Management System (RDBMS)—A computer database application used for general data storage that organizes data into tables consisting of one or more rows of information and one or more columns of the same data. Oracle is an RDBMS.

Remote Procedure Call (RPC)—A call from one host to another host in order to perform a certain Oracle function.

RepCat—See Replication catalog.

Replicated group—A collection of replicated objects that are always updated in a consistent manner. An object group can span multiple schemas, but a replicated object can be a member of only one object group.

Replicated object—A database object that is copied to multiple sites in a distributed environment. Any replica of this object can potentially be updated, and updates made to one replica are applied at all other copies.

Replication catalog—Tables used by the replication facility that contain all the information necessary to maintain the replicated environment. Also called RepCat.

Replication facility—A set of packages that uses RepCat, job queues, and deferred transactions to maintain consistency among replicated schemas.

Rollback segments—Areas of memory that hold users' transactions until the users "commit" their transactions into the database. This is similar to an "undo" in other applications, whereby the transactions can be "rolled back."

S

Schema—The data definitions that comprise a database created with SQL data definition statements such as tables, views, and indexes.

Segment— Any database object that has space allocated to it is called a SEGMENT. A segment consists of one or more EXTENTS allocated within a tablespace.

SGA (System Global Area)—An Oracle database that holds the most commonly used or requested structural information about the database instance.

Snapshot—A means or method of creating a local copy of remotely located data.

SQL—Oracle's Structured Query Language is an ANSI standard language used to manipulate information stored in a relational database.

SQL*Net—Oracle software that allows remote data-access between a user application and Oracle databases, or among multiple databases.

Subscriber—This is a receiver of a replicated database change. Note that a subscriber can also be a publisher in bi-directional schemes.

Synonym—A name assigned to a table or view that can be used thereafter in place of the original name. Generally, synonyms are shorter names that refer to another user's tables so that the qualifier doesn't need to be included.

T

Table— A collection of computer data organized, defined, and stored as rows and columns. This is the basic data storage structure in an Oracle relational database.

Tablespace—Databases have one or more tablespaces, each made of one or more datafiles. Tables and indexes are created within a tablespace.

TAR—Technical Assistance Requests. A TAR is the process of correcting an Oracle-related problem or error through Oracle support.

Trigger—A program in a database that gets called each time a row in a table is INSERTED, UPDATED, or DELETED.

U

Uptime—The amount of time that a computer is available for users to log into and use. In the 24×7 world, uptime should be all the time. (See also downtime for the opposite definition.)

Index

Meeting the Needs of Today's
ERP Professionals

Taking a tailored approach with the larger players in the ERP industry, PRIMA TECH focuses on that

aspect of ERP that each company does best. The niche approach of these books provide quality

materials that keep you abreast of technologies that other publishers may ignore. From the OneWorld™

technology of J.D. Edwards®, to the powerful database of Oracle®, to the e-business solutions of Baan®,

PRIMA TECH provides you with the information you need on today's ERP leaders.